Liturgy and Sacrament, Mystagogy and Martyrdom

# Liturgy and Sacrament, Mystagogy and Martyrdom

Essays in Theological Exegesis

Jeffrey L. Morrow

☙PICKWICK *Publications* • Eugene, Oregon

LITURGY AND SACRAMENT, MYSTAGOGY AND MARTYRDOM
Essays in Theological Exegesis

Copyright © 2020 Jeffrey L. Morrow. All rights reserved. Except for brief quotations in critical publications or reviews, no part of this book may be reproduced in any manner without prior written permission from the publisher. Write: Permissions, Wipf and Stock Publishers, 199 W. 8th Ave., Suite 3, Eugene, OR 97401.

Pickwick Publications
An Imprint of Wipf and Stock Publishers
199 W. 8th Ave., Suite 3
Eugene, OR 97401

www.wipfandstock.com

PAPERBACK ISBN: 978-1-5326-9380-9
HARDCOVER ISBN: 978-1-5326-9381-6
EBOOK ISBN: 978-1-5326-9382-3

*Cataloguing-in-Publication data:*

Names: Morrow, Jeffrey L., author.

Title: Liturgy and sacrament, mystagogy and martyrdom : essays in theological exegesis / by Jeffrey L. Morrow.

Description: Eugene, OR: Pickwick Publications, 2020 | Includes bibliographical references and index.

Identifiers: ISBN 978-1-5326-9380-9 (paperback) | ISBN 978-1-5326-9381-6 (hardcover) | ISBN 978-1-5326-9382-3 (ebook)

Subjects: LCSH: Bible—Criticism, interpretation, etc.—History. | Bible—Hermeneutics. | Bible—Reading.

Classification: BS500 M67 2020 (print) | BS500 (ebook)

Manufactured in the U.S.A.                                              10/09/20

This book is dedicated in loving memory to my grandparents, Walt Hall, Mable Hall, Bernice Freedman, and Morty Morrow.

# Contents

*Acknowledgments* | ix

Introduction | 1

1: Rightly Reading the Sacred Page: A Brief History of Catholic Biblical Interpretation | 6

2: Priestly Humanity in the Temple of Creation: A Liturgical Reading of Genesis 1–3 | 33

3: St. Joseph and the Value of Work: A Sacramental Reading of Genesis 1–3 | 59

4: Heavenly Bread: A Mystagogical Reading of 1 Kings 19 | 78

5: St. Thomas More as Biblical Interpreter: Martyrological Exegesis | 89

Conclusion | 113

*Bibliography* | 119
*Author Index* | 149
*Subject Index* | 157
*Scripture Index* | 159

# Acknowledgments

EACH CHAPTER IN THIS book has its own unique origin. I thought to bring these essays together into this unified volume in light of the constructive nature of each. Much of my scholarship up to this point has been more genealogical and deconstructive, underscoring the history behind modern historical biblical criticism, showing its lack of neutrality and objectivity by way of pointing out its historical, philosophical, and political roots. In contrast to that prior work, the essays in this volume seek to be constructive, pointing the way forward to a fruitful theological exegesis in light of what came in the past.

The first chapter is a revision of my article that was originally published as "*Dei verbum* in Light of the History of Catholic Biblical Interpretation," *Josephinum Journal of Theology* 23, no. 1–2 (2016) 227–49. I wish to thank the *Josephinum Journal of Theology* for permission to reuse this material. I am indebted to many people for essential conversations that contributed greatly to what became this initial article and the present chapter, especially to Eric Johnston, Andrew Jones, and Fr. Pablo Gadenz. Fr. Jared Wicks, SJ, deserves a special word of thanks for his important feedback on an initial draft of the original journal article, based on which I made important revisions. I also owe Bill Murphy and my wife Maria Morrow thanks for their insightful critiques of early versions of what eventually became this chapter.

The second chapter began as part of the conference presentation I made entitled, "Genesis 1–3 in a Liturgical Context: The Role of Liturgy in Christian Theological Interpretation of Scripture," for the Society of Biblical Literature in San Diego, 2007. It was later revised and presented as "Creation and Liturgy: The Liturgical Background of Genesis 1–3," for the Trends of Ancient Jewish and Christian Mysticism Seminar at the University of Dayton in 2008. It was further revised again and presented as "Genesis

## ACKNOWLEDGMENTS

1–3 and the Exultation of All Creation Around God's Throne," at the College Theology Society Annual Meeting at the University of Notre Dame in 2009. It was revised further and published as "Creation as Temple-Building and Work as Liturgy in Genesis 1–3," *Journal of the Orthodox Center for the Advancement of Biblical Studies* 2, no. 1 (2009) 1–13. A small portion of that paper was revised and incorporated into another article which was published as "Work as Worship in the Garden and the Workshop: Genesis 1–3, the Feast of St. Joseph the Worker, and Liturgical Hermeneutics," *Logos* 15, no. 4 (2012) 159–78. I owe both the *Journal of the Orthodox Center for the Advancement of Biblical Studies* and *Logos* thanks for permission to reuse this material here. I owe more people thanks for their assistance at the various stages of research, writing, and revision of what became this chapter than I can put here. The most important discussions I had that informed my conference presentations and initial publications of what became incorporated into this chapter, were with Fr. Silviu Bunta, Scott Hahn, and John Bergsma. I also owe Biff Rocha and Maria Morrow thanks for critiquing and editing various versions of this material, which has benefited the present chapter version.

A portion of the third chapter began as part of the fifth chapter of my doctoral dissertation, "Evangelical Catholics and Catholic Biblical Scholarship: An Examination of Scott Hahn's Canonical, Liturgical, and Covenantal Biblical Exegesis," which I completed at the University of Dayton in 2007. That portion was included in my 2007 Society of Biblical Literature presentation, "Genesis 1–3 in a Liturgical Context," mentioned above, and was revised further and was published electronically through Amazon.com on Kindle, but is no longer available. It was then revised thoroughly, shortened but then expanded to include the material on the Feast of St. Joseph the Worker, and then published as "Work as Worship in the Garden and the Workshop," in the 2012 *Logos* article cited above. This chapter represents a more thorough revision and expansion of that work, and I owe *Logos* thanks for permission to include it here. I need to thank the members of my dissertation committee, my director, William Portier, as well as my readers, William Trollinger, Dennis Doyle, Vincent Branick, and Sandra Yocum. I also owe Fr. Silviu Bunta, Scott Hahn, and John Bergsma thanks for conversations that informed this chapter in its various early stages, and both Biff Rocha and Maria Morrow for their many critiques and helpful comments for revision at various points in the early drafting of what became this chapter.

ACKNOWLEDGMENTS

The fourth chapter initially began as a paper presentation entitled, "Elijah's Resurrection and Mystical Communion with Angelic Bread: 1 Kings 19:3–8 and its Reception," for the Reception History of the Bible: A Colloquium: Biblical Exegesis as Mystical Experience in Judaism and Christianity at Duquesne University in 2010. It was subsequently revised and published as, "'Arise and Eat': 1 Kings 19:3–8 and Elijah's Death, Resurrection and Bread from Heaven," *Journal of the Orthodox Center for the Advancement of Biblical Studies* 3, no. 1 (2010) 1–7. It has here been greatly revised and expanded. I owe the *Journal of the Orthodox Center for the Advancement of Biblical Studies* thanks for permission to reuse material from this article. I owe numerous individuals thanks for their helpful suggestion of sources for my research on what became this chapter, as well as for fruitful conversations that informed my work, especially Gregory Glazov, Fr. Pablo Gadenz, John Bergsma, Brant Pitre, Biff Rocha, Fr. Joseph Kozar, SM, and David Greer. I owe Fr. Bogdan Bucur special thanks for inviting me to present this paper at Duquesne, and for his encouragement. I owe Benjamin Sommer thanks for correcting mistakes I had made initially, and I owe Maria Morrow thanks for editing early versions of what became this chapter. I also owe Brant Pitre thanks for providing me with his work before it was published.

The fifth chapter is an expansion and revision of my earlier article originally published as "Thomas More on the Sadness of Christ: From Mystagogy to Martyrdom," *Heythrop Journal* 58, no. 3 (2017) 365–73. I owe *Heythrop Journal* thanks for permission to reuse this material. I owe thanks to Justin Anderson, Joseph Rice, and Fr. Robert Connor, for fruitful conversations that aided me as I thought through the material for what became this chapter. I also owe Biff Rocha and Maria Morrow thanks for critiquing earlier versions of this work. Maria also read through the entire finished manuscript and made helpful critiques of the penultimate draft. Unless otherwise noted in the footnotes, all English translations are my own.

Finally, I recognize how rare it is to have memories of all four grandparents. I have so many memories of my mother's father, Walt Hall, from sailing, splitting logs in the backyard, or various projects. I sat mesmerized at his feet as a child as he introduced me to works of science and critical thought. I lost Grandpa Hall when I was in my first year of college. My father's mother, Bernice Freedman, was a model grandmother. I spent more time with my Bubbie Bernice than any of my other grandparents. In so many ways she was the loving matriarch of the family. I got to know my

## ACKNOWLEDGMENTS

cousins very well from our time together at "Bubbie Camp," when Bubbie would travel alone with her grandchildren for vacations to famous historical sites, or to water and amusement parks. My father's father, Morty Morrow, always lightened the mood with his constant humor. I always enjoyed visiting him at his home in Pennsylvania. Bubbie and Grandpa Morty passed the same week at the end of my first year during my M.A. program. My mother's mother, Mable Hall, outlived them all. Grandma Hall made it almost to one hundred before she passed away last year. I consider myself blessed to have known all four of my grandparents throughout my childhood and early adult years, and I retain many fond memories of each one. It is in loving memory of my grandparents that I dedicate this volume.

# Introduction

When I teach introductory Scripture courses in the classroom, I typically cover hermeneutics, that is, methods of interpretation, in the first few days. We include a discussion of Pope Emeritus Benedict XVI's now famous essay, from prior to his papacy, "Biblical Interpretation in Conflict,"[1] as well as his comments from after he delivered this lecture, wherein he argued that the way forward in biblical exegesis was to utilize both the best methods of traditional and modern forms of interpretation.[2] We also cover early Patristic exegesis, that form of interpretation in which the earliest Christians engaged Scripture. I find the second and third chapters of Robert Louis Wilken's *The Spirit of Early Christian Thought* very helpful for getting at the spirit of early Christian biblical interpretation.[3] Invariably students ask something along the lines of, "if modern biblical methods are flawed, and there's no simple retreat back to patristic exegesis, then how are we supposed to read the Bible?"

I typically try to clarify that just because modern exegetical methods are flawed—e.g., they are not as objective as they are often portrayed—they still retain many useful insights, and should not be rejected outright, as Benedict XVI himself reiterated time and again. I likewise point out that patristic and medieval methods are flawed too—e.g., there were significant gaps in the historical knowledge of patristic and medieval writers. I teach at a Catholic seminary, so I have the benefit of using the Second Vatican Council's Dogmatic Constitution on Divine Revelation, *Dei Verbum*, and Pope Emeritus Benedict XVI's beautiful and thorough Post-Synodal Apostolic

---

1. Benedict XVI, "Biblical Interpretation in Conflict," 91–126.
2. Stallsworth, "Story of an Encounter," 102–90.
3. Wilken, *Spirit of Early Christian Thought*, 25–79.

Exhortation On the Word of God in the Life and Mission of the Church, *Verbum Domini*, as authoritative sources for instructing how Catholics can and should read Scripture. Moreover, the *Catechism of the Catholic Church*, in numbers 50–141, quite helpfully and eloquently discusses the nature, transmission, and interpretation of divine revelation.

In my scholarship, however, most of my work has been answering the first part of Benedict XVI's call to explore the history of the historical critical method, discovering its limits and pitfalls.[4] I have focused on the seventeenth century roots of the modern historical critical method.[5] I have also spent a little time covering some of the pre-seventeenth century roots of modern biblical criticism.[6] Since beginning my research projects in the seventeenth century, I have also explored this history behind modern historical biblical criticism, in the better known eighteenth and nineteenth centuries.[7] More recently, I have studied how such biblical criticism entered the Catholic world during the modernist controversy, and particularly looking at the pivotal work here of Alfred Loisy.[8] The essays in this present volume, however, represent a constructive approach, an answer to the second half of Benedict's call to develop a theological Catholic biblical

---

4. E.g., Benedict XVI, "Biblical Interpretation in Conflict," 91–126.

5. See works by Morrow, "Methods of Interpreting"; "Lives of Jesus"; *Pretensions*, 35–74, 81–82, 102–3; "Spinoza and the Theo-Political," 374–87; *Theology, Politics, and Exegesis*, 1–51; "Acid of History," 169–80; "*Dei verbum*," 235–38; "Averroism," 1317–40; *Three Skeptics*, 29–149; "Faith, Reason and History," 658–73; "Cut Off," 547–58; "Spinoza's Use," 1–18; "Untold History," 149–55; "Secularization," 20–21; "Historical Criticism," 189–221; "Pre-Adamites," 1–23; "*Leviathan*," 33–54; "French Apocalyptic Messianism," 203–13; "Modernist Crisis," 270–72; "Early Modern," 7–24; "Politics," 534–39; and "Bible in Captivity," 285–99.

6. See works by Morrow, "Lives of Jesus"; *Pretensions*, 11–34, 78–80, 93–94, 100–102; *Theology, Politics, and Exegesis*, 1–15; "*Dei verbum*," 234–35; "Averroism," 1293–317; *Three Skeptics*, 11–29; "Untold History," 145–49; "Secularization," 20; "Modernist Crisis," 267–70; and "Politics," 530–34.

7. See Hahn and Morrow, *Modern Biblical Criticism*; Morrow, "Lives of Jesus"; Morrow, *Pretensions*, 82–90 and 103–6; Morrow, *Theology, Politics, and Exegesis*, 52–73; Morrow, "*Dei verbum*," 238–44; Morrow, *Three Skeptics*, 46–53; Morrow, "Cut Off," 552–54; Morrow, "Secularization," 21–22; Morrow, "Enlightenment University," 897–922; Morrow, "Modernist Crisis," 272–77; and Morrow, "Politics," 539–45.

8. See works by Morrow, "Thy Kingdom Come," 3–13; "Religion and the Secular State," 35–45; *Pretensions*, 84–89; *Alfred Loisy*; "Études Bibliques," 12–32; "Loisy," 1039–41; *Theology, Politics, and Exegesis*, 74–90; "*Dei verbum*," 242–44; "Babylon in Paris," 261–76; "Cut Off," 547–58; "Alfred Loisy et les Mythes Babyloniens," 87–103; "Études Assyriologie," 3–20; "Alfred Loisy's Developmental Approach," 324–44; "Babylonian Myths," 43–62; "Newman," 20–22; and "Modernist Crisis," 273–77.

interpretive method that relies upon the best of both traditional Christian forms of interpretation and of modern methods.⁹

Three of my prior books, *Three Skeptics and the Bible*, *Theology, Politics, and Exegesis*, and *Pretensions of Objectivity*, serve as a sort of trilogy exploring the historical, political, philosophical, and theological roots of modern historical criticism, by bringing together revisions of several of my essays on that topic. I hope *Liturgy and Sacrament, Mystagogy and Martyrdom*, completes those volumes as a more constructive piece. Not long ago I was asked to propose a list and review of the sorts of books I thought a Catholic moral theologian should read on the topic of the Bible and its interpretation, to help inform moral theologians in regard to Catholic biblical interpretation and biblical studies in general, as well as what would serve as good introductory material to Scripture.¹⁰ I focused there on the work of Scott Hahn and Benedict XVI, because I truly believe that their exegetical works point the way forward beyond the impasse between theology and modern biblical studies. In addition to Benedict's *Jesus of Nazareth* trilogy, much of Hahn's scholarly work is illustrative of the exact type of biblical scholarship we need.¹¹ In particular, I am thinking of his scholarly books like *Kinship By Covenant* and *Kingdom of God as Liturgical Empire*.¹² I hope this book will contribute to these same conversations about theological biblical interpretation.

In the first chapter, I take a bird's eye view surveying the long history of Catholic biblical interpretation from the earliest centuries through the present. I spend the majority of the chapter focusing on the nineteenth and twentieth century leading up to the Second Vatican Council, because the point of the chapter is to situate the kind of theological exegesis this book engages within the history behind Vatican II and the post-conciliar exegetical trends. I show the richness of the theological interpretation of the church fathers and medieval theologians like St. Thomas Aquinas and

---

9. This is something I believe Benedict himself has done in his three volumes on *Jesus of Nazareth*.

10. Morrow, "Studies in Scripture," 36–56.

11. Benedict XVI, *Jesus of Nazareth I*, *Jesus of Nazareth II*, and *Jesus of Nazareth III*.

12. Hahn, *Kinship By Covenant*; and Hahn, *Kingdom of God*. There are many other like-minded scholars I could mention here, like John Bergsma, Brant Pitre, Michael Barber, Leroy Huizenga, Nathan Eubank, William Wright, Fr. Pablo Gadenz, and John Kincaid, among others. See, e.g., Bergsma, *Jesus and the Dead Sea Scrolls*; Pitre et al., *Paul*; Barber, *Salvation*; Huizenga, *Behold the Christ*; Eubank, *First and Second Thessalonians*; Wright and Martin, *Encountering the Living God*; and Gadenz, *Gospel of Luke*.

the Victorines. I trace the tragic separation of faith and reason in biblical interpretation, which I have covered in many of my prior works, and I point to the modernist controversy, and its aftermath, as a key to understanding what led to the Second Vatican Council. My exegetical work here fits within the post-conciliar attempts at reading the Bible from the heart of the Church, without ignoring history.

In the second chapter I turn to an examination of Gen 1–3, focusing on the literal sense, but ultimately showing how the clues in the text and in the biblical canon, as well as in Jewish and Christian interpretive traditions, point to our understanding the world God created as a macro temple and humanity as priest stewards created to worship God in the temple of the world. This sets the stage for the sort of liturgical interpretation that I seek to accomplish in this volume.

In chapter three, I turn to the issue of liturgical interpretation, following the work of Hahn and others.[13] I walk through the history of how the Bible was read and understood, primarily in liturgical contexts. I then focus on the various calls from Catholic theologians to read the Bible in a liturgical setting, which provides a natural theological hermeneutic which is canonical in that it encourages the reading of the various parts of Scripture in light of the whole of Scripture. I join these theologians in urging for such a liturgical hermeneutic. I conclude by using the example of Gen 1 in light of its liturgical use in a particular feast, the Feast of St. Joseph the Worker, in order to show concretely what such a liturgical hermeneutic might look like.

In chapter four I consider what a mystagogical interpretation, building on typology, might look like. The specific passage I take as an example is from the Elijah narratives, specifically 1 Kgs 19:3–8. Here I argue that Elijah's "falling asleep" and "arising," only to be greeted by an angel and fed bread and water, are types pointing forward to Jesus' death and resurrection, and to the Eucharist. I ground this typology in what I tentatively argue is the literal sense of the text, wherein I argue that Elijah appears to actually have died and been raised from the dead by the angel, after which he is nourished on heavenly food, akin to the Manna in the Wilderness narratives of the Pentateuch, which strengthens him for his journey to have an encounter with God.

---

13. E.g., Hahn, "Canon, Cult and Covenant," 207–35, *Letter and Spirit*, and "Worship in the Word," 101–36.

INTRODUCTION

My fifth and final chapter addresses what I regard as martyrological exegesis. I use the example of St. Thomas More, who wrote extensive spiritual texts involving the sort of biblical interpretation that I think is helpful in our own day. More's examples become especially powerful when read against the backdrop of his own holy life and physical martyrdom. He thus provides the sort of example of saintly exegesis the Pope Benedict put forward as essential in *Verbum Domini*.[14]

I ended my last book, *Pretensions of Objectivity*, with the following lines: "While more work of analysis for these early biblical critics may be helpful, there is also a need to move forward to a constructive biblical exegesis that benefits from the insights of modern biblical criticism without being beholden to the underlying political motivations that often resulted in false notions of fact and objectivity in the study of the Bible."[15] *Liturgy and Sacrament, Mystagogy and Martyrdom* thus picks up where *Pretensions of Objectivity* left off, in the hopes of moving forward to a constructive biblical exegesis which is historical but also theological.

---

14. Benedict XVI, *Verbum Domini*, no. 48.
15. Morrow, *Pretensions*, 108.

# 1

# Rightly Reading the Sacred Page

## A Brief History of Catholic Biblical Interpretation

BEFORE WE ENGAGE IN theological exegesis, it would be beneficial to review the Church's rich interpretive tradition. In what follows, I provide a cursory overview of the history of Catholic biblical interpretation spanning two millennia. Of necessity such a summary will remain partial, but it will be important for situating the theological exegetical work this volume is attempting to accomplish, in light of the post-Conciliar period context with which this chapter concludes. As we shall see, biblical interpretation developed through the centuries quite naturally with a desire to understand better the Scriptures and thereby facilitate an encounter with the God who authored them. In the modern period, an overemphasis on an anemic reason, increasingly severed from faith, set biblical interpretation on a trajectory that would drive a wedge between attention to history and faith commitments.[1] Within the Catholic world, the Second Vatican Council attempted to provide the outline of a more unified approach, united faith and reason, in a hermeneutic from the heart of the Church.

The Second Vatican Council's Dogmatic Constitution on Divine Revelation, *Dei Verbum*, was an important magisterial document setting forth the Church's teaching, including its discussion of Sacred Scripture, within the context of the Church's tradition and the event of the Council itself. *Dei*

---

1. A number of my earlier books have dealt with this history. See Morrow, *Three Skeptics, Theology, Politics, and Exegesis*, and *Pretensions of Objectivity*. A more thorough treatment of the eighteenth and nineteenth century components to this history are in Hahn and Morrow, *Modern Biblical Criticism*. My recent work, *Alfred Loisy*, deals in part with how this history filtered into the Catholic world at the end of the nineteenth century and dawning of the twentieth century.

*Verbum* synthesized the tradition in a clear and marvelous way, especially taking up the Magisterium's late nineteenth and twentieth century teachings on Scripture regarding a number of related issues. One of these central issues pertained to the interpretation of Sacred Scripture, which is found in paragraph 12 of *Dei Verbum*.[2] In 2010, Pope Benedict XVI issued his post-synodal apostolic exhortation, *Verbum Domini*, which was the most thorough and significant document pertaining to Scripture to come from the Magisterium since the Second Vatican Council. Pope Benedict's broader theological work holds such potential and promise for profoundly shaping the future of Catholic exegesis, and therefore a number of Catholic scholars have commented on its significance, particularly in bridging the gaps of older debates and taking Catholic biblical interpretation forward.[3]

In this chapter, I will begin with a *longue durée*, surveying briefly the first nineteen hundred years. Secondly, I will consider more extensively the dawn of the twentieth century leading up to the Second Vatican Council, and finally I will narrate the trends that have since unfolded in Catholic biblical scholarship. It should be borne in mind, as we approach the Second Vatican Council and the time period afterwards, that Catholic biblical scholars had a difficult road to walk, as many feared censure in the anti-Modernist period, and for a long time were not treated as equals in the wider world of non-Catholic biblical scholarship.[4] My reason for spending so much time on roughly the last century within this two thousand year history is that the remainder of this volume is my attempt at contributing to the post-conciliar theological exegesis, and thus this last period of time serves as the proximate historical context necessary for understanding the work I seek to do.

---

2. On the thornier issues concerning biblical inspiration in *Dei Verbum* no. 11, see all of the articles in *Letter and Spirit* 6 (2010): Hahn, "For the Sake of Our Salvation," 21–45; Betz, "Glory(ing) in the Humility," 141–79; Grisez, "Inspiration and Inerrancy," 181–90; and especially Pitre, "Mystery of God's Word," 47–66; Gadenz, "Magisterial Teaching," 67–91; and Waldstein, "*Analogia Verbi*," 93–140.

3. Studies on this abound, but see, as a very brief list of examples, all of the essays in Carl, *Verbum Domini*, especially Pitre, "*Verbum Domini*," 26–40 and Gadenz, "Overcoming the Hiatus," 41–62; Gadenz, "Jesus the New Temple," 211–30; Waldstein, "Self-Critique," 732–47; Wright, "Patristic Biblical Hermeneutics," 191–207; Wright, "New Synthesis," 35–66; Hahn, *Covenant and Communion*; Hahn, "At the School," 80–115; Hahn, "Hermeneutic of Faith," 415–40; and Hahn, "Authority of Mystery," 97–140.

4. Joseph Ratzinger reflected sympathetically on the difficulties his own biblical studies teachers faced in "Kirchliches Lehramt," 522–29.

## Catholic Exegetes within the History of Biblical Interpretation

### The Earliest Christian Centuries

It has become commonplace to describe early and medieval Christian biblical interpretation in reference to the *quadruplex sensus*, the fourfold sense. In reality, the fourfold sense of Scripture is really composed of two senses, the literal and the spiritual. The literal sense pertained to the sense of the words themselves, whereas the spiritual sense was further subdivided into three, hence a fourfold sense: one literal and three spiritual senses. As with Jewish interpretation, the church fathers evidenced a vast array of exegetical diversity far broader than this fourfold sense.[5] The liturgy is where biblical interpretation was continually born anew and lived. Prayer, and particularly the eucharistic liturgy, has always been the prime setting for biblical interpretation among Christians.[6] Scripture is thus by its very nature liturgical, sacramental, and performative; it is intended primarily for liturgy, where it functions sacramentally and prepares for the sacraments, and then facilitates their efficacious work in our lives, leading to our divinization, or deification.[7]

---

5. For all of its many merits, Henri de Lubac exaggerates both the universality of the *quadruplex sensus*, especially when dealing with the fathers, and also its completely Christian origin untainted by non-Christian exegesis. See, e.g., his comments on patristic exegesis in de Lubac, *Exégèse médiévale*, 171–220. Scholars have increasingly recognized de Lubac's oversimplifications, e.g., Persidok, "Revolucionario," 67–80; and McDermott, "Henri de Lubac's Genealogy," 124–56. Comparable is Smalley's classic work, *Study of the Bible*, which sees the waning of the spiritual sense and the waxing of the literal sense, in the same general time period. More historical precision, at least regarding medieval exegesis, is in Dahan, *Lire la Bible*; and Dahan, *L'Exégèse chrétienne*. Alastair Minnis puts it well in his summation, "the methodologies of medieval exegesis were a lot more flexible and context-specific than has sometimes been allowed." His conclusion that de Lubac (over) emphasized spiritual exegesis, whereas Smalley (over) emphasized the literal sense, is perhaps correct. See Minnis, *Medieval Theory*, xii.

6. On the liturgical context of Christian biblical interpretation throughout church history see, e.g., Olsen, *Reading Matthew*; Levering, *Engaging the Doctrine*, 59–85; Hahn, *Consuming the Word*, 39–47; Farkasfalvy, *Inspiration and Interpretation*, 63–87; Hahn, "Canon, Cult and Covenant," 207–35; Hahn, *Letter and Spirit*; Hahn, "Worship in the Word," 101–36; and Wilken, *Spirit of Early Christian Thought*, xvii–xviii and 25–79.

7. Scott Hahn puts it well when we he writes, "Having formed this understanding—with respect to the ecclesial setting, the patristic traditions, and the privileged liturgical setting for the Word—we begin to discover the *sacramentality* of Scripture and experience its *performative power* precisely as it is proclaimed in the liturgy and then fulfilled in

Quite naturally, Christian exegetes had concern for more than simply the literal sense of the biblical texts. They practiced spiritual interpretation, including typology, in part because this was a form of interpretation already found in the pages of Scripture, but also because it arose from the juxtaposition of texts from the Old and New Testaments at the liturgy when Scripture was proclaimed in the immediate context of the celebration of the Eucharist. Thus Scripture was often read following the two senses, literal and spiritual, with the spiritual divided further into its three subdivisions: allegorical or typological; moral or tropological; and anagogical.[8] This engagement with spiritual and allegorical interpretations, however, did not mean that the literal sense was neglected. Although Origen of Alexandria, for example, was known for allegorical interpretation, this has often been overemphasized; it should not be forgotten that the literal sense was also important for Origen.[9]

St. Augustine was important here in the context of the development of and engagement with the *quadruplex sensus*. He explained biblical interpretation on this model, for example, in his *De doctrina christiana*.[10] St. Augustine's hermeneutic was indebted to the Donatist Tyconius's *Liber Regularum*.[11] St. Thomas Aquinas and other medieval exegetes built upon St. Augustine's hermeneutical model. Here the literal sense was the necessary foundation; without understanding the sense of the words themselves, nothing further could be discovered profitably. Typology could be read from the texts, not because they were biblical, but because history

---

the celebration of the Eucharist. Christ himself is present when God's life-giving word is proclaimed at the Eucharistic celebration. He who is the Way and the Truth and the Life speaks life to us, and, when we listen, we are transformed and renewed by that life-giving Word so that we can walk in His Way and live the Truth.... as the Word is proclaimed and expounded in the Liturgical assembly of the Church, it has *performative power*—it functions *sacramentally* in renewing and elevating the life of the Christian." Hahn, "Introduction," 8.

8. See, e.g., *Catechism of the Catholic Church*, nos. 115–17; Benedict XVI, *Verbum Domini*, nos. 37–41; Waldstein, "*Analogia Verbi*," 129–32; and Benedict XVI, "Handing on the Faith," 32–35.

9. See, e.g., Martens, *Origen and Scripture*, 63–67; Martens, "Origen Against History," 635–56; Vogt, "Origen," 546–47; and Simonetti, *Lettera*, 73–98.

10. St. Augustine's *De doctrina christiana*. On St. Augustine's biblical hermeneutic in *De doctrina christiana*, see, e.g., Burns, "Delighting the Spirit," 182–94; and Weismann, "Principios," 61–73.

11. On Tyconius's *Liber Regularum* see, e.g., Bright, *Book of Rules*. On St. Augustine's use of Tyconius, see, e.g., Tilley, "Understanding Augustine," 405–8; Dulaey, "La sixième Règle," 83–103; and Gaeta, "Le *Regole*," 109–18.

was understood typologically, as part of the divine condescension.[12] As Scott Hahn explains:

> History unfolds, like all creation, according to a single divine plan. Augustine explained that ordinary human writers use words to signify things; but God uses even created *things* to signify things. So not only are the *words* of scripture signs of things that happened in history, but the *very events of sacred history* were fashioned by God as material signs—temporal events and realities that disclose eternal truths.[13]

Michael Fishbane observes, typology is "a disclosure of the plenitude and mysterious workings of divine activity in history."[14] Tropological exegesis applies the Scriptural message to our lives. These moral interpretations lead Scripture's reader or auditor to sanctity, to better their lives on their heavenly pilgrimage. Finally, anagogical interpretation lifts our mind to contemplate the heavenly realities we hope to contemplate for eternity.

## Medieval Diversity and Synthesis

The exegetical trends of the earlier Christian centuries continued in the medieval period. Pope St. Gregory the Great's *Moralia in Iob* became one of the most influential medieval works pertaining to biblical interpretation.[15] His primarily tropological reading of the Book of Job represents an important example of the spiritual sense of Scripture in the medieval period. In the twelfth century, the *Glossa Ordinaria* was produced, amassing together the interpretations of the church fathers alongside the biblical text to aid the work of interpretation. This was one of the major projects of the twelfth century, which saw a number of important developments in the history of medieval biblical exegesis.

---

12. On Jewish and Christian notions of the divine condescension or accommodation, see, e.g., Benin, *Footprints of God*. Francis Martin, among others, recognizes that typological exegesis, and the spiritual sense more generally, are grounded more in a particular theological understanding of history than in any literary hermeneutical theories on how to read and interpret texts. See, e.g., Martin, "Election," 865–71.

13. Hahn, *Letter and Spirit*, 23.

14. Fishbane, *Biblical Interpretation*, 352.

15. On Pope St. Gregory the Great's *Moralia in Iob*, see, e.g., Greschat, *Die Moralia in Job*; Wilken, "Interpreting Job Allegorically," 213–26; Catry, *Paroles de Dieu*, 38–58; and Penco, "La dottrina," 170–201.

The twelfth century proved momentous in the history of medieval theology and biblical interpretation, not only because of the *Gloss*, but for a number of other highly influential works which emerged then. Also in the twelfth century Peter Comestor's *Historia scholastica* and Peter Lombard's *Libri quattuor sententiarum*, his famous *Sentences*, were immensely influential.[16] Linking Comestor's *History*, Lombard's *Sentences*, and Gratian's *Decretum* (also in the twelfth century), David Luscombe remarks that they "were the most enduring manuals produced in the Middle Ages for teaching and learning biblical history, theology, and canon law."[17] In fact, the great Medievalist Stephen Brown comments that:

> The 1253 university statutes at Oxford, confirming actually existing practice, indicate that a student could attain his degree in theology . . . by one of three routes: (1) he could study the Bible, a practice that usually entailed writing commentaries, using earlier exegetical efforts, on at least one book of the Old Testament and one book of the New Testament; (2) he could present a commentary on Peter Comestor's *Scholastic History* . . . ; (3) he could comment on the *Sentences* of Peter Lombard . . . . The same options in practice were available even earlier in Paris . . . .[18]

Regarding Comestor's *Historia scholatica*, Christopher Ocker and Kevin Madigan suggest that it was "perhaps the most broadly influential work of biblical scholarship in late medieval Europe."[19]

A real exegetical diversity existed, but the liturgical context remained important. There were varying emphases, but we might say that a sort of synthesis emerged with the Victorines and later with the work of St. Thomas Aquinas.[20] With St. Thomas Aquinas we have an example of biblical

---

16. The influence of Lombard and his *Sentences* is well known. On Comestor, his work, and its reception, see, e.g., Clark, *Making of the Historia Scholastica*; Luscombe, "Place of Peter Comestor," 27–45; Dahan, "Les exégèses," 49–87; Clark, "Le cours," 243–66; Delmas, "Le réception," 267–87; Lobrichon, "Le Mangeur," 289–312; Clark, "Commentaries of Stephen Langton," 373–93; Clark, "Commentaries on Peter Comestor's *Historia scholastica*," 301–446; and Morey, "Peter Comestor," 6–35. On the dual importance of both Lombard and Comestor see, e.g., Clark, "Peter Comestor," 85–142.

17. Luscombe, "Peter Comestor," 137.

18. Brown, "Intellectual Context," 193–94.

19. Ocker and Madigan, "After Beryl Smalley," 95.

20. On the biblical exegesis of the Victorines like Hugh of St. Victor, Richard of St. Victor, Andrew of St. Victor, and those influenced by them like Stephen Langton, see, e.g., all of the essays in Bataillon et al., *Étienne Langton*, especially Berndt, "Étienne Langton," 125–63, Dahan, "Les commentaires," 201–39, Bellamah, "Lament of a Preacher,"

exegesis that would become paradigmatic in the Catholic Church. This is evidenced not only by the Council of Trent's use of St. Thomas's form of biblical interpretation, but also in the Thomistic understanding of biblical interpretation evidenced in the *Catechism of the Catholic Church*'s discussion of the interpretation of Sacred Scripture, which in turn affects the presentation of that same topic in Pope Benedict XVI's *Verbum Domini*.[21] St. Thomas latched onto the earlier *quadruplex sensus* and systematized it. In many of his own works, e.g., his commentaries on Job and on Isaiah, St. Thomas focuses exclusively on the *sensus literalis*.

## Hermeneutics Forged in the Battles of Modernity

### Early Modern Theo-Political Exegesis

At the end of the medieval period, in the Renaissance or early modern period, just prior to the time we have come to know as the Reformation, the retrieval of classical sources took on an explicit importance. Of particular importance is the famous move *ad fontes*, with an emphasis on original languages, textual criticism, and a general honing of Philological tools and

---

327–52, and Nielsen, "Langton's Questions," 623–44; Taylor Coolman, *Theology of Hugh of St. Victor*, 124–37; all of the essays in Berndt, *Bibel und Exegese*, especially Iversen, "Lex est umbra," 83–103, van 't Spijker, "Ad commovendos," 215–34, Stammberger, "Die Exegese," 235–57, Mégier, "Zur Artikulation," 335–61, Nakamura, "Schriftauslegung," 363–89, Berndt, "Exegese des Alten Testaments," 423–41, Thomson, "English Reception," 527–37, and Egger, "Viktorinische Exegese," 539–55; van 't Spijker, "Literal and the Spiritual," 225–48; Knoch, "Exegese und Dogmatik," 1–11; Taylor Coolman, "*Pulchrum Esse*," 175–200; Ocker, *Biblical Poetics*, 31–48; Berndt, "School of St. Victor," 467–95; and Smalley, *Study of the Bible*, 83–195.

21. On St. Thomas's biblical interpretation, see, e.g., all of the essays in Roszak and Vijgen, *Reading Sacred Scripture*, especially Dahan, "Thomas Aquinas," 45–70, Reinhardt, "Thomas Aquinas," 71–90, Holmes, "Participation," 91–114, Narváez, "Intention," 141–70, Bellamah, "Interpretation," 229–56, Levering, "Old Testament," 349–74, Ramage, "In the Beginning," 481–506, Keating, "Exegesis," 507–30, and Baglow, "Principle(s)," 531–54; all of the essays in Levering and Dauphinais, *Reading Romans*, especially Boyle, "On the Relation," 75–82, Taylor Coolman, "Romans 9–11," 101–12, Hahn and Kincaid, "Multiple Literal Sense," 163–82, Healy, "Aquinas's Use," 183–95, Levering, "Aquinas on Romans 8," 196–215, Waldstein, "Trinitarian," 274–87, and Wilken, "Origen," 288–301; all of the essays in Dauphinais and Levering, *Reading John*, especially Boyle, "Authorial Intention," 3–8, Brown, "Theological Role," 9–22, Emery, "Biblical Exegesis," 23–61, Levering, "Does the Paschal Mystery," 78–91, and Waldstein, "Analogy," 92–114; Baglow, "Rediscovering," 137–46; Baglow, "Sacred Scripture," 1–26; Boyle, "Theological Character," 276–83; Baglow, *"Modus et forma"*; and Boyle, "Thomas Aquinas," 92–104.

skills.[22] Many of these trends continued in the Reformation, including the emphasis on original languages.[23] When discussing Reformation exegesis, the Protestant phrase *sola Scriptura* quickly comes to mind, with priority on the texts themselves. Here it is helpful to remember Jaroslav Pelikan's observation in his important volume on the history of the development of doctrine in the Reformation era, namely that, "Despite their protestations of 'sola Scriptura,' the Reformers showed that the 'Scriptura' has never been 'sola.'"[24] Each community which emerged through the Reformation, and, indeed, even the leading figures themselves, set up a tradition of interpretation (as well as of practice, devotion, etc.), which conditioned the reception of Scripture, its role in Christian life, and how it was to be read.

Moreover, these traditions were not absent politics. Travis Frampton reminds us that:

> the Reformation was, at heart, politically engendered. What were the *protests* of Magisterial Reformers, if not political? Did Catholicism or Protestantism represent the *kingdom* of God on earth—and if the latter, which of its divergent forms would be representative? What part were churches of the Reformation to have in the numerous, religiously disparate European states?[25]

Only recently has politics become intellectually disentangled from "religion"—newly redefined as a generic category of private beliefs and/or voluntary communal practices—and even now, this only goes for the secularized west.[26]

---

22. On the many exegetical developments during this time period, see, e.g., all of the pertinent essays in Sæbø, *Hebrew Bible/Old Testament II*, especially Sæbø, "From the Renaissance," 21–45, Rasmussen, "Bridging the Middle Ages," 76–93, Catto, "Philosophical Context," 106–22, Vanderjagt, "*Ad fontes*," 154–89, Rummel, "Textual and Hermeneutical Work," 215–30, and Mesguich, "Early Christian," 254–75; Reventlow, *Epochen der Bibelauslegung III*; and Shuger, *Renaissance Bible*, 1–53.

23. See, e.g., the helpful chapters pertaining to late medieval/early modern to Reformation periods in Hahn and Wiker, *Politicizing the Bible*, 17–59 on Marsilius of Padua and William of Ockham, 61–115 on John Wycliffe, 117–46 on Machiavelli, 147–219 on Martin Luther, and 221–55 on the English Reformation.

24. Pelikan, *Reformation of Church and Dogma*, vii.

25. Frampton, *Spinoza and the Rise of Historical Criticism*, 13.

26. We see the complexity of the pre-modern situation in Jones, *Before Church and State*; Cavanaugh, *Myth of Religious Violence*, 123–80; and Cavanaugh, "Fire Strong Enough," 397–420. On the changing understanding of "religion" from antiquity to the modern period see, e.g., Morrow, "Religion and the Secular State," 25–45; Cavanaugh, *Myth of Religious Violence*, 57–122; Feil, *Religio 1*; Feil, *Religio 2*; Feil, *Religio 3*; Feil,

These political aspects became clearer in the seventeenth century exegetical endeavors, especially the biblical work of interpreters like Isaac La Peyrère, Thomas Hobbes, Baruch Spinoza, and Fr. Richard Simon.[27] Increasingly, the work of these figures has been identified as laying the foundations of modern historical biblical criticism. Although Hobbes and Spinoza are more known for their work in early modern political philosophy, their two most famous political works—Hobbes's *Leviathan* and Spinoza's *Tractatus theologico-politicus*—are as much about the Bible, including biblical interpretation and the narrative of salvation history contained therein, as politics; their politics drove their exegesis, which in tautological turn ostensibly supported their politics. Often Fr. Simon is put forward as a more faithful alternative to Spinoza, and yet, in many ways, he subtly furthered Spinoza's skeptical exegetical program.[28]

In 1993, Jon Levenson wrote,

> It is no coincidence that the early pioneers of biblical criticism—Hobbes, Spinoza, Richard Simon—lived in the aftermath of the Thirty Years' War. Through the famous formula *cuius regio, eius religio* (whoever's realm, his religion), the Treaty of Westphalia (1648), which ended that war, established the superiority of the state over religion in fact and provided a hospitable climate for a theory to the same effect.[29]

William Cavanaugh's 1995 article, "'A Fire Strong Enough to Consume the House': The Wars of Religion and the Rise of the State," and his more recent 2009 monograph, *The Myth of Religious Violence: Secular Ideology and the Roots of Modern Conflict*, have done important work bringing attention to the ways in which the so-called seventeenth century "wars of religion"

---

*Religio* 4; Asad, *Formations of the Secular*, 181–201; Asad, *Genealogies of Religion*, 37–45; and Feil, "From the Classical," 31–43.

27. On the seventeenth-century biblical hermeneutics of La Peyrère, Hobbes, Spinoza, and Simon, see, e.g., Morrow, *Pretensions*, 35–54; Morrow, *Theology, Politics, and Exegesis*, 16–41; Morrow, *Three Skeptics*, 54–149; Hahn and Wiker, *Politicizing the Bible*, 285–423; Pietsch, *Isaac La Peyrère*; Bernier, *La critique du Pentateuque*; Gibert, *L'invention critique*; Müller, *Richard Simon*; Malcolm, *Aspects of Hobbes*, 383–431; Popkin, "Millenarianism and Nationalism," 74–84; Preus, *Spinoza and the Irrelevance*; Woodbridge, "Richard Simon," 193–206; Mirri, *Richard Simon*; and Zac, *Spinoza*.

28. On this see especially Morrow, *Theology, Politics, and Exegesis*, 36–41; Hahn and Wiker, *Politicizing the Bible*, 395–423; Barthélemy, *Studies in the Text*, 60–62; Mirri, *Richard Simon*, 29–84; and Auvray, "Richard Simon," 201–14.

29. Levenson, *Hebrew Bible*, 117.

affected the theological landscape.[30] Even more so, this affected the early formation of the methods of historical biblical criticism, especially as laid out in the seventh chapter of Spinoza's *Tractatus theologico-politicus*.[31] This is significant and is part of what William Portier calls a "pattern of subordination." As Portier elaborates, "The Peace of Westphalia of 1648 fixed the political map of Europe in a configuration of confessional states. With the multiplicity of sovereignties came the tendency to established churches or state religions which viewed the church as a department of state and bishops as its functionaries."[32]

Andrew Jones's important volume, *Before Church and State: A Study of Social Order in the Sacramental Kingdom of St. Louis IX*, more than any other work, has shown how inextricably bound together were notions, motives, and actions, we have learned to separate as sacred and secular.[33] In medieval Christendom, temporal rulers often had real, albeit imperfect, and sometimes perfidious, concern for things sacred. At the same time, members of the ecclesiastical hierarchy and of religious orders were frequently interested in temporal matters, and not always because of their own sinfulness, but rather because they saw the world as an important location where the Kingdom of God is made present in the here and now. Moreover, they saw themselves as in part stewards of God pertaining to temporal concerns, just as kings and princes saw themselves as having a sacred duty, not only to govern rightly, but also to enforce Church laws and lead others to live virtue.

What took place during the Reformation and beyond was not simply about matters of private belief, specific doctrines, etc., but rather concerned the organization of the temporal order itself. In such a context, exegesis often served the court, German, papal, or other. William of Ockham evidences the exegesis of a biblical *peritus*, a specialist, as superior to the Magisterium.[34] This trend continued in the Reformation, with its *de facto* focus

---

30. Cavanaugh, *Myth of Religious Violence*, 3-13, 15-56, and 123-230; and Cavanaugh, "Fire Strong Enough," 397-420.

31. For the political context of conflicts like the Thirty Years' War's effect on nascent modern biblical criticism see especially Morrow, *Three Skeptics*; and Hahn and Wiker, *Politicizing the Bible*, 259-75, 280-86, 289-92, 296, 300, 302, 310-12, 336-38, 362-64, 378-93, 400-403, and 425-541. The best critical edition of the Latin text of Spinoza's *Tractatus theologico-politicus* is Spinoza, *Œuvres III*.

32. Portier, "Church Unity," 32.

33. Jones, *Before Church and State*.

34. Ockham uses this language in a number of important places, e.g., when he speaks

on the individual interpreter over and against the Magisterium. By mid-seventeenth century, the more skeptical criticisms of La Peyrère, Hobbes, and Spinoza, took the focus on the individual further, using reason as the ostensible guide instead of faith—an anemic reason severed from and opposed to faith.[35] The great biblical scholar Moshe Goshen-Gottstein identified this time period, and these figures, as a pivotal turning point in this history of biblical scholarship.[36] These intellectuals received the skeptical traditions of the past and progressively erected a method that would serve as the foundation for modern historical biblical criticism of the future.

As we shall see, not all of this is bad, but neither is it neutral and absent ambiguity. La Peyrère and Hobbes took prior skeptical traditions of doubting the origin, authorship, and composition of various biblical books, not because of some reasoned hermeneutical approach, but because it aided and abetted their political positions. Politics and biblical interpretation had a long history.[37] For Spinoza political concerns were of the utmost importance in his *Tractatus theologico-politicus*, which, as the title makes clear, was his theological *political* tractate. Yet he relied upon some of the same more skeptical, and even polemical, traditions of the past, likely including those stemming from medieval Muslim biblical criticism.[38] Spinoza, however, is the individual arguably most responsible for creating a rigorous historical method for engaging in modern biblical criticism. Simon took Spinoza further, systematizing the detection of textual and related difficulties in the biblical writings. These laid the foundation upon which the next two

---

of the specialists or experts in the Scriptures (*periti in scripturis*) in William of Ockham, *Dialogus*, part 3, tract 1, book 3, ch. 9.

35. All of these cases are a bit more complex, especially that of Hobbes, who continued to subordinate the individual's interpretation to that of a higher authority, namely, the sovereign, or any experts (however expert or inexpert they be) the sovereign appointed. See, e.g., his comments in *Leviathan*, III.38 and III.42. Hobbes maintained the centrality of "reason," however, and he measured reason by geometry, which he saw as the ultimate expression of reason. See, e.g., Hobbes, *Leviathan*, I.4. The most thorough critical edition of *Leviathan*, which includes Hobbes's own Latin translation, is the three-volume, Malcolm, *Thomas Hobbes*.

36. Goshen-Gottstein, "Textual Criticism," 376.

37. On the history of the intimacy of politics and biblical exegesis, particularly of the Old Testament and particularly in the early modern period, see, e.g., Nelson, *Hebrew Republic* and all of the essays in Schochet et al., *Political Hebraism*, especially Neuman, "Political Hebraism," 57–71; Perreau-Saussine, "Why Draw a Politics," 90–106; Lorberbaum, "Spinoza's Theological–Political," 167–90; and Remer, "After Machiavelli," 207–30.

38. See, e.g., Lazarus-Yafeh, *Intertwined Worlds*; Freedman, "Father of Modern Biblical Scholarship," 31–38; and Arnaldez, "Spinoza et la pensée arabe," 151–74.

centuries would build. In their groundbreaking work, *Politicizing the Bible*, Scott Hahn and Benjamin Wiker brought needed attention to the ways in which the exegesis of figures from Marsilius of Padua through John Toland, from the fourteenth through seventeenth centuries, laid the groundwork for what would emerge in the Enlightenment and beyond.[39]

## Enlightenment Criticism

The eighteenth and nineteenth centuries continued these trends, but in general with less overtly skeptical motivations.[40] In some instances, as with Jean Astruc, they attempted to counter the skeptical exegesis of the past. Astruc attempted to defend the Mosaic authorship of the Pentateuch by countering the attempts of Spinoza et al. to place the Pentateuch in the post-exilic period. He pointed to the Samaritan Pentateuch, which is virtually identical, containing the same passages source critics usually attribute to different documentary sources.[41] He also came up with a method to detect, mainly in Genesis, earlier sources upon which Moses may have relied. As Aulikki Nahkola explains, "It is in Astruc's work that we see the first systematic, if embryonic, presentation of the procedures for determining

39. See Hahn and Wiker, *Politicizing the Bible*; Morrow, *Pretensions*, 10–34 and 55–74; and Morrow, *Theology, Politics, and Exegesis*, 1–15.

40. For the broader political contexts to the work of these and other exegetes working in the eighteenth and nineteenth centuries, see especially Hahn and Morrow, *Modern Biblical Criticism*; Kurtz, "Way of War," 1–19; Hahn and Wiker, *Politicizing the Bible*, 546–65; Rohls, "Historical," 31–63; Legaspi, *Death of Scripture*; Sheehan, *Enlightenment Bible*; Pasto, "When the End," 157–202; Farmer, "State *Interesse*," 15–49; Simon, "History As a Case-Study," 168–96; Levenson, *Hebrew Bible*, 106–26; and Momigliano, "Religious History," 49–64. For the political context in nineteenth-century Germany that conditioned the reception of modern historical biblical criticism there, see especially Gross, *War Against Catholicism*.

41. This was argued more forcefully later in Munro, *Samaritan Pentateuch*. Wilhelm Martin Leberecht de Wette cleared the way for renewed late-dating of the Pentateuch to the post-exilic period, by positing uninterrupted relations between northern and southern Israel, thus accounting for the Samaritan appropriation of alleged southern as well as northern documentary sources, when they might be expected only to have northern pre-exilic sources, now usually seen as the Elohist, at least among continental European source critical scholars. See de Wette, *Beiträge*, 216. Johann Severin Vater had mentioned this prior to de Wette, but it was de Wette who re-narrated the history such that it cleared the way for the later arguments of Julius Wellhausen et al. More recently, some scholars have been pushing segments of the Pentateuchal material increasingly earlier in the second millennium, e.g., Berman, "CTH 133," 25–46; Binder, "Joseph's Rewarding," 44–64; Hoffmeier, *Ancient Israel in Sinai*; and Bergsma, "Jubilee," 225–46.

compositional layers in biblical traditions, which became the hallmark of Old Testament criticism for nearly two centuries, as well as an articulation of the presuppositions on which these procedures are based."[42]

Michael Legaspi has shown, in his important work *The Death of Scripture and the Rise of Biblical Studies*, how eighteenth century biblical scholarship, particularly in the work of Johann David Michaelis at the University of Göttingen, was transformed into modern biblical studies shorn from any theological moorings.[43] The study of the Sacred Page no longer was seen as the heart of theology (or sacred theology's soul, in the later words of *Dei Verbum*), but rather became a secular cultural historical study.

Despite the many gains in understanding of the Bible's ancient Near Eastern environment, historical background, etc., that were made during the nineteenth century, one element, inherited from prior more skeptical generations, that was characteristic of modern biblical criticism in the nineteenth century, was the Bible's de-Judaizing and de-Catholicizing. The hypothetical history behind the Bible and its composition tended to be read through post-Enlightenment Protestant lenses, eschewing anything that sounded sacrificial, priestly, cultic, etc. Ritual, covenants, sacrifices, the Temple/tabernacle, etc., were assumed to be late post-exilic fabrications ordered to the *realpolitik* of the priestly class newly thrust into power after returning from Babylon.

Perhaps the greatest example of this is in the work of Julius Wellhausen who, for example, assumed tabernacles and accounts of their construction must be late. We now know that this is unnecessary from the perspective of comparative analysis, since the biblical accounts of the construction of the tabernacle and the temple have very early parallels throughout the ancient Near East, from Mesopotamia to Egypt.[44] Wellhausen, of course, despite having competence in and considering for a time a change of careers to Assyriology, operated in a near vacuum when it came to studying the Old Testament.[45] Increasingly, a New Kingdom Egyptian background is being supported for the Pentateuch and Joshua over and against Wellhausen et al.'s supposition of an exilic Babylonian

---

42. Nahkola, "*Memoires* of Moses," 204. See also Nahkola, *Double Narratives*.

43. See Legaspi, *Death of Scripture*; and Morrow, *Theology, Politics, and Exegesis*, 52–73.

44. See, e.g., Hoffmeier, *Ancient Israel*, 193–222; Hurowitz, *I Have Built You*; and Hurowitz, "Priestly Account," 21–30.

45. See Machinist, "Road Not Taken," 469–531.

or post-exilic context.[46] Although versions of Wellhausen's compositional theory (whose roots lie in the earlier eighteenth century works of Astruc and Johann Gottfried Eichhorn) remains the primary form in which Pentateuchal compositional theories are taught, there has been a long tradition of scholarly dissent from an immensely wide variety of backgrounds. Limiting ourselves to those who maintained an earlier primary unified compositional theory, we find the Orthodox Jewish Italian immigrant to Israel Umberto Cassuto, the secular American born Jewish scholar Cyrus Gordon, the German born Catholic Augustin Bea, and the Anglican Roger Norman Whybray.[47] Of the four, it was only the Catholic Bea who held to the more traditional Mosaic authorship of the Pentateuch. Cassuto followed Spinoza et al and held the Pentateuch's composition to date from Ezra. Whybray dated it to the sixth century.

### The Era of Rationalist and Modernist Biblical Criticism

Within the Catholic world of the nineteenth century leading up to the First Vatican Council, the controversies surrounding biblical interpretation and inspiration, which had been raging for several centuries, brought issues specifically concerning the nature of biblical inspiration to the fore and initiated a series of theological works concerning that topic.[48] Shortly after the First Vatican Council ended in 1870, issues concerning biblical interpretation in the Catholic world would come to a head in what would eventually be known as the Modernist Crisis.[49]

---

46. E.g., Walton, *Genesis 1*, who concedes that while an Egyptian context fits some aspects better, a Babylonian context fits others aspects better; Hoffmeier, *Ancient Israel*; Hoffmeier, *Israel in Egypt*; Hoffmeier, "Structure of Joshua 1–11," 165–79; Currid, "Examination," 18–40; Younger, *Ancient Conquest Accounts*; and Hoffmeier, "Some Thoughts," 39–49.

47. See Bea, *De Pentateucho*; Cassuto, *La Questione*; Gordon, "Higher Critics," 3–6; and Whybray, *Making of the Pentateuch*. Many others could be added, e.g., Kaufmann, "Probleme," 35–47; Kaufmann, *Religion of Israel*; Kitchen, "Pentateuchal Criticism"; Wenham, "Coherence," 336–48; Kikawada, "Double Creation," 43–45; Wiseman, *Ancient Records*; and Kikawada and Quinn, *Before Abraham Was*; Rendsburg, *Redaction of Genesis*.

48. E.g., see the discussion in Burtchaell, *Catholic Theories*, especially 8–87.

49. On the history of Modernism and the Modernist Crisis, see especially Morrow, *Alfred Loisy*, 11–30; Portier, *Divided Friends*; Izquierdo, "Cómo se ha entendido," 35–75; all of the essays in Jodock, *Catholicism Contending with Modernity*, especially by Jodock, "Introduction I," 1–19; Jodock, "Introduction II," 20–28; Lease, "Vatican Foreign Policy,"

The most significant Catholic exegete embroiled in this controversy was Alfred Loisy.[50] Loisy, as with a number of other biblical scholars and Catholic intellectuals of the late nineteenth and early twentieth century, was beginning to appropriate the very same methods of modern historical biblical criticism that had begun flourishing in Protestant universities, especially in Germany.[51] Loisy learned this suspect form of biblical criticism directly from Ernest Renan. It was while teaching Scripture at the Institut catholique in Paris that conflict intensified. In partial response to Loisy's work on exegesis, both inside and outside the classroom, Pope Leo XIII promulgated the first papal encyclical devoted to sacred Scripture, *Providentissimus Deus*, which was issued on November 18, 1893.[52] The very day Leo's encyclical was published, Loisy was removed from the Institut catholique's faculty. Eventually, the Holy Office of the Inquisition would censure propositions it saw as Modernist, and Pope St. Pius X would famously condemn Modernism as the "synthesis of all heresies," in his 1907 papal encyclical *Pascendi Dominici Gregis*. Both of these documents had Loisy in mind, as the archival work on their (particularly *Lamentabili Sane Exitu*'s) drafting has made clear, and Loisy was excommunicated the following year.[53]

Like previous situations where biblical interpretation and politics were entangled, the anti-Modernist policies then in place had numerous political factors, as scholars have pointed out before.[54] William Portier noted the Church's anti-Modernism was part of a much longer "chronicle

---

31–55; Misner, "Catholic Anti-Modernism," 56–87; Daly, "Theological and Philosophical," 88–112; Tavard, "Blondel's *Action*," 142–68; Hill, "Politics of Loisy's," 169–90; and Talar, "Innovation and Biblical Interpretation," 191–211; Talar, *(Re)reading*; Colin, *L'audace*; O'Connell, *Critics on Trial*; García de Haro, *Historia teológica*; and Poulat, *Histoire*.

50. On Loisy's exegesis see, e.g., Morrow, *Alfred Loisy*; Morrow, "Thy Kingdom Come," 3–13; Morrow, "Études Bibliques," 12–32; Talar, "Between Science and Myth," 27–41; Zumstein, "Alfred Loisy," 43–58; Amsler, "Les sources," 93–105; Hill, *Politics of Modernism*, 59–89; Talar, "Innovation and Biblical Interpretation," 191–211; and Théobald, "L'exégèse catholique," 391–92, 396–403, 418–21, 425, and 432–38.

51. On this history in its broader context, regarding especially the issue of biblical inspiration, see, e.g., Morrow, *Pretensions*, 75–91.

52. See, e.g., Hill, "Leo XIII," 40, 47, 51, 53, and 56; and O'Connell, *Critics on Trial*, 133 and 135.

53. See, e.g., Arnold, "Roman Magisterium," 159–69; Arnold and Losito, *Lamentabili sane exitu*; Arnold and Losito, *La censure*; and Arnold, "Lamentabili sane exitu," 24–51.

54. See, e.g., Portier, *Divided Friends*, 7–12 and 38–57; and Gary Lease's (less sympathetic-to-the-Magisterium) account in his essay, "Vatican Foreign Policy," 31–55.

of Catholicism's protracted and ambivalent struggle with liberal secular states...."[55] Anti-Modernists were concerned with more than just how the Bible was interpreted: "Intransigent Catholic opponents of the Kingdom of Italy viewed the incursion of Loisy and Tyrrell into Italy as the intellectual arm of a broader secularizing movement in politics and culture."[56] There was a political side as well to those criticized as Modernist, and this is perhaps no clearer than with Loisy himself, who supported the French secular state over and against Pius X, and also hope to be selected as bishop of Monaco, when the skeptic Prince Albert of Monaco named him as one of three candidates.[57]

Contra O'Connell's comment that in the US the controversy over Modernism "caused hardly more than a ripple," Portier's extensive work in this regard has proved a helpful corrective.[58] O'Connell follows the conventional scholarly wisdom that "Modernism" was basically consigned to Italy and France, whereas Portier's work on the American dimension to the Modernist controversy complicates this narrative. The aftermath of the Modernist crisis was far-reaching in its debilitating effects. It is difficult for many of us who grew up in, or entered, the Catholic world after Vatican II to realize the full pathos of the Modernist conflict. Portier explains how, "the modernist crisis ripped through Catholic intellectual life like a tragic storm. But its havoc cut to a level deeper than the merely intellectual. *Pascendi* forced people to take sides. Agonized personal decisions put colleagues at odds and set friend against friend. Censured priests questioned fellow clergy or pious laymen who escaped censure."[59]

The priest Umberto Benigni erected an informal institute, the Sodalitium Pianum, which functioned as a clandestine organization bent on eradicating modernism by making public anonymous denouncements, stealing and leaking documents, as well as other unsavory methods.[60] For-

---

55. Portier, *Divided Friends*, 14.

56. Portier, *Divided Friends*, 44.

57. See, e.g., Hill, "Loisy's *L'Évangile*," 88–89; Hill, "Loisy's 'Mystical Faith,'" 73–94; Hill, *Politics of Modernism*, 154–59, 164–72, and 175–78; Hill, "Politics of Loisy's," 169–90; Hill, "French Politics," 521–36; O'Connell, *Critics on Trial*, 236–51; and O'Connell, "Bishopric of Monaco," 26–51.

58. See O'Connell, *Critics on Trial*, 355 for his comment. Regarding Portier's work, see especially Portier, *Divided Friends*.

59. Portier, *Divided Friends*, 4.

60. On Begnini and the Sodalitium Pianum, see, e.g., Portier, *Divided Friends*, 42–45; O'Connell, *Critics on Trial*, 361–65; and Poulat, *Intégrisme*.

mally suppressed by Pope Benedict XV, Benigni's organization wreaked havoc on the lives of priests. As O'Connell explains, "the sodality provided an opportunity for all those who cared to label as Modernists their bishops, parish priests, professors, local editors, or indeed anyone with whom they disagreed. No one was safe .... The files of the sodality eventually bulged with the names of such alleged malefactors, whose guilt was maintained simply by the fact that they had been denounced."[61] Joseph Ratzinger, future Pope Benedict XVI, wrote of the time, "The danger of a narrow-minded and petty surveillance is no figment of the imagination, as the history of the modernist controversy demonstrates."[62]

## The Path to Vatican II and a New Era in Catholic Exegesis

This history is important for many reasons, not least of which is understanding the currents that led to the Second Vatican Council, but also how that Council has been received. The three major currents of revivals and renewals—the patristic, the biblical, and the liturgical—that grew prior to the Council, must be understood within the context of the broader controversies of the time. These *ressourcement* movements grew amidst controversies over the role of the laity in the Church as well as the Church's combat of modernism and its juridical infrastructures that were set in place to prevent modernism from surviving and spreading. The modernist controversy conditioned Catholic appropriation of historical biblical criticism.

In the context of biblical interpretation, a number of Magisterial pronouncements emerged. In 1920 Pope Benedict XV released his papal encyclical on Scripture, *Spiritus Paraclitus*, which, among other things, emphasized the importance of traditional patristic and medieval exegesis. Prior to Vatican II, the Pontifical Biblical Commission, which was then a formal part of the Magisterium, issued a full thirty documents dealing with the Bible.[63] A number of the points affirmed in these documents have been seen as controversial, to say the least: the affirmation of Mosaic authorship of the Pentateuch, the unity of the Book of Isaiah, that the Apostle John wrote the Fourth Gospel, etc. In 1971, Pope St. Paul VI removed the Pontifical Biblical Commission from its place as an organ of the Magisterium, and transformed

---

61. O'Connell, *Critics on Trial*, 363.

62. Benedict XVI, *Nature and Mission of Theology*, 66.

63. On the history of the Pontifical Biblical Commission see, e.g., Vanhoye, "Passé et présent," 261–75.

its role to a merely advisory one. Henceforth, the Pontifical Biblical Commission's documents have had no authority over Catholics.

The status of the documents that the Commission issued prior to 1971 (the last of these was in 1964), when it was a formal part of the Magisterium, is contested. The decisions are clearly no longer enforced, as the Second Vatican Council and much that came in its wake, removed the juridical structures that had been in force from the anti-Modernist measures erected during St. Pius X's reign. The reason for the contested status of these earlier pre-1971 decisions originates from a number of different statements.

In 1907, along with the Holy Office's *Lamentabili* and Pius X's *Pascendi*, Pius X also issued his papal encyclical *Praestantia Scripturae*, in which he declared that the Pontifical Biblical Commission's decrees were perpetually binding. To date, no formal statement from the Magisterium has rescinded Pius's comments here. Since *Praestantia* focuses on doctrinal matters, however, the remaining question would be which portions of those statements constituted matters of doctrine. In 1955, Athanasius Miller, then secretary to the Pontifical Biblical Commission, and Arduin Kleinhans, then assistant secretary to the Pontifical Biblical Commission, published journal articles as private scholars, in which they mentioned that the Pontifical Biblical Commission's earlier statements were no longer in force.[64] Most Catholic theologians and Bible scholars, including Pope Emeritus Benedict XVI, now seem to take the position of Miller and Kleinhans.

Miller's and Kleinhans's interpretations were grounded in their understanding of Pope Pius XII's 1943 papal biblical encyclical *Divino Afflante Spiritu*, commemorating the fiftieth anniversary of Leo XIII's *Providentissimus Deus*. Too often, this encyclical has been read as a complete rupture from what came before, particularly contrasted with Leo's document. An example of this overly sharp dichotomy between the two encyclicals is the English translation of Augustin Bea's, *La Storicità Dei Vangeli*.[65] In the English edition, *Divino Afflante* is identified as the "magna carta" of

---

64. Miller, "Das neue biblische," 49–50; and Kleinhans, "De nova Enchiridii," 63–65.

65. Bea, *La Storicità*. This work is translated into English as Bea, *Study of the Synoptic Gospels*. Notice the differences in titles: Bea's original title reads: "*The Historicity of the Gospels*," whereas the English translation renders it: "*The Study of the Synoptic Gospels*." There are numerous differences between the English translation and the original Italian, and not merely differences one would expect in a translation. For example, portions are excised and a number of "glosses" are added without drawing attention to them. For more details on this, see Morrow, "Evangelical Catholics," 230n121. The differences noticed here are unique to the English edition. Nothing comparable can be found in the French translation (Bea, *L'historicité*), nor in the German translation (Bea, *Die Geschichtlichkeit*).

biblical studies, whereas in Bea's original Italian, Bea identifies both *Providentissimus* and *Divino* as the "magna carta" of biblical studies (*Providentissimus* is not mentioned a single time in the English translation).⁶⁶ Bea, as has been pointed out by many scholars, was one of the main drafters of *Divino*.⁶⁷ Nonetheless, *Divino*, while affirming the teachings of *Providentissimus*, did take a more positive approach to modern critical methods, while maintaining the predecessor's cautions—it should be remembered that Leo's *Providentissimus* was also more positive towards modern scholarly methods than is often remembered. These pre-*Dei Verbum* magisterial documents closed with the Commission's 1964 document, *Sancta Mater Ecclesia*, on the historical truth of the Gospels.

The years immediately leading up to the Council witnessed more controversy, even though the specter of modernism had apparently disappeared. Controversies, especially in Rome and in the United States, continued. Historian Gerald Fogarty recounts that from the year 1955 leading up all the way to the beginning of the Council in 1962 was a sort of Americanist controversy redivivus. In Rome, the tension was high over the removal and then reinstatement of two professors of the Pontifical Biblical Institute, Max Zerwick and Stanislaus Lyonnet.⁶⁸

## "The Council's Biblical Hermeneutic: A Directive to be Appropriated"⁶⁹

### The Second Vatican Council's Dogmatic Constitution on Divine Revelation: *Dei Verbum*

In *Verbum Domini*, reflecting on *Dei Verbum* paragraph 12, concerning Catholic biblical interpretation, Benedict XVI remarked:

> Against this background, one can better appreciate the great principles of interpretation proper to Catholic exegesis set forth by the Second Vatican Council.... On the one hand, the Council emphasizes the study of literary genres and historical context as basic

---

66. Compare Bea, *La Storicità*, 8–9 with Bea, *Study of the Synoptic*, 10–11.

67. Viviano, *Catholic Hermeneutics*, 15; Schelkens et al., *Aggiornamento?*, 108; O'Malley, *What Happened at Vatican II*, 116; Vereb, "Because He Was a German!", 123 and 208; and Fogarty, *American Catholic Biblical Scholarship*, 235.

68. See, e.g., Fogarty, *American Catholic Biblical Scholarship*, 254–55 and 258–323.

69. Benedict XVI, *Verbum Domini*, title of the subheading before no. 34.

elements for understanding the meaning intended by the sacred author. On the other hand, since Scripture must be interpreted in the same Spirit in which it was written, the Dogmatic Constitution indicates three fundamental criteria for an appreciation of the divine dimension of the Bible: 1) the text must be interpreted with attention to *the unity of the whole of Scripture*; nowadays this is called canonical exegesis; 2) account is to be taken of the *living Tradition of the whole Church*; and, finally, 3) respect must be shown for *the analogy of faith* . . . . The Synod Fathers rightly stated that the positive fruit yielded by the use of modern historical-critical research is undeniable. While today's academic exegesis, including that of Catholic scholars, is highly competent in the field of historical-critical methodology and its latest developments, it must be said that comparable attention needs to be paid to the theological dimension of the biblical texts, so that they can be more deeply understood in accordance with the three elements indicated by the Dogmatic Constitution *Dei Verbum*.[70]

Thus, Benedict's subtitle, indicating that *Dei Verbum*'s interpretive "directive" remains yet "to be appropriated."

Pope Benedict's comments on *Dei Verbum* here are quite helpful.[71] The first part of *Dei Verbum* 12 underscores the importance of careful attention to the mind of the biblical writers and the related areas of investigation, namely genre, history, and culture. Much of the historical methods of biblical interpretation necessarily investigate these areas. Whereas the second part of *Dei Verbum* 12 focuses on the issue of interpreting Scripture in light of the Spirit in which it was written, which *Dei Verbum* identifies with the Bible's content and unity, the living tradition, and the Magisterium. This second part, as Benedict mentioned, is the area in most need of growth. As we shall see, however, there has been some development here over these past fifty years.

---

70. Benedict XVI, *Verbum Domini*, no. 34.

71. For more on the background of *Dei Verbum* and its teaching on biblical interpretation, see, e.g., Kruggel, "Scripture, Tradition, and the Magisterium,"; Martin, "Revelation," 55–75; Farkasfalvy, "Inspiration," 77–100; Dulles, "Vatican II," 17–26; Bieringer, "Biblical Revelation," 25–58; Burigana, *La Bibbia*; Burigana, "La commissione," 27–61; McGovern, "Divine Origin," 98–179; Tábet, "Cristología," 299–324; Benedict XVI, "Dogmatic Constitution," 155–66; Grillmeier, "Divine Inspiration," 199–246; Benedict XVI, "Sacred Scripture," 262–72; Grelot, "Commentaire," 345–80; and Bea, *La Parola*.

## Catholic Biblical Exegesis Since the Council

By and large, Catholic scholarship since the Council has represented cutting edge appropriation and deft mastery of, as well as pioneering work in, historical biblical criticism. The history of the Pontifical Biblical Institute in Rome is just one significant example of this.[72] Indeed, on the occasion of the celebration of the Institute's one hundredth anniversary, the Orthodox Jewish biblical scholar James Kugel remarked on "the tremendous impact that the Institute has had on biblical studies worldwide . . . . its own faculty and students . . . together have helped shape the course of contemporary biblical scholarship. Indeed, it is hard to imagine what the history of this scholarship would look like without the work of [some of these scholars] . . . ."[73]

In the US, Catholic biblical scholars had an uphill battle to fight prior to the Council.[74] On the one hand, they were not permitted fully to engage with the same sort of historical (source, form, and eventually redaction) biblical criticism with which their Protestant compatriot biblical scholars were then engaging. On the other hand, Protestant scholars often held Catholic biblical scholarship in suspicion because of the earlier decrees coming from the Pontifical Biblical Commission and the Papal Magisterium. Thus, Catholic biblical scholars were often limited in terms of academic freedom, and their scholarship was not taken seriously by Protestant counterparts who viewed them as biased and limited. Yet many important Catholic scholars working prior to the Council deserve mention for the advances they made under such conditions. These would certainly include, among many others, Edward Arbez, the Sulpician biblical scholar who helped found, and serve as its first President, the Catholic Biblical Association of America.[75]

---

72. On the history of the Pontifical Biblical Institute in Rome see especially all of the essays in *Parole del Centenario*; and Gilbert, *Pontifical Biblical Institute*.

73. This quotation is taken from Kugel's actual presentation, which is available online as "One Hundred Years," on the Pontifical Biblical Institute website and also on the Society of Biblical Literature website. A published version, which differs slightly from the presentation copy, can be found as Kugel, "One Hundred Years," 79–87.

74. For a more detailed look at the history of biblical scholarship in the US, see, e.g., Morrow, "Fate of Catholic Biblical Interpretation," 41–59; and Fogarty, *American Catholic Biblical Scholarship*.

75. On Arbez, see, e.g., Morrow, "Fate of Catholic Biblical Interpretation," 50; Fogarty, *American Catholic Biblical Scholarship*, 180, 194–95, and 222–23; Kauffman, *Tradition and Transformation*, 207, 227–28, and 278; Hill, "Edward Philip Arbez," 72–75; and Hill, "Reverend Edward P. Arbez," 113–24.

The Catholic Biblical Association of America played an important role in shaping contemporary biblical scholarship. Much like the Pontifical Biblical Institute, the work of the CBA members has impacted the broader field of modern biblical scholarship, and especially English-speaking scholarship. Beyond the NAB, and now NABre, translation of the Bible, the CBA has been responsible for the *Catholic Biblical Quarterly* and both the *Jerome* and the *New Jerome Biblical Commentary*.[76]

John L. McKenzie was a key Catholic biblical scholar during the time leading up to the Council. McKenzie, and many of the other CBA Catholic scholars—including R.A.F. MacKenzie—pushed the envelope on engaging historical biblical criticism during this post-*Divino Afflante Spiritu* period leading up to Vatican II. Other notable Catholic biblical scholars willing to risk their careers to explore the benefits of historical criticism included Roland Murphy, William Moran, Barnabas Ahern, Mitchell Dahood, Louis Hartman, and Carroll Stuhlmueller. Each of these individuals, in their own way, contributed greatly to the burgeoning revolution in Catholic biblical scholarship that was seen in the wake of Vatican II, wherein Catholic biblical scholars, who had prior been viewed as working only within the confines of the early anti-Modernist Magisterial decrees, became, quite rapidly, at the forefront of modern biblical scholarship, now competitive with Protestant counterparts.

Two of the foremost giants of Catholic biblical scholarship who dominated the post-conciliar period, with roots prior to the Council, are Raymond Brown and Joseph Fitzmyer.[77] Reflecting on his days studying the New Testament as a doctoral student at Harvard University, under Rudolf Bultmann's leading disciple in the US, Helmut Koester, Michael Waldstein remarked, "... I invested much time in studying Brown's [1966] commentary [on John's Gospel]. Particularly in comparison with Bultmann, I found it to be a work of refreshing sanity and common sense in its use of the tools of historical criticism. I also found deep theological insight in it."[78] Both

---

76. On the work of the CBA see, e.g., Morrow, "Fate of Catholic Biblical Interpretation," 50–52; and Fogarty, *American Catholic Biblical Scholarship*, 222–80 and 344–48.

77. On Brown and Fitzmyer see, e.g., Morrow, "Fate of Catholic Biblical Interpretation," 54; Witherup, "Raymond E. Brown," 1–26; Donahue, "Joseph A. Fitzmyer," 63–83; Waldstein, "*Analogia Verbi*," 93–140; Dunn, "Raymond Brown," 531–51; Ossandón Widow, "Raymond E. Brown," 337–56; Witherup, "Incarnate Word," 238–52; Witherup and Barré, "Biography," 253–90; Duffy, "Ecclesial Hermeneutic," 37–56; and Fogarty, *American Catholic Biblical Scholarship*, 257–58.

78. Waldstein, "*Analogia Verbi*," 108.

Brown and Fitzmyer had followed the path, not then uncommon among Catholic biblical scholars, of studying doctoral work in biblical and ancient Near Eastern Studies, at non-Catholic research institutes—in this case, under William Foxwell Albright at Johns Hopkins University.[79]

Brown's work as a biblical scholar can be roughly divided into three periods: (1) the first period from 1955–1971; (2) the second period 1971–1985; (3) the third period 1985–1998. The first period is from 1955, after writing his dissertation in Theology on the *sensus plenior* of Scripture, and commencing doctoral work in Scripture, and ends with his faculty position at Union Theological Seminary.[80] This was the period that would see Brown's influential two volume Anchor Bible Commentary on the Gospel of John, which remains to this day, arguably one of the finest modern commentaries on that Gospel.[81] Fitzymer's work, like Brown's, was exemplary in its use of Jewish sources (like the Dead Sea Scrolls) as important for understanding the New Testament and its background. These two scholars have been recognized internationally, not only as two leading Catholic biblical scholars, but two leading biblical scholars, period.

## Catholic Engagements with Postmodern Hermeneutics

Although historical critical exegesis has remained a forte of Catholic biblical scholarship in the post-Vatican II period, already in the 1970s, Catholic biblical scholars were moving beyond historical criticism into other postmodern forms of exegesis, like feminist and liberationist exegesis, and more recently postcolonial. Numerous scholars could be mentioned here, and some examples include the work of Elizabeth Schüssler Fiorenza, Fernando Segovia, and Sandra Schneiders.[82] The inclusion of these more recent forms of exegesis in the Pontifical Biblical Commission's 1993 *The Interpretation*

---

79. On this trend, see, e.g. Morrow, "Fate of Catholic Biblical Interpretation," 54; and Morrow, "Evangelical Catholics," 194–200.

80. Brown, *Sensus Plenior*.

81. Brown, *Gospel According to John*. These volumes were initially published in the Anchor Bible Commentary series from Doubleday, before Yale University Press took over that series.

82. E.g., Schneiders, *Jesus Risen*; Segovia, "Postcolonial Biblical Criticism," 91–101; Segovia, "Postcolonial Criticism," 194–237; Segovia, "Liberation Hermeneutics," 106–32; Schneiders, *Written That You May Believe*; Schüssler Fiorenza, *Jesus and the Politics*; Schneiders, *Revelatory Text*; Schüssler Fiorenza, *Sharing Her Word*; Schüssler Fiorenza, *Bread Not Stone*; and Schüssler Fiorenza, *In Memory*.

*of the Bible in the Church*, shows how much broader Catholic exegesis has become in the post-conciliar period.[83]

### Catholic Biblical *Scholarship* or *Catholic* Biblical Scholarship?

In 1998, Catholic biblical scholar Luke Timothy Johnson famously asked the question, "What's Catholic about Catholic biblical scholarship?"[84] Thus began a published dialogue with Roland Murphy.[85] Reflecting on this conversation in a later version of his essay, Johnson writes:

> From the middle of the 19th century to the middle of the 20th century, the phrase "Roman Catholic biblical scholarship" would have been regarded by many as oxymoronic: it may have been Roman Catholic, but was it really scholarship? At the end of the 20th and the beginning of the 21st century, however, the phrase is equally oxymoronic: no one doubts the quality of the scholarship, but in what sense is it any longer "Catholic"?[86]

The specific *Catholicity* of Catholic biblical scholarship had become a major debate. Indeed, Carolyn Osiek took this as the starting point for her discussion in her presidential address, not as president of the Catholic Biblical Association, but rather as president of the Society of Biblical Literature. She entitled her address, "Catholic or catholic? Biblical Scholarship at the Center."[87]

The need for a uniquely *Catholic* biblical scholarship has been recognized outside of Catholic scholarly circles, and is noted, e.g., by Kugel in his address on the Pontifical Biblical Institute's centenary, as when he comments: "the one thing that has been relatively neglected (and I stress the *relatively*) at the PBI has been the charge given to it by its first founder [Pius

---

83. Pontifical Biblical Commission, *Interpretation of the Bible*, Part I, section E, subsection 1 deals with liberationist hermeneutics, and Part I, section E, subsection 2 pertains to feminist hermeneutics. On the PBC's *The Interpretation of the Bible in the Church* see especially Williamson, "Catholic Principles," 327–49; Williamson, "Place of History," 196–226; Williamson, *Catholic Principles*; and Fitzmyer, *Biblical Commission's Document*.

84. Johnson, "So What's Catholic," 12–16. He had already written of a "crisis" in Catholic biblical scholarship in Johnson, "Crisis," 18–21.

85. Murphy, "Historical Criticism," 4 and 29; Johnson, "Glass," 30; Johnson, "Imagining," 165–80; Johnson, "An Inexhaustible Text," 26–29; Murphy, "What Is Catholic," 112–19; and Johnson, "How Not to Read," 22–26.

86. Johnson, "What's Catholic," 4.

87. Osiek, "Catholic or catholic," 5–22.

X], the mission to somehow seek to think about modern biblical scholarship in the context of Church tradition and traditional exegesis....modern scholars ought to reevaluate the Church's so-called pre-modern approach to Scripture."[88] Kugel's comments concern specifically the biblical scholarship at the Pontifical Biblical Institute, but they can be applied to Catholic biblical scholarship since the Council more generally.

These comments pertain more broadly speaking to what Benedict XVI, as Joseph Ratzinger, already identified at the end of the 1980s as a "conflict of biblical interpretation."[89] Ratzinger famously identified the often unrecognized philosophies—some antithetical to Christianity—undergirding much of historical criticism as practiced by Catholics, Protestants, and Jews alike.[90] This has been noted by non-Catholic scholars as well, perhaps most notably the Jewish scholars James Kugel and Jon Levenson.[91] Ratzinger continued his cautions as Pope, most importantly in his post-synodal apostolic exhortation, *Verbum Domini*, where he wrote, under the subheading, "The danger of dualism and a secularized hermeneutic":

> The lack of a hermeneutic of faith with regard to Scripture entails more than a simple absence; in its place there inevitably enters another hermeneutic, a positivistic and *secularized hermeneutic* ultimately based on the conviction that the Divine does not intervene in human history.... A philosophical hermeneutic is thus imposed, one which denies the possibility that the Divine can enter and be present within history.[92]

## "A New Era in Theological Exegesis":[93]
### The Development of a Sacramental Hermeneutic

In his three volume work *Jesus of Nazareth*, Pope Benedict XVI provided a glimpse into his answer to the problem of a one-sided biblical

---

88. Kugel, "One Hundred Years."

89. Benedict XVI, "Biblical Interpretation in Conflict," 91–126. On this important essay see Waldstein, "Self-Critique," 732–47; and Hahn, *Covenant and Communion*, 25–40.

90. This has been pointed out by others independently, especially Waldstein, "*Analogia Verbi*," 93–140; Waldstein, "Foundations of Bultmann's Work," 115–45; and Blank, *Analyse und Kritik*.

91. Kugel, *How to Read*; and Levenson, *Hebrew Bible*.

92. Benedict XVI, *Verbum Domini*, no. 35.

93. Ouellet, *Relevance and Future*, 36.

hermeneutic within the world of Catholic biblical scholarship.[94] Neither strictly postmodern, nor exclusively concerned with the *letter* in historical critical fashion, Benedict avoided the Scylla of spiritual and pastoral interpretations severed from history and from the literal sense of Scripture, as well as the Charybdis of dead historical interpretations leaving the desiccated and dissected bones of Scripture in its analytical wake. As he tells us in the first volume:

> The main implication of this for my portrayal of Jesus is that I trust the Gospels. Of course, I take for granted everything that the Council and modern exegesis tell us about literary genres, about authorial intention, and about the fact that the Gospels were written in the context, and speak within the living milieu, of communities. I have tried, to the best of my ability, to incorporate all of this, and yet I wanted to try to portray the Jesus of the Gospels as the real, 'historical' Jesus in the strict sense of the word. I am convinced ... that this figure is much more logical and, historically speaking, much more intelligible than the reconstructions we have been presented with in the last decades.... the way I look at the figure of Jesus goes beyond what much contemporary exegesis ... has to say.[95]

It was in speaking of Ratzinger's volumes on Jesus that Cardinal Marc Ouellet spoke of the emergence of "a new era of theological exegesis" that he believed was beginning to dawn.[96]

A younger generation of Catholic biblical scholars, many of whom are converts from Protestant Christianity, can be found turning to this Ratzingerarian mode of exegesis, which attempts to combine the best of traditional patristic and medieval exegesis and the best insights of modern historical biblical interpretation; this was the sort of exegesis with which we began this chapter. What we might speak of as a "new" sacramental hermeneutic is developing, where these biblical scholars attempt to read the Scriptures with the best tools of the critical scholarship in which they were trained, guided by the Church's Magisterium and rich exegetical traditions, all the while keeping their eyes on the ultimate purpose of biblical interpretation—namely our sanctification and divinization.[97] The liturgi-

---

94. Benedict XVI, *Jesus of Nazareth I*; Benedict XVI, *Jesus of Nazareth II*; and Benedict XVI, *Jesus of Nazareth III*.

95. Benedict XVI, *Jesus of Nazareth I*, xxi–xxiii.

96. Ouellet, *Relevance and Future*, 36.

97. On this important development in contemporary Catholic biblical scholarship,

cal and sacramental context (and often content) of Scripture plays a key role within these newer developments. In recent years, the St. Paul Center for Biblical Theology, which Scott Hahn founded and for which I serve as a senior fellow, has gathered together a host of these scholars with the purpose of equipping priests to become biblically fluent and the Catholic laity to be biblically literate.[98] The number of major established scholars published in the journal *Letter & Spirit*, as well as the contributions from an ever-increasing number of junior scholars trained in biblical interpretation at prestigious institutions is a testament to the trend toward reuniting the historical critical method with spiritual and pastoral concerns, while also reaching beyond the academy for the benefit of the laity in popularized versions of academic work.

The Second Vatican Council's discussion of biblical interpretation in paragraph 12 of *Dei Verbum* which provides a basic blueprint for authentically Catholic biblical exegesis, is most helpfully situated within the broader historical context of the question of biblical interpretation within the Catholic Church. When this is done, we can see how *Dei Verbum* provides a rich synthesis of the Church's long tradition of interpreting Scripture. The last fifty years since Vatican II have seen Catholic biblical scholars come into their own as first-rate Bible scholars, recognized as such by their non-Catholic peers across the globe. Catholic biblical scholarship has excelled at attempting to uncover the historical, cultural, political, literary, and philological context, emphasized in the first part of *Dei Verbum* 12. Although in some ways, the second part of *Dei Verbum* 12 remains, "a directive to be appropriated," there is work being done in this regard. I intend the remainder of this volume to be one small contribution to this broader and important project. I believe the future is bright for Catholic biblical scholarship as it seeks to unite letter and spirit in biblical interpretation, as *Dei Verbum* envisioned. The diversity of skills and methods among Catholic biblical scholars is an asset to the field of Catholic biblical scholarship, as well as to biblical scholarship more generally. Now that we have covered the necessary historical background to the changes in theological exegesis within the Catholic world over the past two millennia, we are prepared for the exegetical work that comes in the remainder of this book.

---

focusing on the work of Benedict XVI and Scott Hahn, see Morrow, "Studies in Scripture," 36–56.

98. See the St. Paul Center for Biblical Theology website: https://stpaulcenter.com/.

# 2

# Priestly Humanity in the Temple of Creation

## A Liturgical Reading of Genesis 1–3

IN THE LAST CHAPTER, we surveyed the long history of biblical interpretation in the Catholic world, focusing on the past roughly a century of exegesis. In what remains of this volume, I will include examples of theological exegesis in the spirit of the Second Vatican Council's guidelines and in the spirit of what I take Marc Ouellet's comments about "a new era in theological exegesis."[1] In this chapter, I will focus on the clues found in the literal sense of the text of Gen 1–3. When early Christian, and especially Jewish, exegetes read Gen 1–3, often highly speculative allegorical interpretations followed. This is especially the case with Jewish Midrashic literature. Adam was sometimes envisioned as a priest offering incense sacrifices in the Garden of Eden. Yet I would argue that such Midrashic exegesis has roots in the various clues that can be pieced together from the literal sense of the text itself.

In short, I will argue that Gen 1–3, in its account of creation and fall event, presents the world as a temple, a place of worship, and humanity is depicted using priestly (among other, e.g., royal) imagery. Thus, in Gen 1–3 the cosmos emerges as one large temple, and the Garden of Eden can then be understood as a sort of Holy of Holies, and the human person as made for worship, for liturgy. The very content and structure of Gen 1–3 is in a very real sense liturgical, with the seventh day emphasized as creation's high point.[2]

---

1. Ouellet, *Relevance and Future*, 36.
2. See Weinfeld, "Sabbath, Temple and the Enthronement," 501–12; and Wenham,

## Overview: The Liturgical *Sitz im Leben* of Gen 1-3

For many of our contemporary readers, unfamiliar with the history of Jewish and Christian interpretive traditions concerning Gen 1-3, the notion of God creating the world as a temple is far from obvious. This is perhaps especially the case because in our cultural context, we are encouraged to look to Genesis in light of contemporary debates concerning science, as in controversies over evolution, creationism, intelligent design, etc., as if the main point of Gen 1 was to answer the question, "How?", as in, "How did God create the world?" The "what?" and the "why?" of creation were often more important to ancient interpreters. What did God create? The world as temple and humanity as God's priestly stewards over creation. Why did God create? Worship. Or, in the famous words of the *Baltimore Catechism*, in response to the question, "Why did God make you?", comes the reply: "God made me to know Him, to love Him, and to serve Him in this world, and to be happy with Him forever in the next."[3] As we shall see below, worship and service are related, particularly in the Hebrew Old Testament.

In addition to this line from the *Baltimore Catechism*, it is worthwhile taking a look at what the contemporary *Catechism of the Catholic Church* has to say about the purpose of creation, with which the *Catechism* opens in its very first paragraph:

> God, infinitely perfect and blessed in himself, in a plan of sheer goodness freely created man to make him share in his own blessed life. For this reason, at every time and in every place, God draws close to man. He calls man to seek him, to know him, to love him with all his strength. He calls together all men, scattered and divided by sin, into the unity of his family, the Church. To accomplish this, when the fullness of time had come, God sent his Son as Redeemer and Saviour. In his Son and through him, he invites men to become, in the Holy Spirit, his adopted children and thus heirs of his blessed life.[4]

---

"Sanctuary Symbolism," 19-25. Wenham's essay has been reprinted in the easily accessible volume, Hess and Tsumura, *"I Studies Inscriptions,"* 399-404. Throughout this chapter, I will be citing Wenham's text from the original publication, but I will follow the later Eisenbrauns volume in transliterating the Hebrew according to the Society of Biblical Literature's guidelines, for stylistic purposes.

3. *Baltimore Catechism*, question 6.
4. *Catechism of the Catholic Church*, no. 1.

Thus, the very purpose for creation, as the *Catechism* explains, is that we "share" in God's "own blessed life." The sort of sacramental worship envisioned in the next few chapters, is the primary way this very participation in God's life is facilitated, at least as understood by Catholics and other sacramental Christian churches. The remainder of this chapter will explore how Gen 1–3 depicts the world as a macro-temple, and humanity as created for liturgical worship as cosmic-priests on earth, which further suggests a liturgical *Sitz im Leben* for Gen 1–3.[5]

Ever since Henning Bernhard Witter (1711) and Jean Astruc (1753) scholars have argued for two different sources underlying Gen 1–3.[6] The first portion, namely, Gen 1:1—2:3, is usually taken as the later Priestly account (P), whereas the second portion, Gen 2:4—3:24, is understood as an earlier Yahwistic account (J).[7] A century after Astruc, Hermann Hupfeld (1853) became the first to isolate the Priestly source (which he called the "older Elohist"), even though a long tradition had already developed for over a century distinguishing between the two accounts of creation.[8]

These foundational source critical distinctions notwithstanding, liturgical concerns link both accounts in their final form, which is the only form we can be sure ever existed. Form critics like Moshe Weinfeld have underscored

---

5. See the important discussion in Pitre, "Jesus, the New Temple," 56–63.

6. Witter, *Jura Israelitarum*; and Jean Astruc's anonymously published *Conjectures sur les mémoires*. Although the original printing of Astruc's work lists Brussels as the location, it appears that it was in fact published in Paris. A more recent edition of Astruc's work is now available, Astruc, *Conjectures sur la Genèse*. For the history of the role double narratives played in Pentateuchal source criticism, see Nahkola's important work, *Double Narratives*.

7. What is less well known is that in contrast to their predecessors in the previous century (like Isaac La Peyrère, Thomas Hobbes, Baruch Spinoza, and Richard Simon), who denied the substantial Mosaic authorship of the Pentateuch based upon their historical and philological analyses, a number of eighteenth century scholars who built upon these earlier works (particularly Simon's) and further paved the way for modern Pentateuchal source criticism, including Astruc and Johann David Michaelis, and who understood Genesis to have come from different sources, adhered to the traditional Mosaic authorship of Genesis, as well as of the rest of the Pentateuch. These scholars simply held that Moses used sources in his composition. The irony is that a number of twentieth-century scholars who argued for a theory of single authorship for Genesis, like Umberto Cassuto, Gary Rendsburg and Roger Whybray, denied Mosaic authorship, dating Genesis anywhere from the tenth century (Rendsburg) to the sixth century BC (Whybray). See Astruc, *Conjectures sur la Genèse*; Michaelis, *Einleitung*; Cassuto, *Documentary Hypothesis*; Rendsburg, *Redaction of Genesis*; and Whybray, *Making of the Pentateuch*.

8. Hupfeld, *Die Quellen*. On this history see, e.g., Hahn and Morrow, *Modern Biblical Criticism*, 97–152.

numerous priestly and liturgical elements in the first creation account, which we will describe in more detail below.⁹ The emphasis on the seventh day reflects priestly concerns for Sabbath observance.¹⁰ Not only is the seventh day the narrative climax, but there is a sevenfold dimension to the three formulae involved in creation: fulfillment, description and approval.

The priestly and liturgical nature of the creation account is further indicated by its many parallels with the priestly account of the construction of the tabernacle, which is portrayed as the chief liturgical structure in Exodus.¹¹ As we shall see below, there are nearly identical Hebrew phrases linking both passages, and both are structured with the heptadic pattern of the number seven.¹² When it comes to the heptadic pattern of the account of the building of the tabernacle, Scott Hahn mentions that:

> In the Sinai covenant we see an obvious recapitulation of the heptadic patterning of Gen 1. God's glory covers Sinai for six days and on the seventh he calls Moses from the cloud of his glory (Exod. 24:16). The divine blueprint for the Tabernacle is given in a series of seven divine addresses. The instructions for the making of the priests' vestments are punctuated by seven affirmations of Moses' obedience to God's command. The Tabernacle is built according to divine command and seven times we are told that Moses did "as the Lord had commanded him."¹³

---

9. Weinfeld, "Sabbath, Temple and Enthronement," 501–12. See also Bauks, "Genesis 1," 333–45; Kearney, "Creation and Liturgy," 375–87; and Blenkinsopp, "Structure of P," 275–92.

10. Scholars have long noted the preponderance of the number seven, and its multiples, within Gen 1:1—2:3: from the number of words in a single verse (e.g. 1:1 and 1:2) to the repetition of specific words (e.g. ' ĕlōhîm "God" and ' ereṣ "earth") to the repetition of specific phrases (e.g. kî-ṭôb "it was good," with a special emphasis the seventh time it is written: wĕhinēh-ṭôb m' ōd "and it was very good"). Umberto Cassuto probably pushes this line of reasoning too far. See his extensive discussion in Cassuto, *Commentary on the Book of Genesis I*, 13–15. See also Levenson, *Creation*, 67–68. Levenson, although critical of Cassuto here, concedes the basic point concerning Gen 1:1—2:3's structure based on the number seven. I will discuss this in more detail below.

11. Fletcher-Louis, *All the Glory of Adam*, 23, 63 and 76; Levenson, *Sinai and Zion*, 142–43; Weinfeld, "Sabbath, Temple and Enthronement," 502–3 and 502n5; Kearney, "Creation and Liturgy," 375–78 and 385–86; and Blenkinsopp, "Structure of P," 275–92.

12. Weinfeld, "Sabbath, Temple and Enthronement," 503.

13. Hahn, "Christ, Kingdom, and Creation," 124.

Moreover, Crispin Fletcher-Louis's textual analysis of Sirach indicates that Sirach relies upon a tradition of interpretation that assumes the parallels between creation and tabernacle construction.[14]

Unsurprisingly, in the biblical canon these accounts orient readers toward the construction of the temple in Jerusalem under King Solomon.[15] This passage parallels those of Genesis and Exodus, primarily inasmuch as the account is based upon a heptadic sevenfold structure.[16] This practice of connecting creation stories with temple-building extends beyond the Hebrew tradition. Scholars of the ancient Near East have shown how temples were often connected to acts of creation, from the Akkadian *Enuma Elish* to the Sumerian Gudea Cylinders.[17] As John Bergsma explains, "In the ancient Near East it was an almost universal commonplace that any given temple mystically represented the great 'cosmic mountain' that was the first to break above the primordial waters of the abyss at creation, and rose to form the habitable land."[18]

Although the priestly character of Gen 1:1—2:3 has been well established for over a century, some scholars like Gordon Wenham have also emphasized priestly and liturgical elements in Gen 2 and 3, which we will discuss further below in this chapter.[19] This is particularly the case with the

---

14. Fletcher-Louis, *All the Glory of Adam*, 76–77.

15. Bunta, "Yhwh's Cultic Statue," 234; and Levenson, "Temple and the World," 286–89. For parallels between the accounts of the tabernacle construction in Exodus and the temple construction in 1 Kgs see especially Hurowitz, *I Have Built You*; and Hurowitz, "Priestly Account," 23–25.

16. Hahn, "Christ, Kingdom, and Creation," 125; Levenson, *Sinai and Zion*, 142–45; Levenson, "Temple and the World," 286–89; and Levenson, "Paronomasia," 131–35.

17. Averbeck, "Sumer," 89, 95–96, 116 and 118–21; Watts, "On the Edge," 145, 146 and 148; Averbeck, "Ritual Formula," 37, 51–54, 51n46, 54n50, 64–66 and 64n71; and Janowski, *Gottes Gegenwart*, especially the chapter entitled, "Tempel und Schöpfung: Schöpfungstheologische Aspekte der priesterschriftlichen Heiligtums Konzeption," 214–46. For an English translation of the *Enuma Elish* see the translation by Benjamin R. Foster in Hallo and Younger, *Context of Scripture I*, 391–402. For an English translation of the Gudea Cylinders see the translation by Richard E. Averbeck in Hallo and Younger, *Context of Scripture II*, 418–33. Loren Fisher has commented further on the connection between the number seven and ancient Near Eastern temple building projects, Fisher, "Temple Quarter," 40–41. See also Hurowitz, *I Have Built You*, 288n1 and 296n1.

18. Bergsma, "Cultic Kingdoms," 55. See also Watts, "On the Edge," 139; Hoffmeier, "Sacred" 171–77; and Hoffmeier, "Some Thoughts," 46.

19. Wenham, *Genesis 1–15*, 64 and 86; and Wenham, "Sanctuary Symbolism," 19–25. A more accessible copy of this essay has been reprinted in Hess and Tsumura, *"I Studied Inscriptions"*, 399–404. In this chapter I will cite from the original version.

imagery found in Gen 2 and 3 that form associations with the tabernacle and temple: e.g. Adam is told to ' *ăbād* "work" and *shāmār* "guard" the garden (2:15) using precisely those two verbs which in the Pentateuch *only* occur together again with the task the Levites are given in their tabernacle service (Num 3:7–8; 8:26; and 18:5–6); the depiction of God walking back and forth in both the Garden of Eden (Gen 3:8) and moving back and forth in the tabernacle (Lev 26:12 and Deut 23:14), both involve forms of the verb *hālāk*; cherubim in the garden (Gen 3:24) are reminiscent of the cherubim images on the ark of the covenant (e.g. Exod 25:18–20, 22; 37:7, 9; and Num 7:89) as well as in the temple's holy of holies (e.g. 1 Kgs 6:27–28 and 8:6).[20] When we turn to *Wirkungsgeschichte*, or reception history, we find that the Adamic and Edenic traditions are linked in Ezek 28's treatment of the king of Tyre as well as Sir 24's handling of Gen 1–3 which Sirach appears to read as a unified whole.[21] These connections between the temple in Jerusalem and Eden are further elaborated in later Second Temple and Rabbinic literature.[22] Hahn explains that:

> The link between the Temple and creation is manifested also in various Edenic motifs associated with the Temple. . . . Eden was atop a mountain . . . and characterized by abundant gold, precious gems . . . flowering trees, and cherubim. Most of these elements are incorporated by Solomon into the design and decoration of

---

20. Bloch-Smith, "Solomon's Temple," 85 and 87–88; and Wenham, "Sanctuary Symbolism," 19–25, especially 20–23. Cherubim imagery abounds in priestly contexts. Not only do we find them carved on the ark of the covenant and in the temple's inner sanctuary, but they are also artistically depicted on the curtains within the Tabernacle (Exod 26:31; 36:8, and 35) and in the temple we even find them carved on the walls of various rooms as well as on the inner sanctuary's doors and on the panels of moveable stands (1 Kgs 6:29, 32, 35; 7:29, and 36).

21. Gosse, "Les traditions," 424–26; Callender, *Adam in Myth*, 89, 100–103, 132 and 210; Stager, "Jerusalem," 183–94; Himmelfarb, "Temple and the Garden of Eden," 63, 65–66 and 75; and Levenson, *Theology of the Program*, 21–36. See also Fletcher-Louis, *All the Glory of Adam*, 78 for his argument that Sirach reads Gen 1–3 in a more unified way.

22. Ben-Dov, *Head of All Years*, 204–05; Hultgren, *From the Damascus Covenant*, 492n67; Beale, *Temple and the Church's Mission*, 67 and 67n90–91; Bloch-Smith, "Solomon's Temple," 88 and 91; Anderson, *Genesis of Perfection*, 46–50, 56–57, 61–62 and 122; Swartz, "Ritual about Myth," 135–55; Bloch-Smith, "Who Is the King of Glory," 18–31; Stager, "Jerusalem," 183–94; and Wise, "4QFlorilegium," 126–32. For the *Wirkungsgeschichte* of this tradition within other Jewish (and also Christian) interpretive traditions, see, e.g. Targum Neofiti of Gen 2:15, Targum Pseudo-Jonathan of Gen 2:7, Pirke de Rabbi Eliezer 11 and 12, and Breshit Rabbah of Gen 14:8.

the Temple.... The sacred river that flows from Eden... is later associated with Mount Zion, site of the Temple.[23]

Gen 1–2 specifically depicts Adam as a royal priest, or priest-king.[24] Adam not only is given the priestly command to guard and work the garden (2:15), but also royal dominion (1:28).[25] This view of Adam specifically as high priest of creation, becomes quite commonplace in later Jewish tradition, where the Jewish high priest is interpreted as a new Adam, and thus a cosmic priest of creation.[26] The human person thus emerges as created for the purpose of worship. Sin becomes understood as a failure to correspond to God's grace as priest kings. In the words of Fagerberg, "The fall is the forfeiture of our liturgical career."[27]

The poetic Priestly framework and symmetry of Gen 1:1–2:3 has led one scholar to describe its theme as the "Cosmic Liturgy of the Seventh Day."[28] It is for these and similar reasons that Weinfeld identifies the liturgy as Gen 1's *Sitz im Leben*.[29] The world itself is depicted as a macro temple, and the temple in later biblical and post-biblical traditions is depicted as a microcosm of the world.[30] As Hahn explains:

23. Hahn, "Christ, Kingdom, and Creation," 126.

24. Fletcher-Louis, "Jesus as the High Priestly 1," 165n38.

25. For a reading of Adam and Eve as cosmic priests on earth, see Fagerberg, "Divine Liturgy," 108. For parallels between Adam's royal role and the later reign of King David, see Hahn, "Christ, Kingdom, and Creation," 127–28. Earlier Hahn explains that, "... Adam is portrayed in biblical texts as king over all creation, and similar language and imagery is also applied to David" (122).

26. Fletcher-Louis, "Jesus as the High Priestly 2," 76; Fletcher-Louis, "Jesus as the High Priestly 1," 159 and 159n8; Fletcher-Louis, "God's Image," 81–99. In his essay, "Temple Cosmology," 69–113, Fletcher-Louis shows how Aaron's responsibilities with the menorah for the Tamid offering (Exod 27:20–21 and 30:7–8) parallel God's role in creation (Gen 1:3–5). Moreover, as Brant Pitre shows, the Jewish high priest was understood within second temple Judaism as embodying both the temple itself and the entire created cosmos, which was symbolized in the priest's liturgical vestments. Pitre, "Jesus, the New Temple, and the New Priesthood," 61.

27. Fagerberg, "Liturgical Asceticism," 208. Writing further on the same page, Fagerberg explains, "God expelled us from the environs of the tree of life lest we be eternally disfigured."

28. Vervenne, "Genesis 1," 48.

29. Weinfeld, "Sabbath, Temple and Enthronement," 508–10.

30. Ben-Dov, *Head of All Years*, 204; Janowski, *Gottes Gegenwart*, 214–46; Wenham, "Sanctuary Symbolism," 19–20; Levenson, "Temple and the World," 283–84; and Weinfeld, "Sabbath, Temple and Enthronement," 506, 506n2 and 508. See also Gregory Beale's comments regarding the correspondence of the regions in the Edenic narrative with

the close correspondence between the building of the Tabernacle and the creation of the cosmos indicates that the tabernacle-building is a recapitulation of creation, and thus the tabernacle is in some sense a *microcosm*, a small embodiment of the universe. Conversely, we may conclude that the universe is a *macro-tabernacle*, a cosmic sanctuary built for the worship of God.[31]

In light of the preceding comments on the Priestly character of the final form of Gen 2–3, we might extend Weinfeld's insight and speak of the final form of Gen 1–3 as having its *Sitz im Leben* in communal liturgy and worship. Fletcher-Louis sums up well the overarching message thus: "creation has its home in the liturgy of the cult."[32]

## The Sevenfold Structure of Creation in Gen 1

In the remainder of this chapter, I will unpack in more detail the points I brought up above in the overview concerning the liturgical context to Gen 1–3, beginning with the sevenfold or heptadic structure of Gen 1. The number seven is important for the form and content of Gen 1 as the number of perfection in the ancient Near East, the number relating to covenant, and of course, the number of the day known as the Sabbath, the pinnacle of creation.[33] As was already noted above, Gen 1:1 contains seven words: *běrē'šît bārā' 'elōhîm 'ēt haŝāmayim wě' ēt hā' āreṣ*. Gen 1:2 has fourteen words, seven times two. Furthermore, significant words in this passage occur in multiples of seven: God (35 times, i.e., seven times five), earth (21 times, i.e., seven times three), heavens/firmament (21 times), "and it was so" (7 times), and "God saw that it was good" (7 times).[34]

---

specific regions of the temple in Beale, *Temple and the Church's Mission*, 74–75.

31. Hahn, "Christ, Kingdom, and Creation," 125. Continuing further on the same page, he writes, "The same heptadic patterning of the Tabernacle construction narrative is recapitulated in the building of Solomon's Temple . . . . now the Temple of the Davidic covenant recapitulated . . . [creation]. The Temple is a microcosm of creation, the creation a macro-temple." On the connection between Gen 1–3 and the later tabernacle and temple, see Hahn, "Christ, Kingdom, and Creation," 122–28; Hahn, "Canon, Cult and Covenant," 213–15; and Hahn, "Worship in the Word," 106–10.

32. Fletcher-Louis, *All the Glory of Adam*, 63.

33. On the number seven as the number of perfection in the ancient Near East, see Cassuto, *Commentary on the Book of Genesis I*, 12–13; and Meyers, *Tabernacle Menorah*, 107.

34. Wenham, *Genesis 1–15*, 6.

The heptadic structure is sufficiently apparent and many scholars have commented upon it. Umberto Cassuto and Jon Levenson disagree on a number of points, but their comments on this heptadic structure are worth quoting at great length. Cassuto has the following to say:

> After the introductory verse (i 1), the section is divided into *seven* paragraphs, each of which appertains to one of the seven days. An obvious indication of this division is to be seen in the recurring sentence, *And there was evening and there was morning, such-and-such a day*. Hence the Masoretes were right in placing an open paragraph . . . after each of these verses . . . . Each of the three nouns that occur in the first verse and express the basic concepts of the section, viz *God* [' *Elōhīm*] *heavens* [*šāmayim*], *earth* [' *ereṣ*], are repeated in the section a given number of times that is a multiple of *seven*: thus the name of *God* occurs thirty-five times, that is, five times *seven* . . . ; *earth* is found twenty-one times, that is, three times seven; similarly *heavens* (or *firmament*, *rāqīaʿ*) appears twenty-one times . . . . The ten sayings with which, according to the Talmud, the world was created . . . that is, the ten utterances of God beginning with the words, *and* . . . *said*—are clearly divisible into two groups: the first group contains *seven* Divine fiats enjoining the creation of the creatures . . . ; the second group comprises three pronouncements that emphasize God's concern for man's welfare . . . . Thus we have here, too, a series of *seven* corresponding dicta . . . . The terms *light* and *day* are found, in all, *seven* times in the first paragraph, and there are *seven* references to *light* in the fourth paragraph . . . . *Water* is mentioned *seven* times in the course of paragraphs two and three . . . . In the fifth and sixth paragraphs forms of the word *ḥayyā* . . . occur *seven* times . . . . The expression *it was good* appears *seven* times (the seventh time—*very good*) . . . . In the *seventh* paragraph, which deals with the *seventh* day, there occur the following three consecutive sentences (three for emphasis), each of which consists of *seven* words and contains in the middle the expression *the seventh day: And on* THE SEVENTH DAY *God finished His work which He had done, and He rested on* THE SEVENTH DAY *from all His work which He had done. So God blessed* THE SEVENTH DAY *and hallowed it* . . . . The words in the seventh paragraph total thirty-five—five times *seven*.[35]

After these lengthy observations, Cassuto concludes, "To suppose that all this is a mere coincidence is not possible . . . . This numerical symmetry

---

35. Cassuto, *Commentary on Genesis Part I*, 13–15. See also, Cassuto, "La creazione," 47–49.

is, as it were, the golden thread that binds together all the parts of this section . . . ."[36] Cassuto even argues that Gen 2–3 exhibits this focus on the number seven. He writes:

> a clear indication of the unity of the section . . . is to be seen in the numerical symmetry based on the number *seven* that we find in this section just as we encountered it in the story of creation . . . . Here, too [chapters 2–3], the words that express the fundamental concepts of the passage recur a given number of times—*seven* times, or a multiple of *seven*. The name Eden occurs, together with *qedhem* ["east"], seven times; the names ʾ*ādhām* and ʾ*īš* [both mean "man"] appear altogether twenty-eight times, that is, four times *seven*; the word ʾ*īš* and its synonyms ʿ*ēzer* ["helper"] and *ṣēlāʿ* ["rib"] are used twenty-one times, that is, three times *seven*; so, too, we find twenty-one examples of words derived from the root ʾ*ākhal* ["eat"] (*seven* in the very paragraph describing the sin, iii 1–7). Likewise, the verb *lāqaḥ* ["take"], which is given special emphasis in a number of verses . . . occurs, all told, *seven* times in the course of the section. And when I sought to break up the section into paragraphs, according to the logical division of the contents, there naturally emerged *seven* paragraphs.[37]

At this point, it is well worth turning to Levenson who is quite critical of Cassuto here. Levenson's points are important precisely because, despite being so critical of Cassuto, Levenson agrees in substance with many of the former's main points, particularly concerning the sevenfold structure of Gen 1. Levenson's comments, although lengthy, are worth quoting, as when he writes:

> Hardly limited to the seven days in which the action takes place, groups or multiples of seven appear throughout the passage. The first verse, for example, consists of seven words; the second, of fourteen. Of the three dominant terms of v. 1—"God," "heaven," and "earth"—the first occurs thirty-five times in Genesis 1:1—2:3, the second and third of total of twenty-one times each. In the description of the first day, "light" is mentioned five times and "day" (which 1:5 defines as its synonym), twice: the total is again seven. In the passages devoted to the fifth and sixth days, the word *ḥayyâ* ("living thing," "alive") occurs a total of seven times. The expression *kî ṭôb* ("that it was good") appears seven times; mysteriously omitted on the second day, it occurs twice on the

---

36. Cassuto, *Commentary on Genesis Part I*, 15.
37. Cassuto, *Commentary on Genesis Part I*, 94.

third and the sixth, the last time with extra force ("very good"). The paragraph devoted to the seventh day consists of thirty-five words, twenty-one of which form three sentences of seven words, each of which includes the expression "the seventh day." ... the first sentence of the paragraph includes five words, that is, two fewer than we expect, but that the last sentence, which follows the three heptads, consists of nine words and thus compensates for the deficiency of the incipit, leaving us with five sentences that average seven words apiece for a total of thirty-five.... even if one demurs on ... [Cassuto's more controversial points, he] is surely right to conclude his discussion of the significance of seven in Genesis 1:1—2:3 with the remark that "it is impossible to think that all this is nothing but coincidence."[38]

Of course, Cassuto and Levenson are far from alone in these observations. Wenham observes, "The number seven dominates this opening chapter in a strange way."[39] He notes further that Gen 2:1–3 makes reference to the seventh day three times, in three separate sentences composed of seven words each. This focus on seven highlights the unique status of the seventh day.[40] Moreover, although we find ten divine announcements and eight divine commands in Gen 1:1—2:3, there are three formulae grouped in sevens. In order to retain this sevenfold structure, certain formulae are actually omitted where we might expect them, namely the fulfillment formula in 1:20, the description of the act in 1:9, and the approval formula in 1:6-8.[41] In Gen 1:6-8 there is no approval formula "God saw that it was good." Gen 1:9 omits any description of the act whatsoever. Finally, Gen 1:20 omits the fulfillment formula, "and it was so." The significance of these omissions is underscored by the fact that in the LXX these missing formulae are included. The sevenfold structure of the Hebrew text is thus lacking in the LXX which prefers to complete the various formulae.[42]

38. Levenson, *Creation*, 67–68.
39. Wenham, *Genesis 1-15*, 6.
40. Wenham, *Genesis 1-15*, 7 (see also 34–35).
41. Wenham, *Genesis 1-15*, 6. See also, Cook, "Septuagint of Genesis," 317. Earlier Wenham describes these formulae which characterize Gen 1: "(1) announcement of the commandment, 'And God said' (10 times ... ); (2) order, e.g. 'Let there be ... ' (8 times ... ); (3) fulfillment formula, e.g. 'And it was so' (7 times ... ); (4) execution formula or description of act, e.g. 'And God made' (7 times ... ); (5) approval formula 'God saw that it was good' (7 times ... ); (6) subsequent divine word, either of naming or blessing (7 times ... ); (7) mention of the days (6/7 times ... )." See Wenham, *Genesis 1-15*, 6.
42. Wenham, *Genesis 1-15*, 6; and Cook, "Septuagint of Genesis," 318 and 320.

The careful attention to a sevenfold structure indicates that Genesis in its final form is a liturgical text.[43] We may go further and state that, in fact, Gen 1 reads as a sort of liturgical hymn.[44] Levenson cautions that:

> Genesis 1 also has a certain liturgical flavor, but its style is far from hymnic. Indeed, in vivid contrast with Psalm 104, the first chapter of the Torah exhibits an austere self-control: no burst of praise here, no expression of the author's feelings, no heartfelt petition, but only a highly regular and repetitive description of the *process* of creation, step by step, day by day, without sound or color. The tone is didactic; the chapter teaches a lesson about the organization and rulership of the world. Its concern is not praise, but order, and the lesson, as we shall soon see, is one that has practical implications.[45]

In general, I agree with Levenson's comments here, but I would want to temper them by maintaining a form of hymnic structure still visible in Gen 1, precisely in its "highly regular and repetitive description of the *process* of creation." As we shall see below, the process of temple construction in, e.g., the Gudea Cylinders, is hymnic (although the Gudea Cylinders contain many more hymnic features than Gen 1). I believe that Gen 1 retains a basic hymnic structure in its final form, although clearly not as evident as in Ps 104, as Levenson points out. Consider Weinfeld's comments:

> The recurring formulas: "And he saw that it was good", "and it was evening and it was morning", are a type of refrain which imparts to the chapter a liturgic character. We know today that the Babylonian Creation Epic *Enuma Elish* was customarily read in ceremonies in the sanctuary, whereas the Persians recited their Theogony while sacrificing (Herodotus I, 132). Also in Israel (at least in Second Temple times) the priestly courses [*mšmrot*] and the [*ʾnšy mʿmd*] who met at the time sacrifices were being offered in Jerusalem, customarily read portions from the account of creation, and on the sixth day they recited [*wyklû hšmym*] Gen. 2:1).[46]

---

43. Fletcher-Louis, "Worship of Divine Humanity," 123. See also Callender, *Adam in Myth*, 23, where he writes, "When isolated from its present literary context of the Pentateuch, the repetitive nature of Gen 1:1–2:4a suggests a liturgy, for which it may, in fact, have been used at some point."

44. Vervenne, "Genesis 1," 48; and Maly, "Israel," 13.

45. Levenson, *Creation and the Persistence of Evil*, 58.

46. Weinfeld, "Sabbath, Temple and Enthronement," 510. Weinfeld may be criticized here for assuming that an early Second Temple tradition lies behind the Mishnah's and the Tosefta's comments here, but it is at the very least plausible, and may possibly be supported by a potential trace of this in Theophrastus who wrote about Jewish practices

Gen 1 does seem to be a liturgical text in some sense.⁴⁷ Creation unfolds as a "cosmic liturgical celebration" culminating on the seventh day.⁴⁸

## The Tabernacle as a New Creation

The emphasis on the number seven is far from the only important liturgical element in the creation narrative in Genesis. The connections between the tabernacle and creation, where creation unfolds like the construction of the tabernacle and where the tabernacle's construction is depicted as a new creation, is another important liturgical background to Gen 1–3. As we mentioned in the overview that began this chapter, numerous parallels exist between the seven days of creation and Moses's construction of the tabernacle in the Exodus.⁴⁹ The tabernacle's consecration process lasted seven days, indicating another heptadic pattern also connected to the Sabbath ordinances. Furthermore, key verbal correspondences exist between Moses's construction of the tabernacle in Exod 39–40 and God's creation of the world in Gen 1.⁵⁰

---

during the Second Temple period, as Weinfeld cites in his essay (510n5). Eventually, of course, as Weinfeld points out, "The festive reading of [*wyklû hšmym*] (Gen. 2:1) was incorporated into the Amidah prayer of the Sabbath Eve . . ." (511).

47. Weinfeld, "Sabbath, Temple and Enthronement," 510. See also 508–9; and Bunta, "Likeness of the Image," 64.

48. Balentine, *Torah's Vision*, 63. On page 66 he writes, "the Torah presents worship as the goal of creation." Writing further, on page 81, Balentine explains that, "The Torah's vision begins with the liturgy of creation . . . . In the liturgy of Gen 1–2, the crucial intersection between the ordered world *qua* ritual world and the relational world is the seventh day (Gen. 2:1–3)."

49. Wenham, *Genesis 1–15*, 35; Blenkinsopp, "Structure of P," 275–92; Haran, "Priestly Image," 191–222; Kearney, "Creation and Liturgy," 375–78 and 385–86; Blenkinsopp, *Prophecy and Canon*, 56–69; Cassuto, *Commentary on Genesis Part I*, 62; Cassuto, *Commentary on the Book of Exodus*, 476–77, 483; Levenson, *Sinai and Zion*, 142–43; Levenson, "Temple and the World," 286–87; Fletcher-Louis, *All the Glory of Adam*, 23, 63, 76; Kline, *Images of the Spirit*, 37–38, 41; Beale, *Temple and the Church's Mission*, 60n73, 61; Balentine, *Torah's Vision*, 64, 67–68, 138–40; Bauks, "Genesis 1," 342–43; Levenson, *Creation*, 78, 83–86; Anderson, *Genesis of Perfection*, 200–202; Weinfeld, "Sabbath, Temple and Enthronement," 502–3 and 502n5; and Wenham, "Sanctuary Symbolism," 23. This has been picked up by more popular authors as well, e.g., Hahn, *Father Who Keeps*, 52–53; and Barber, *Singing in the Reign*, 41. Joseph Ratzinger likewise noticed this point several years ago in his *Spirit of the Liturgy*, 26–27.

50. Levenson, *Sinai and Zion*, 143; Balentine, *Torah's Vision*, 67–68; Levenson, *Creation*, 85–86; Weinfeld, "Sabbath, Temple and Enthronement," 503; Kearney, "Creation and Liturgy," 375.

Meredith Kline has pointed out that:

> The Sabbath motif that informs Genesis 1:1–2:3 is prominent in the account of the tabernacle. The completion of the project is related in a concluding summary (Exod. 40:33; cf. 39:43) that echoes the seventh day conclusion of the creation record in Genesis 2:2. The promulgation of the Sabbath ordinance marks the close of the fiat-command section (31:12–17) and the beginning of the fulfillment section (35:2, 3). And the consecration of the cult is a seven-day process.... The Spirit who structured the cosmic temple in the beginning by divine wisdom was also the primary builder of the tabernacle, present and acting through Bezalel and Oholiab, whom he filled and endued with the wisdom of craftsmanship. In this connection the creative naming theme of Genesis 1 also emerges.[51]

Perhaps the most helpful comparisons were provided by Weinfeld in his description of similar Hebrew phrases between creation in Gen 1–2 and the construction of the tabernacle in Exodus. As can be seen, the Hebrew phrases are either identical or nearly identical in each passage. They include the following:

1. Gen 1:31 ["And God saw all that He had made, (*kăl ' ašer ' aśah*), and found it (*wĕhinēh*) very good"]; Exod. 39:43 ["And when Moses saw that they had performed all the tasks (*kăl hamĕlā' kāh*)—as the LORD had commanded, so they had done (*wĕhinēh ' aśû ' ōtāh*)"].

2. Gen 2:1 ["The heaven and the earth were completed (*wayĕkulû*) and all (*wĕkăl*) their array"]; Exod 39:32 ["Thus was completed all (*watēkĕl kăl*) the work of the Tabernacle of the Tent of Meeting"].

3. Gen 2:2 ["God finished the work which He had been doing (*wayĕkăl ' elōhîm . . . mĕla' kĕto ' ašer ' āśāh*)"]; Exod 40:33 ["When Moses had finished the work (*wayĕkăl mōšeh ' et hamĕlā' kāh*)"].

4. Gen 2:3 ["And God blessed . . . (*wayĕbārek*)"]; Exod 39:43 ("And Moses blessed (*wayĕbārek*) them"].

5. Gen 2:3 ["And sanctified it (*wayĕqadaš*)"]; Exod 40:9 [" . . . and to sanctify (*wĕqidašĕtā*) it and all its furnishings"].[52]

---

51. Kline, *Images of the Spirit*, 38.

52. Weinfeld, "Sabbath, Temple and Enthronement," 503 (I slightly modified the order of the Hebrew words and ellipsis in the Gen 2:2 reference to more closely reflect the Hebrew text of Genesis, and I slightly modified Weinfeld's English translations of Exod 39:43 and 40:9 to more closely reflect the Hebrew).

Fletcher-Louis's summary of the significance of this correspondence is highly significant. He writes:

> [There exists] a set of literary and linguistic correspondences between creation (Genesis 1) and the tabernacle (Exod 25–40) .... the seven days of creation in Genesis 1 are paired with God's seven speeches to Moses in Exodus 25–31 .... Each speech begins "The Lord spoke to Moses" (Exod 25:1; 30:11, 16, 22, 34; 31:11, 12) and introduces material which corresponds to the relevant day of creation. Most transparently, in the third speech 30:16–21 there is commanded the construction of the bronze laver. In the Solomonic temple this is called simply the "sea" and in P it matches the creation of the sea on the third day of creation in Genesis 1:9–11. Similarly, the seventh speech (Exod 31:12–17) stresses the importance of the Sabbath for Israel, just as Genesis 2:2–3 tells us how God rested on the seventh day. In the first speech to Moses Aaron's garments and his ordination are described and stress is placed upon his duty to tend the menorah at the evening and morning sacrifice (Tamid) (27:20–21; 30:7–8) .... the golden and jewel-studded garments which Aaron wears are, generally, best understood as the Israelite version of the golden garments worn by the gods of the ancient Near East and their statues. This means that Aaron is dressed to play the part within the temple-as-microcosm theatre that God plays within creation. Indeed, the fact that in this *first* speech Aaron is twice told to tend the temple lampstand and offer the Tamid sacrifice means that he is to police the first boundary—between day and night, light and darkness— which God creates on the first day of creation (Gen 1:3–5).[53]

In light of these overwhelming parallels, Fletcher-Louis concludes, "Obviously, these correspondences mean that creation has its home in the liturgy of the cult and the Tabernacle is a mini cosmos."[54]

## The Temple as New Tabernacle and as New Creation

The parallels between creation and the tabernacle are also mirrored in the parallels between the seven days of creation and Solomon's construction

---

53. Fletcher-Louis, *All the Glory of Adam*, 63. See also 70–71 and 71n51. Weinfeld as well notes that the tabernacle in Jewish interpretation was often seen as a microcosm of the universe ("Sabbath, Temple and Enthronement," 506 and 506n2).

54. Fletcher-Louis, *All the Glory of Adam*, 63.

of the Jerusalem temple, which itself was a new tabernacle.[55] Absent are the striking verbal correspondences, yet there remains cosmic symbolism in the temple construction.[56] Levenson helpfully details these correspondences, including the following connections:

1. The construction of the Solomonic Temple in Jerusalem takes seven years to complete (1 Kgs 6:38). In Lev 25:3–7, the seventh year is called a Sabbath, thus forming a connection between the seven days of the week and the seven years of, in the case of Lev, agricultural labor, but in the case of 1 Kgs, architectural labor.

2. The Temple dedication occurs during the Feast of Tabernacles, which was a seven day festival (Deut 16:13) which fell on the seventh month of the year (1 Kgs 8:2).

3. Solomon's speech during the Temple's dedication included seven petitions (1 Kgs 8:31–53).

4. The concept of *měnûḥāh* also links the Temple with creation. Rest occurs at the completion of each project (Ps 132:13–14—associates the experience of the Temple with rest). In fact, 1 Chr. 22:9 claims that the reason Solomon and not David was instructed to build the Temple was because Solomon was a "man of rest" (*' îš měnûḥāh*) and of peace (*šlm*) as his name (*šlmh*) implies.[57]

Hence, we see an association with the Jerusalem Temple and creation in Genesis; the Temple's construction was depicted as a new creation, and the Temple was seen as a microcosm of world.[58] This connection between temple-building and creation has a broader ancient Near Eastern context, to which we now turn.

---

55. Levenson, *Sinai and Zion*, 142–45; Bunta, "Yhwh's Cultic Statue," 234 and 239; Beale, *Temple and the Church's Mission*, 61; Levenson, *Creation*, 78; Levenson, "Paronomasia," 135–38; Levenson, "Temple and the World," 286–89; Kearney, "Creation and Liturgy," 378. This has been picked up by more popular authors as well, e.g., Hahn, *Father Who Keeps His Promises*, 44–45 and 51–53; Barber, *Coming Soon*, 16; and Barber, *Singing in the Reign*, 41.

56. Levenson, *Sinai and Zion*, 143.

57. Levenson, 143–44. See also, Levenson, "Paranomasia," 131–35.

58. Levenson, *Sinai and Zion*, 133–35, 140–45; Levenson, "Temple and the World," 283–84; Fletcher-Louis, *All the Glory of Adam*, 62, 64–65, 64–65n35; Levenson, *Creation*, 87–99; Weinfeld, "Sabbath, Temple and Enthronement," 506 and 508; Wenham, "Sanctuary Symbolism," 19–20; and Fishbane, *Text and Texture*, 12.

PRIESTLY HUMANITY IN THE TEMPLE OF CREATION

## Creation as Temple in the Ancient Near East

This association between Temple and creation is not unique to the Genesis text, nor is the heptadic structure unique to that text. In fact, temples throughout the ancient Near East often had cosmological connotations.[59] Throughout the ancient Near East, the building of a temple often accompanied creation, as we find, e.g., in the *Enuma Elish*.[60] One of the best examples of ancient Near Eastern temple building is found in the Sumerian Gudea Cylinders. The Gudea Cylinders depict the construction of the temple as a liturgical act, the temple building and dedication are essentially a step by step ritual process.[61] Richard Averbeck notes that, "Ritual actions and processes saturate the text and, in fact, structure it."[62] Averbeck explains that:

> The Gudea Cyls., therefore, have affinities with the Sumerian Temple Hymns—a genre that we know was already active in the Old Sumerian literary tradition, long before the time of Gudea—but should *not* be subsumed under the genre category. Rather, they recount, albeit in poetic style and with some hymnic interludes, the construction and consecration of the temple with special emphasis upon the ritual nature of the temple building process.[63]

Writing further, Averbeck elaborates:

> the structure of the composition is a reflex of the ritual nature of the composer's (and probably also Gudea's) historical conception (and experience) of the temple building and dedication processes . . . . The "recurring statement" (*i.e.*, ritual formula) which moves

---

59. Meyers, *Tabernacle Menorah*, 172; Beale, *Temple and the Church's Mission*, 51–58, 61–66, 63n78 and 128; Kearney, "Creation and Liturgy," 384 and 384n22; Levenson, *Creation*, 80, 82; Levenson, "Temple and the World," 287–88; and Weinfeld, "Sabbath, Temple and Enthronement," 507.

60. Weinfeld, "Sabbath, Temple and Enthronement," 501. See also Kearney, "Creation and Liturgy," 384 and 384n22.

61. Averbeck, "Sumer," 89, 95–96, 116, and 118–21; Averbeck, "Ritual Formula," 37, 51–54, 51n46, 54n50, 64–66, and 64n71; and Averbeck, "Preliminary Study," 44–121, 268–398, and 407–579.

62. Averbeck, "Sumer," 95. In this passage, he also notes that, "This is not the case in the parallel biblical accounts. It is true that the dedication procedures for the tabernacle and temple in the Bible involved elaborate ritual procedures, but that in no way compares with the obsessive concern for ritual guidance and confirmation in the Cylinders." See also 118.

63. Averbeck, "Ritual Formula," 53–54.

the story-line along is both a ritual and literary formula and should be taken seriously by those who are willing to see the text for what it is: a hymnic and, at the same time, step-by-step ritualistic description of a ruler's pious involvement in the process of building a temple in ancient Sumer.[64]

Although he does not connect this to the creation account of Gen 1, the description parallels this passage on a number of points.[65] For example, consider the following based on Averbeck's treatment of the Gudea Cylinders:

1. Temple building connected with fertility (Gudea Cylinder A i 5–9, xi 5–11; Gen 1:22).[66]

2. Temple building in connection with wisdom (Gudea Cylinder A i 12–14; Gen 2:9, 17).[67]

3. Divine call or permission to build a temple (Gudea Cylinder A i 19; Gen 1:1, 3, 6, 9, 11).[68]

4. Construction of temple following all the details of a divinely revealed plan (Gudea Cylinder A i 20–21; Gen 1:3, 6, 9, 11, 14–15, 20, 24, 26).[69]

5. Tireless commitment to temple building (Gudea Cylinder A vi 11–13; Gen 1:1–2:3).[70]

6. "Pronouncement of blessing on temple" (Averbeck suggests Gudea Cylinder A xx 27–xxi 12; Gen 2:3).[71]

7. Building temple on raised region like mountain (Gudea Cylinder A xxi 19–23 [later traditions associate Eden with a raised mountain, and sometimes Mount Zion is associated with Eden]).[72]

8. "Laudatory descriptions of the temple" (Gudea Cylinder A xxv 24–xxix 12; Gen 1:4, 10, 12, 18, 25, 31).[73]

---

64. Averbeck, "Ritual Formula," 64n71.
65. Averbeck, "Sumer," 119–21.
66. Hallo and Younger, *Context of Scripture II*, 419n4.
67. Hallo and Younger, *Context of Scripture II*, 419n6.
68. Hallo and Younger, *Context of Scripture II*, 419n8.
69. Hallo and Younger, *Context of Scripture II*, 419–20n9, 426n43, 426n44.
70. Hallo and Younger, *Context of Scripture II*, 421n16, 426n42, 427n50.
71. Hallo and Younger, *Context of Scripture II*, 428n55.
72. Hallo and Younger, *Context of Scripture II*, 428n56.
73. Hallo and Younger, *Context of Scripture II*, 429n59.

9. Temple completion's announcement (Gudea Cylinder B ii 14–iii 1; Gen 1:31, 2:1).[74]

10. Seven-day temple dedication (Gudea Cylinder B xvii 18–19; Gen 2:1–3).[75]

11. Association of temple building with kingship (Gudea Cylinder B xxiii 18–xxiv 8 [Adam is sometimes interpreted in light of royal terms, as a king, and furthermore, the king of Tyre is associated with Adam in Ezek 28]).[76]

12. Divine selection and commissioning of king (Gudea Cylinder A xxiii 25–29 [relates to Adam's creation in the later interpretation that associates Adam with kingship]).[77]

Ancient Near Eastern temples beyond Sumer also served as places for divine rest.[78] In the ancient Near East temples were sometimes further associated with gardens.[79] The parallels here with the creation of the cosmos in Gen 1 are evident, especially the pattern of the number seven.[80] As Loren Fisher notes, the ancient Near East's convention of describing temple construction in terms of seven, means we should not be surprised that creation in Genesis is heptadic: "One must speak of ordering the cosmos in terms of seven even as the construction of the microcosm must be according to the sacred number."[81] Creation in Genesis, we may conclude, is described as a temple; it is constructed as an ancient Near

---

74. Hallo and Younger, *Context of Scripture II*, 432n74.

75. Hallo and Younger, *Context of Scripture II*, 432n74.

76. Hallo and Younger, *Context of Scripture II*, 433n79.

77. Hallo and Younger, *Context of Scripture II*, 429n57. All of these examples are found in Averbeck, "Sumer," 119–21.

78. Beale, *Temple and the Church's Mission*, 66; and Weinfeld, "Sabbath, Temple and Enthronement," 501–2. Weinfeld cites the example of Egyptian, Assyrian, and Sumerian literature for this theme ("Sabbath, Temple and Enthronement," 502 and 502n4).

79. Beale, *Temple and the Church's Mission*, 128; Callender, *Adam in Myth*, 50, 54, 59; and Levenson, "Temple and the World," 297.

80. John Currid likewise notes that God is depicted in Gen 1 as creating the world the way a craftsperson or builder would construct a building. See Currid, *Ancient Egypt*, 43 and 64.

81. Fisher, "Temple Quarter," 40–41.

Eastern temple would be constructed.[82] The divine fiats are, in the words of Kline, "architectural directives."[83]

## The Garden of Eden as the Inner Sanctuary and the Human Person as Created for Worship

So far we have looked at the poetic heptadic structure that provides clues that the author attempted to portray the creation of Gen 1 as related to the construction of a temple. This has both canonical parallels—as with Moses's construction of the tabernacle at Sinai and Solomon's construction of the Temple on Zion—as well as extra-biblical ancient Near Eastern parallels, such as the Gudea Cylinders. What remains to be seen is the implications of this on understanding the creation of humanity and thus the human vocation. The creation and fall account in Gen 2–3 depicts the Garden of Eden as the Holy of Holies, and this has implications for our understanding of humanity's purpose. In this section, I will first discuss Eden's image as an Inner Sanctuary and then discuss human beings as *homo liturgicus*, liturgical humanity made for worship.[84]

Gregory Beale notes that the distinction of regions of creation described by Genesis are similar to those later found in the Temple. The heavens represent the Holy of Holies, the earth represents the inner sanctuary, and the sea represents the outer court. Beale's comments are worth quoting in full:

> It may even be discernable that there was a sanctuary and a holy place in Eden corresponding roughly to that in Israel's later temple. The Garden should be viewed as not itself the source of water but adjoining Eden because Genesis 2:10 says, "a river flowed out of Eden to water the Garden". Therefore, in the same manner that ancient palaces were adjoined by gardens, [quoting John Walton] "Eden is the sources of the waters and [is the palatial] residence of God, and the garden adjoins God's residence." Similarly, Ezekiel 47:1 says that water would flow out from under the holy of holies in the future eschatological temple and would water the earth around. Similarly, in the end-time temple of Revelation 22:1–2

---

82. Kline, *Images of the Spirit*, 20–21, 35; Kline, *Kingdom Prologue*, 17–19, 21; Levenson, *Creation*, 84; and Weinfeld, "Sabbath, Temple and Enthronement," 501.

83. Kline, *Kingdom Prologue*, 19.

84. I am borrowing the phrase, "*Homo liturgicus*," from Hahn, "Worship in the Word," 106.

there is portrayed "a river of the water of life . . . coming *from the throne of God and of the Lamb*" and flowing into a garden-like grove, which has been modeled on the first paradise in Genesis 2, as has been much of Ezekiel's portrayal. If Ezekiel and Revelation are developments of the first garden-temple . . . then Eden, the area where the source of water is located, may be comparable to the inner sanctuary of Israel's later temple and the adjoining garden to the holy place. . . . Eden and its adjoining garden formed two distinct regions. This is compatible with . . . [the] identification of the lampstand in the holy place of the temple with the tree of life located in the fertile plot outside the inner place of God's presence. Additionally, "the bread of the presence", also in the holy place, which provided food for the priests, would appear to reflect the food produced in the Garden for Adam's sustenance . . . . the land and seas to be subdued by Adam outside the Garden were roughly equivalent to the outer court of Israel's subsequent temple . . . . Thus, one may be able to perceive an increasing gradation in holiness from outside the garden proceeding inward: the region outside the garden is related to God and is "very good" (Gen. 1:31) in that it is God's creation (= the outer court); the garden itself is a sacred space separate from the outer world (= the holy place), where God's priestly servant worships God by obeying him, by cultivating and guarding; Eden is where God dwells (= the holy of holies) as the source of both physical and spiritual life (symbolized by the waters).[85]

Other indications of this similarity appear in the text. In Gen 3:8, for example, God walks back and forth (using a form of *hlk*) in Eden, which is also how God's presence is described in the tabernacle in Lev 26:12 and Deut 23:14.[86]

In examining the rest of the biblical canon, we find other evidence that points to intentionality in these parallels that make creation appear as a temple. The Temple, and Mount Zion in general, are frequently associated with Eden, and in some instances actually identified with Eden. Ezek 28's discussion of the king of Tyre is perhaps the most famous example where Mount Zion, and the Temple, are associated with Eden.[87] Sirach also associates Eden with the

---

85. Beale, *Temple and the Church's Mission*, 74–75.

86. Beale, *Temple and the Church's Mission*, 66, 72n101; and Wenham, "Sanctuary Symbolism," 20.

87. Wenham, *Genesis 1–15*, 64; Bunta, "Yhwh's Cultic Statue," 224; Fletcher-Louis, "Worship of Divine Humanity," 126; Himmelfarb, "Temple and the Garden of Eden," 65–66; Levenson, *Sinai and Zion*, 128–29; Meyers, *Tabernacle Menorah*, 150; Fletcher-Louis,

Temple and tabernacle, where the Temple is the new Eden.[88] Fletcher-Louis's comments here, in regard to Sir 24, are particularly intriguing. Following the lead of Hartmut Gese, Fletcher-Louis suggests that:

> ... Sirach 24:3–6 follows the order of the first three days of creation as described in Genesis 1: the pre-creation chaos over which hovers God's primeval spirit (Genesis 1:2, cf. Sirach 24:3); the creation of the "intellectual light" (Genesis 1:3–5, cf. Sirach 24:4); the "delimiting of the cosmos by the firmament and the abyss" (Genesis 1:9–10, cf. Sirach 24:6) .... [These comments] can be developed considerably, and, indeed, Sirach 24:3–22 as a whole emerges as a complex reflection upon Genesis 1 and Exodus 25–31 .... in Sirach 24:3 there is an allusion to the creation by the word of God in Gen 1:3 (cf. 1:6, 11, 14, etc.) and the spirit over the primeval waters in Gen 1:2 .... [The cloud in which Wisdom dwells in Sirach 24:4 provides light, but, furthermore,] its changing appearance demarcates the boundary between day and night (Exod 13:21–22; 40:38; Num 14:14; Deut 1:33; Neh 9:12, 16, 19; Isa 4:5) in a way parallel to the appearance of light on the first day of creation according to Genesis .... in the next verse Wisdom is located in the "vault of heaven" and the "depths of the abyss", the two upper and lower extremities created on day 2 according to Genesis 1:6–8. In Sirach 24:6a Wisdom rules "over the waves of the *sea*, over all the *earth*" ....[89]

Fletcher-Louis continues, explaining that the vegetative symbolism of Sir 24:12–17 is inspired by the third day of creation when plants emerge. Halfway through this discussion of creation, Sirach switches to discuss the cult in the wilderness and then at Zion, to show where Wisdom will find rest. Sirach has just alluded to the first three days of creation in Gen 1, but instead of continuing with the fourth through sixth days of creation (sun, moon, living creatures, etc.), Fletcher Louis explains:

---

*All the Glory of Adam*, 18–19; Gage, *Gospel of Genesis*, 50n3; Callender, *Adam in Myth*, 89, 100–103, 132, 210; Levenson, *Theology of the Program*, 21–36; Beale, *Temple and the Church's Mission*, 75–76, 76n110; Gosse, "Les traditions," 424–26; and Levenson, *Creation*, 74, 93. Fletcher-Louis writes that, "The office of high priest was thought to recapitulate the identity of the pre-lapsarian Adam. This goes back at least as far as Ezekiel 28:12ff. where the prince of Tyre wears precious stones which are simultaneously those worn by the *Urmensch* in the garden of Eden and those of the Aaronic ephod according to Exodus 28" ("Worship of Divine Humanity," 126).

88. Himmelfarb, "Temple and the Garden of Eden," 63 and 75; Fletcher-Louis, *All the Glory of Adam*, 64, 74–75, 75n63; Gese, "Wisdom," 23–57, esp. 32–33; Gese, *Essays on Biblical Theology*, 196; and Sheppard, *Wisdom as a Hermeneutical*, 22–27.

89. Fletcher-Louis, *All the Glory of Adam*, 76–77.

> [Sirach instead] gives us in verse 15 those elements in the tabernacle order which correspond to the fourth and fifth days of creation: first he compares Wisdom's growth to the cinnamon, choice myrrh and fragrance of Israel's sacred incense . . . , and then to galbanum, onycha, stacte and frankincense of the sacred oil . . . . Finally, the hymn climaxes with an invitation to Wisdom's banquet . . . which is reminiscent of God's abundant provision of food for humanity in Genesis 1:28–30. The final verse looks forward to the Edenic existence of Adam and Eve in Genesis 2–3 (which is developed in the rest of chapter 24).[90]

According to Fletcher-Louis, Sirach does this because he knows of the intratextuality between Gen 1 and Exod 25–31. Writing further, Fletcher-Louis concludes, "In a chapter so redolent with themes from Genesis 1–3 this [Sirach 24:22] must be an allusion to the curse on Adam and Eve's labour on their exit from the garden (Gen 3:19) and the first couple's freedom from shame before their temptation and fall (Gen 2:25)."[91]

The intratextuality between Gen 1:1—2:2 and Exod 25–31 that Fletcher-Louis believes Sirach assumes, is as follows:

1. Day 1 of creation (Gen 1:3–5: heavens and the earth, light and darkness) corresponds to Speech 1 in the Exodus passage (Exod 25–29: tabernacle structure = heavens and earth, taking care of menorah/tamid sacrifice/incense offering = evening and morning).

2. Day 2 of creation (Gen 1:6–8: upper and lower waters separated) corresponds to Speech 2 in Exodus (Exod 30:11–16: the census and the half-shekel).

3. Day 3 of creation (Gen 1:9–13: land separated from sea, growth of plants) corresponds to Speech 3 in Exodus (Exod 30:17–21: bronze laver = sea).

4. Day 4 of creation (Gen 1:14–19: sun, moon, stars) corresponds to Speech 4 in Exodus (Exod 30:22–33: holy oil—myrrh, calamus, cinnamon, cassia, which are used to anoint cultic objects and priests).

5. Day 5 of creation (Gen 1:20–23: living creatures in air and sea) corresponds to Speech 5 in Exodus (Exod 30:34–38: holy incense—stacte, onycha, galbanum, frankincense).

---

90. Fletcher-Louis, *All the Glory of Adam*, 77–78.
91. Fletcher-Louis, *All the Glory of Adam*, 78.

6. Day 6 of creation (Gen 1: 24-31: land animals and humans in God's image) correspond to Speech 6 in Exodus (Exod 31:1-11: Bezalel is filled with the Spirit of God).

7. Day 7 of creation, the Sabbath (Gen 2:1-3), corresponds to Speech 7 in Exodus, which concerns the Sabbath (Exod 31:12-17).[92]

In addition to the connections Sirach seems to imply between creation in Genesis and the Exodus account of the construction of the tabernacle, elsewhere in the canon, and especially in light of later Jewish interpretations, there appear clear connections between the temple and creation. The Temple was often described with garden-like elements, further associating it with Eden and creation in general.[93] Eden in turn was seen as a prototype of the Temple.[94] As Lawrence Stager remarks, "the original Temple of Solomon was a mythopoeic realization of heaven on earth, of Paradise, the Garden of Eden."[95] Some of the other elements important in this connection include the presence of cherubim and the eastward-facing entrance. One might mention in addition that the tabernacle and temple menorah were stylized as a symbol of the tree of life. Wenham concludes: "Thus in this last verse of the narrative there is a remarkable concentration of powerful symbols that can be interpreted in the light of later sanctuary design . . . . These features combine to suggest

---

92. Fletcher-Louis, *All the Glory of Adam*, 76.

93. Stager, "Jerusalem," 189; Monson, "Temple of Solomon," 7; Fletcher-Louis, *All the Glory of Adam*, 19, 64-65, 67; Gage, *Gospel of Genesis*, 49-61, 57; Kline, *Images of the Spirit*, 41; Callender, *Adam in Myth*, 51-54; Beale, *Temple and the Church's Mission*, 71-72, 78n119; Gosse, "Les traditions," 424-26; Levenson, *Creation*, 90-99, esp. 98-99; Anderson, *Genesis of Perfection*, 46-48, 50, 56-57, 61, 79-80, 122-24, and 213-14; and Wenham, "Sanctuary Symbolism," 19. Fletcher-Louis writes that, "The close association of temple and paradise is widespread in post-biblical texts including those cherished at Qumran (e.g. *Jub.* 3:8-14, 27; 1QHa 16:4-37; 4Q500 frag. 1; 4Q265 7 ii 11-17). It is already enshrined in the narrative of Genesis 2-3 which draws heavily on the symbolism and traditions of the Temple, including something like Ezekiel 28:12-19)" (*All the Glory of Adam*, 19).

94. Hultgren, *From the Damascus Covenant*, 492n67; Beale, *Temple and the Church's Mission*, 26, 79-80; Callender, *Adam in Myth*, 41, 50; Kline, *Kingdom Prologue*, 32; and Wise, "4QFlorilegium," 103-32, esp. 126-32. Beale concludes that, "The cumulative effect of the . . . parallels between the Garden of Genesis 2 and Israel's tabernacle and temple indicates that Eden was the first archetypal temple, upon which all of Israel's temples were based" (79-80). In a similar vein, Kline explains that, "the garden of Eden was a microcosmic, earthly version of the cosmic temple and the site of a visible, local projection of the heavenly temple" (*Kingdom Prologue*, 32).

95. Stager, "Jerusalem," 191.

that the garden of Eden was a type of archetypal sanctuary, where God was uniquely present in all his life-giving power."[96]

If Eden is the Holy of Holies in God's Temple of creation, the implication is that humanity, created for this inner sanctuary, is best understood as *Homo liturgicus*. Living in the Holy of Holies, humanity is called to give worship to God in all thoughts, words, and deeds. When we look at the Genesis account of Eden, we find other instances of people portrayed as created for worship. Adam, for example, is told to "till" (from the root '*bd*) and "keep" (from the root *šmr*). When *šmr* and '*bd* occur together in the Old Testament (Num 3:7–8; 8:25–26; 18:5–6; 1 Chr 23:32; Ezek 44:14) they refer to keeping/guarding and serving God's word and also they refer to priestly duties in the tabernacle. In fact, *šmr* and '*bd* only occur together again in the Pentateuch in the descriptions in Numbers for the Levites' activities in the tabernacle.[97] Such an association reinforces the understanding of Adam as a sort of priest-king, or even high priest, who guarded God's first temple of creation, as it were.[98] In light of this discussion, therefore,

---

96. Wenham, *Genesis 1–15*, 86. See also Wenham, "Sanctuary Symbolism," 19.

97. Beale, *Temple and the Church's Mission*, 66–67, 81; and Wenham, "Sanctuary Symbolism," 21. This has been picked up in more popular literature, e.g., Hahn, *First Comes Love*, 56 and 65; and Hahn, *Father Who Keeps*, 58–59. Beale's comments about how rabbinic literature treated Adam's duties in the Garden are insightful. He explains that, "The Aramaic translation of Genesis 2:15 (*Tg. Neofiti*) underscores this priestly notion of Adam, saying that he was placed in the Garden 'to toil in the Law and to observe its commandments' (language strikingly similar to . . . Numbers [3:7–8; 8:25–26; 18:5–6] . . . . Verse 19 of this Aramaic translation also notes that in naming the animals Adam used 'the language of the sanctuary'" (*Temple and the Church's Mission*, 67). Beale writes further, "Indeed, *Tg. Pseudo-Jonathan Genesis* 2:7 says that God created Adam partly of 'dust from the site of the sanctuary' . . . . *Pirke de Rabbi Eliezer* 11 and 12, and *Midrash Rabbah Genesis* 14:8 [among other texts], . . . all affirm that Adam was created at the site of the later temple, which was also at Eden or was apparently close to it . . ." (67n90). Finally, "*Midrash Rabbah Genesis* 16:5 interprets Adam's role in Gen. 2:15 to be one of offering the kinds of 'sacrifices' later required by the Mosaic Law" (67n91). For mention of the way the Midrash treats these terms, see also Wenham, "Sanctuary Symbolism," 21.

98. Beale, *Temple and the Church's Mission*, 68, 70, 78n118, 81–121; Anderson, *Genesis of Perfection*, 122–24; Kline, *Kingdom Prologue*, 42–43, 54; Scroggs, *Last Adam*, 43–44; and Wenham, "Sanctuary Symbolism," 21. Beale writes, "While it is likely that a large part of Adam's task was to 'cultivate' and be a gardener as well as 'guarding' the garden, that all of his activities are to be understood primarily as priestly activity is suggested not only from the exclusive use of the two words in contexts of worship elsewhere but also because the garden was a sanctuary . . ." (68). Furthermore, as Kline explains, when we read Gen 2 in its canonical context, we find that, "The Creator had prepared in Eden an earthly replica of his heavenly dwelling as the holy place where man would fulfill his priestly office" (54).

what we find in Gen 1–3 is creation unfolding as the construction of a divine temple, the Garden of Eden as an earthly Holy of Holies, and the human person created for liturgical worship. The implications are that by their labors, prayer, and rest, humanity is to mediate God to the world, and consecrate the world to God. We will return to this theme in the next chapter as we explore it in light of one of a specific liturgical context in which a portion of this reading comes up in the lectionary.

# 3

# St. Joseph and the Value of Work

## A Sacramental Reading of Genesis 1–3

THE DISCIPLINE OF THEOLOGY is in dire straits because of the fragmentation of the theological disciplines. The most tragic of all is arguably the chasm between theology and biblical studies. Throughout Christian history, theologians were nothing other than interpreters of Scripture. The challenge today of reuniting theology and the Bible, of making biblical studies more theological and theology more biblical, is an urgent one, and hence one of the purposes of this present volume. David Fagerberg explains that, "Our task is to let the connection between liturgy, Scripture and theology be a path to a thickened understanding of each of them. That is what we have ceased doing because we no longer see these three in the light of the singular mystery of God."[1]

In this context, the Church's liturgy emerges as an important site for studying Scripture, and for making such study theological. This present chapter is a modest attempt at contributing to the reunification of the Bible and theology by highlighting the promise contained in a liturgical hermeneutic for accomplishing this goal. In the previous chapter, we took a look at Gen 1–3 as a text with liturgical concerns. As a concrete example for the present chapter, I have thus chosen the theme of work as worship within Gen 1–3, as

---

1. Fagerberg, "Theologia Prima," 55. Writing further, in the context of Reformation debates, he contends that, "There is a problem with allowing these fault lines to continue. It just may be that a particular scroll only blooms if it remains securely rooted in the whole Scripture; and the whole Scripture may only be intelligible if read as the marching orders for a liturgical procession; and the theology that comes from this liturgical life is about participation in the life of God. Liturgy, Scripture, and theology must be seen in light of the mystery of God" (57).

read in light of a particular liturgical feast, the Feast of St. Joseph the Worker.[2] I begin with a lengthy discussion of the historical and theological reasons for reading Scripture liturgically.[3] I conclude by picking up on the theme of work as worship in Gen 1–3, which we saw in the prior chapter, as read and experienced in the context of the Feast of St. Joseph the Worker to show what such a liturgical hermeneutic might look like.

## Scripture's Living Environment in the Church's Liturgy

Priestly elements regarding liturgy and worship in Genesis, like those we encountered in the last chapter, are not the only, nor even the primary reason for reading the creation account in the context of liturgy; the lived history of Christians throughout two millennia provides another reason for reading the Bible liturgically. More than simply noticing themes and associations concerning liturgy and worship within specific biblical narratives, studying and meditating upon biblical passages as they appear juxtaposed within the Church's liturgy is a rich reservoir from which theological insights may be gained and the streams of salvation history may be imbibed to provide spiritual nourishment. This is the primary way the Christian faithful have encountered Scripture alive in the tradition up to the present.[4]

In his influential exegetical work *Moralia in Job*, Pope St. Gregory the Great wrote, "the divine word .... Indeed, is almost a kind of river, so to speak, in which both the lamb walks, and the elephant swims."[5] The specific context for Pope St. Gregory's comments here is the question of biblical interpretation. Gregory discusses the *sensus literalis* as well as allegorical interpretation, and then he uses the above analogy to highlight how Scripture is sufficiently rich to allow people of different spiritual stages and intellectual capacities to benefit from it. Although his *Moralia in Job* is much neglected at present, it left an indelible mark upon medieval

---

2. For a more thorough treatment of this theme, see Morrow, "Genesis 1–3."

3. For a more thorough argument and description of a liturgical hermeneutic, see Hahn, "Canon, Cult and Covenant," 207–35; Hahn, "Worship in the Word," 101–36; and Hahn, *Letter and Spirit*.

4. Morrow, *Three Skeptics*, 139–49.

5. From chapter 4 of Gregory's dedicatory letter, "Epistola In qua operis sui tempus, occasionem, divisionem, institutum ac dicendi et interpretandi modum explicat," to his *Moralia in Job*.

biblical interpretation.⁶ Ever since the publication of Henri de Lubac's four volume *Exégèse médiévale* (1959–1964) there has been a growing interest in the kind of patristic and medieval biblical exegesis represented by such works as Gregory's *Moralia*.⁷ What is sometimes neglected in these studies, however, is the role liturgy played in forming the primary context for such theological biblical interpretation.⁸ Indeed, for Gregory and his confrères Scripture alone was not the sacred river to which he referred in his analogy; rather, the divine word encountered primarily in its sacred liturgical setting was the living stream by which Christians were nourished at both tables: the table of the word and the table of the altar.⁹

In the subsections that follow, I describe how the majority of Christians have quite naturally used the liturgy as the main context for biblical interpretation, particularly before the invention of the printing press. I also discuss the shift that occurred with the invention of moveable type and with the advent of the modern period when the Bible became viewed primarily as a book, i.e., a written text. Finally, I discuss how a liturgical or sacramental hermeneutic can aid a theological reading of Scripture by providing a natural canonical and Christological framework for interpreting the Sacred Page. The work of Scott Hahn and Pope Benedict XVI serve as my primary interlocutors because I believe that no one has addressed the liturgy as a key setting for biblical interpretation as much as they have.

### Liturgy as the Place of Biblical Interpretation

Arguably, no popular author has made the point about Scripture's natural setting being the liturgy as frequently and forcefully as Hahn, who, in both lay-oriented and scholarly venues, has consistently pressed for a new liturgical or sacramental hermeneutic, and at the same time, has begun to engage

---

6. Pope St. Gregory's *Moralia in Job* was one of the most influential theological texts in the West before the time of St. Thomas Aquinas, and yet, no complete translation of this mammoth work exists in any modern language. For the significance of Gregory's *Moralia* see Wilken, "Interpreting Job," 213–26.

7. De Lubac, *Exégèse médiévale*. For English translations of the first three volumes, see De Lubac, *Medieval Exegesis 1*, *Medieval Exegesis 2*, and *Medieval Exegesis 3*.

8. See especially section four in the sixth chapter of De Lubac, *Exégèse médiévale II*.

9. I am indebted here to Wilken's article, "Allegory," 11–21, as well as to two of his presentations, "Bread from Both Tables"; and "Interpreting the Bible." See also Morrow, *Three Skeptics*, 139–49.

in such exegesis.[10] In fact, Hahn has issued a clarion call to Bible scholars and theologians alike, urging for the recovery and development of a liturgical reading of Scripture, what he now calls a sacramental hermeneutic.[11] One commonality of these proposals is the importance they place on interpreting Scripture in light of the liturgy. The liturgy was the primary context for biblical hermeneutics in the early periods. As Hahn explains, "the ordinary place of biblical interpretation was the church, and the ordinary time was the liturgy."[12] This is significant, since, as Robert Louis Wilken forcefully asserts: "any effort to mount an interpretation of the Bible that ignores its first readers is doomed to end up with a bouquet of fragments that are neither the book of the church nor the imaginative wellspring of Western literature, art, and music. Uprooted from the soil that feeds them, they are like cut flowers whose vivid colors have faded."[13]

Although such a proposal might seem relevant only to those Christians who, like Catholics, Lutherans, Anglicans, Eastern and Oriental Orthodox, and others, share a liturgical heritage that closely resembles the Christian form of worship St. Justin Martyr described in the second century, a liturgical hermeneutic may be fruitfully engaged by Christians of all liturgical traditions, albeit more so by some than others.[14]

---

10. Hahn is by no means alone here. Brant Pitre, John Bergsma, and Michael Barber are just a few of the names of more recent scholars who are continuing, in both popular and scholarly venues, to engage in the type of exegesis Hahn is urging. See, e.g., Barber, "Historical Jesus and Cultic Restoration,"; Barber, *Coming Soon*; and Barber, *Singing in the Reign*.

11. E.g., Hahn, *Kingdom of God*; Hahn, "Liturgy and Empire," 13–50; Hahn, "Temple, Sign, and Sacrament," 107–43; Hahn, "Christ, Kingdom, and Creation," 113–38; Hahn, "Canon, Cult and Covenant," 207–35; Hahn, "Scripture and the Liturgy," 648–53; Hahn, *Letter and Spirit*; Hahn, "Worship in the Word," 101–36; Hahn, "Covenant, Cult, and the Curse-of-Death," 65–88; and Hahn, "Kingdom and Church," 294–326.

12. Hahn, *Letter and Spirit*, 9. This notion of Scripture's liturgical context has Jewish roots. See Stewart, *Priests of My People*, who specifically argues for the sacrificial nature of the Mass of the early Christians, and of the early Christian priesthood itself as consciously being viewed as the continuation of the Jewish Levitical priesthood. See also Cavalletti, "Memorial and Typology," 69–86.

13. Wilken, *Spirit of Early Christian Thought*, xvii. On the importance of such a liturgical interpretation for the earliest Christians, see especially chs. 2 and 3 of Wilken's book.

14. I am referring to the passage in Justin, *1 Apol.* 61, 65–67, as cited by Wilken in his *Spirit of Early Christian Thought*, 28–29, where we read: "On the day called Sunday all who live in the cities or in the country gather at one place and the memoirs of the apostles or the writings of the prophets are read as long as time permits. When the reader has finished, the one who is presiding instructs us in a brief discourse and exhorts us to

Benedict XVI wrote, "The Church's liturgy being the original interpretation of the biblical heritage has no need to justify itself before historical reconstructions: it is rather itself the standard, sprung from what is living, which directs research back to the initial stages."[15] And elsewhere, Ratzinger explained that the liturgy is "the place of encounter with Jesus. It is above all in the liturgy that Jesus is among us, here it is that He speaks to us, here He lives.... the liturgy is the true, living environment for the Bible and... the Bible can be properly understood only in this living context within which it first emerged."[16]

## From Communal Worship to Private Reading: How the Bible Became a Book

There has been much talk in recent years about canonical biblical interpretation. Although Christians for two millennia have been reading books of the Bible in light of other books of the Bible found within the biblical canon, the conscious modern return to such a reading is often associated with the Yale School in the US, and especially with the work of Brevard Childs.[17] In its 1993 recommendation for Catholic biblical interpretation, the Pontifical Biblical Commission mentioned the importance of such canonical reading.[18] It is important to recognize, however, that the canon

---

imitate these noble things. Then we all stand up together and offer prayers.... When we have finished the prayer, bread is brought forth, and wine and water, and the presiding minister offers up prayers and thanksgiving to the best of his ability, and the people assent, saying the Amen; after this the consecrated elements are distributed and received by each one. Then a deacon brings a portion to those who are absent. Those who prosper, and who so wish, contribute what each thinks fit. What is collected is deposited with the presiding minister who takes care of the orphans and widows, and those who are in need because of sickness or some other reason, and those who are imprisoned, and the strangers and sojourners among us."

15. Benedict XVI, *Church, Ecumenism and Politics*, 84–85. See also Hahn, *Covenant and Communion*, 137–85; and Hahn, "Authority of Mystery," 112.

16. Benedict XVI, "Introduction," xii.

17. E.g., Childs, "Canon in Recent Biblical," 33–57; and Childs, *Old Testament Theology*. See Pope Benedict XVI's comments: "the individual writings [*Schrifte*] of the Bible point somehow to the living process that shapes the one Scripture [*Schrift*]. Indeed, the realization of this last point some thirty years ago led American scholars to develop the project of 'canonical exegesis.'" Ratzinger/Benedict XVI, *Jesus of Nazareth I*, xviii, as well as the rest of his comments concerning canonical exegesis through page xix.

18. Pontifical Biblical Commission, "Interpretation of the Bible in the Church," no. IC1. In this same section, the PBC mentions Brevard Childs by name. The subtitle for

itself was formed for the purpose of determining precisely which texts should be read in the sacred liturgy.[19]

Crucial to this view is a reconsideration of seeing the Bible as a book. Before the invention of the printing press, Scripture was not viewed as a book in the modern sense of the word, nor did most Christians encounter it as a book.[20] Prior to the invention of the printing press at the end of the 15th century, most Christians encountered Scripture in liturgical contexts, especially at the Eucharistic liturgies, and therefore the liturgy was the privileged location for biblical interpretation.[21] Even as late as the 16th century, Bibles tended to be prohibitively expensive for average families to own.[22] In our present age too, even with the ubiquity of computers and smart phones, the liturgy remains the primary context of Christian encounter with Scripture and of scriptural interpretation.

Prior to the printing press, however, even those monks and scribes in the monasteries and scriptoria who had more ready access to the Sacred Page in the medieval period, had the liturgical cycle in their bones. They frequented the Eucharistic liturgy regularly and their lives were regulated by the liturgical seasons. In fact, their entire days were punctuated by their communal praying of the Divine Office. In such an environment,

---

most of the translations of this section of the PBC's document call this canonical reading a "canonical approach" (e.g. German *Kanonischer Zugang*, Italian *Approccio canonico*, Portuguese *Abordagem canônica*). Interestingly, only the German translation adds the gloss *Kanonkritik* (roughly "canonical criticism"). Online versions of this text are available from the Vatican website. Unfortunately, the Vatican website does not yet have an official Latin, the original French, nor an English translation of this text online.

19. See, e.g., Hahn, "Canon, Cult and Covenant," 209–10; Hahn, "Worship in the Word," 102–3; McDonald, "Identifying Scripture," 420, 423, 432–34 and 439; and Sanders, *From Sacred Story*, 162.

20. Morrow, *Three Skeptics*, 139–49; Legaspi, *Death of Scripture*, 18–25; Candler, *Theology, Rhetoric, Manuduction*, 9n19, 10, 13, 15, 30, 33, 74, 76–77, 79, 119, and 160; Pickstock, *After Writing*, 161n139; and Duffy, *Stripping of the Altars*, 420 and 450.

21. Morrow, *Three Skeptics*, 139–49; Candler, *Theology, Rhetoric, Manuduction*, 7, 9, 15, 18, 27, 38–39, 50, 66, 74, 77n17, 77–82, 151–60, and 162; D'Costa, *Theology in the Public Square*, 112–13, 119–22, 132–33, and 138; Huizinga, *Autumn of the Middle Ages*; Illich, *In the Vineyard*, 69 and 82; Pontifical Biblical Commission, "Interpretation of the Bible in the Church," nos. IIIB2, IIIB3, and IVC1; Duffy, *Stripping of the Altars*, 420 and 467; Benedict XVI, *Church, Ecumenism and Politics*, 84–85; Benedict XVI, *God and the World*, 157; Benedict XVI, *Spirit of the Liturgy*, 169 and 207–9; Stallsworth, "Story of an Encounter," 118; and Ong, *Presence of the Word*, 269.

22. Morrow, *Three Skeptics*, 139–49; Reventlow, *History of Biblical Interpretation 4*, 130; and van der Coelen, "Pictures for the People," 185–205.

the liturgy could not but become an important context for their Scripture study.[23] The full panoply of senses was often involved in such liturgical encounters, as Talal Asad explains:

> the divine word, both spoken and written, was necessarily also material. As such, the inspired words were the object of a particular person's reverence, the means of his or her practical devotions at particular times and places. The body, taught over time to listen, to recite, to move, to be still, to be silent, engaged with the acoustics of words, with their sound, feel, and look. Practice at devotions deepened the inscription of sound, look, and feel in his sensorium . . . . The proper reading of the scriptures that enabled her to *hear* divinity speak depended on disciplining the senses (especially hearing, speech, and sight).[24]

Such a holistic sensory appropriation of Scripture liturgically was facilitated by the fact that these Christians were never far removed from the liturgy, but rather, the liturgy informed their whole lives. Peter Candler writes:

> Even when sufficient literacy is achieved by the medieval monk so as to permit reading privately in one's cell, this form of engagement with the text is never abstracted from a rigorous daily routine of matins, masses, vespers, and so on. Lectio divina is, however "private" reading might be, always a matter of reading and interpreting not just communally but liturgically . . . . It is not a possibility for such religious to abstract their reading from the liturgical cycle of daily masses and annual feasts, the use of the entire body, hands, knees, lips, tongue, ears, not to mention the eyes, all of which the reading of such texts requires.[25]

Writing further, Candler notes:

> there is the question of the way in which the Scriptures are present in the life of the Church. In the early and high Middle Ages, the Scriptures are present not primarily as a physical object, but rather preeminently in the memory. The Scriptures, as they are

---

23. Candler, *Theology, Rhetoric, Manuduction*, 7, 152–55 and 162; Turner, *Eros and Allegory*, 162; and Illich, *In the Vineyard*, 82. For a more detailed discussion on how this played out in medieval monasteries and the schools, see Leclercq's classic study, *L'Amour*. An English edition is available as *Love of Learning*.

24. Asad, *Formations of the Secular*, 37–38.

25. Candler, *Theology, Rhetoric, Manuduction*, 7. See also Leclercq, *L'Amour*; and Illich, *In the Vineyard*, 82.

read, and importantly, heard, by the congregation over the course of the liturgical year, are assigned to certain times in the calendar, and over the course of a year the Scriptures in their entirety may be read aloud each week, and over the course of a year, the average monk would have heard each Psalm at least fifty-two times.[26]

All of this began to change with the invention of the printing press. As Candler explains, "After the invention of moveable type, the sense of 'the book' becomes attenuated to refer to sheets of paper bound together within a leather cover, a physical object which can be bought or sold, carried in one's pocket, read at home, opened and read at will."[27] Eamon Duffy's study of the English Reformation epitomizes this transformation.[28] In the English Reformation, the State began to encourage parishioners to read their Bibles in English, and formerly Latin prayer books were printed in English with revised prayers.[29] With regard to the new prayer books, people "recognized that the prayer-book was merely one element in a programme which affected their religious life at every level, the dissolution of the elaborate symbolic framework within which the life of the communities had been shaped for generations. There was far more at stake than the merits of English or Latin in liturgy . . . ."[30] Reading the Bible in English became a means of showing support for the State and a way of criticizing the traditional liturgy. Groups of parishioners would bring their English Bibles to the liturgy, and would read their Bibles out loud during the Mass, in protest of the traditional liturgy and in support of the newer State reforms.[31] Duffy explains that, "New pieties were forming, and something of the old sense of the sacred was transferring itself from the sacramentals to the scriptures."[32]

### The Liturgy Unites Canonical and Christological Readings

Centuries later, we too can benefit from reading and praying the Bible in light of the liturgy, especially because of how the sacred texts in the liturgy

---

26. Candler, *Theology, Rhetoric, Manuduction*, 77.
27. Candler, *Theology, Rhetoric, Manuduction*, 76.
28. Duffy, *Stripping of the Altars*.
29. Duffy, *Stripping of the Altars*, 398, 406, 412, 450, and 486.
30. Duffy, *Stripping of the Altars*, 467.
31. Duffy, *Stripping of the Altars*, 420.
32. Duffy, *Stripping of the Altars*, 586.

provide new contexts for biblical interpretation.[33] The liturgical calendar, liturgical time, liturgical gestures, liturgical objects, liturgical art and architecture, all of these things affect how one reads Scripture.[34] By these and other means, the liturgy trains Christians to read Scripture in a certain way, forming particular habits of thought. As Candler explains: "the ability rightly to read the biblical texts is an art learned not through the strenuous exercises of a solitary mind, but rather from the use of the Scriptures in the liturgy, not to mention the larger liturgical apparatus of high medieval culture, which must include art, architecture, political relations, the mechanics of local commerce, and so forth."[35]

One of the most significant benefits of such a context is in facilitating Christological interpretations. Reading Scripture in the liturgy is a natural way to read the Bible Christologically, with Jesus as the key to reading the Old Testament as a Christian text. The liturgy is a privileged site for linking biblical interpretation with prayer. Furthermore, the liturgical juxtaposition of Scripture passages provides unique contexts for biblical interpretation, facilitating a reading which unites the Old and New Testaments.

The liturgy is likewise an important site for theology. The lectionary and the liturgical calendar are all important sites for theological reflection, inquiry, and biblical interpretation.[36] Again, Ratzinger comments that, "The reading of Scripture . . . reaches its highest point when the Church listens to the word of God in common in the sacred liturgy and

---

33. Wilken, "Allegory," 15; and Wilken, "In Dominico Eloquio," 849. For an example of how this worked in the early church, see the chs. 2 and 3 of Wilken, *Spirit of Early Christian Thought*.

34. On liturgical time, see Candler, *Theology, Rhetoric, Manuduction*, 151–52 and 155–56; Candler, "Liturgically Trained Memory," 433; D'Costa, *Theology in the Public Square*, 119–22; Levering, *Sacrifice and Community*, 92, 171, and 190; Corbon, *Wellspring of Worship*, 179–88; Benedict XVI, "End of Time," 4–5, 18, and 22; Cavanaugh, "Eucharistic Sacrifice," 599; Cavanaugh, *Torture and Eucharist*, 222–29 and 269; Benedict XVI, *Spirit of the Liturgy*, 53–61 and 92–111; and Pickstock, *After Writing*, 139 and 220–23. On liturgical gestures, see Candler, *Theology, Rhetoric, Manuduction*, 162. On liturgical objects, see Candler, 158–59. On liturgical art and architecture, see Candler, 152–55 and 157; Jones, *Hermeneutics of Sacred Architecture*; Carruthers, *Craft of Thought*; Baldovin, *Urban Character*; Heitz, "Architecture et liturgie," 30–47; and Mâle, *Gothic Image*.

35. Candler, *Theology, Rhetoric, Manuduction*, 50.

36. D'Costa, *Theology in the Public Square*, 132–33; Fagerberg, "Theologia Prima," 55–67; Fagerberg, *Theologia Prima*, IX, 2, 41–42, 66, 78–79, 81, and 109; and Fagerberg, "Liturgical Asceticism," 202–14.

within this framework itself experiences the active presence of the Logos, the Word in the words."[37]

Furthermore, liturgical concerns were the primary motivations for creating an official canon of Scripture. The canon was formed to decide which sacred texts should be read in the Church's official liturgical celebrations. In fact, one of the primary ways in which books were determined as suitable for inclusion in the canon was by their prior presence in the Church's liturgy.[38] Most Christians did not own their own personal copies of the Bible, nor did they have access to written copies, since the printing press was not invented and facilitating the widespread dissemination of hard copies of the scriptural texts until the end of the fifteenth century, and even then things changed only gradually. The canon determined which books were acceptable to be read together in the Church's communal worship.

The canon of Scripture as used in the liturgy created a special theological hermeneutic. In the Church's liturgy, the sacred events of salvation history, as set forth in the texts of Scripture, are made present to the community gathered in worship, and to each individual in the community.[39] As Hahn writes, "The liturgy draws the believer into the drama of the divine economy, not as a spectator, but as a participant. The stream of salvation history cascades from generation to generation through the course of the divine liturgy."[40]

Central to Hahn's affirmation of the need for a liturgical hermeneutic is his claim that this was the primary hermeneutic of Christians since the dawn of the first millennium. He explains, "To read scripture 'with the

---

37. Benedict XVI, "Sacred Scripture," 271. See also the Second Vatican Council's Dogmatic Constitution *Dei Verbum* nos. 21 and 23. In no. 21 *Dei Verbum* explains that Scripture is revered "most especially in the sacred liturgy" (Latin text from Tanner, *Decrees of the Ecumenical Councils II*). In no. 23 *Dei Verbum* highlights the importance of actually studying liturgy along with studying Scripture. In no. 25 *Dei Verbum* underscores the necessity of prayer for Scripture study. On the importance of the liturgy for encountering and understanding Scripture, also see John Paul II, "Address Commemorating," no. 4; and John Paul II, *Scripturarum Thesaurus*, no. 1.

38. Wilken, *First Thousand Years*, 43; Hahn, "Canon, Cult and Covenant," 209–10; Hahn, "Worship in the Word," 102–3; Childs, "Canon in Recent Biblical Studies," 33–57; Childs, *New Testament*; McDonald, *Formation*, 246–49; McDonald, "Identifying Scripture,", 420, 423, 432–34, and 439; Sanders, *From Sacred Story*, 162; and Stuhlmueller, *Thirsting for the Lord*, 102.

39. Hahn, "Canon, Cult and Covenant," 208, 211, and 228–29; and Hahn, *Letter and Spirit*, 48–49 and 92.

40. Hahn, *Letter and Spirit*, 93.

church' was to read it or hear it in the liturgy. Apostolic and patristic exegesis took place not primarily in the classroom or in the monastic cell, but in the public reading and proclamation of scripture in the liturgy."[41] The liturgy continues to provide a rich theological context for Scripture. The various Scripture passages from the Old and New Testaments are paired together in unique ways, relate to each other in liturgical time, and, read at the Church's liturgy, they provide a specific theological hermeneutic in the Church's life.

The liturgy places texts together and thereby creates associations in the minds of the hearers and readers at the Church's liturgical celebrations. This provides Christological connections, in other words, the Old Testament passages are read in light of the New Testament passages, and especially the Gospel passages.[42] Denys Turner observes that, "Even today, in a Sunday eucharistic liturgy, the placing of readings from the Old and New Testaments in immediate succession within the Liturgy of the Word has the effect of provoking the reading of one in terms of the other in a manner which would have been familiar, through daily practice, to the mediaeval monk."[43]

Mystagogy is the key concept that makes the sacred liturgy such a unique location for uniting prayer and interpretation. Mystagogy is not simply that time after Easter when the newly baptized participate fully in the Church's liturgical and sacramental life, but rather sums up our entire post-baptismal life. Mystagogy is our immersion in the sacred Christian mysteries, which we initiate in the sacred liturgy, which is, in Fagerberg's words, "our trysting place with God."[44] The Eucharist brings to completion the work begun in us through Scripture. Mystagogy, then, is our continued experience living the sacramental life.[45] Catholic biblical exegesis should be

---

41. Hahn, *Letter and Spirit*, 142. Writing on page 144, Hahn elaborates, "Liturgy is the place where the stream of salvation history runs swift and clear—sweeping Christians into the current of the divine and sacramental economy." And again, "Liturgy is the place where God's people have always gone to hear the covenant and to renew the covenant, with all their heart and mind, soul and body."

42. As Hahn points out, "The interpreter of the Bible enters into a dialogue with a book that is itself an exegetical dialogue—a complex and highly cohesive interpretive web in which the meaning of earlier texts is discerned in the later texts, and in which later texts can only be understood in relation to ones that came earlier" (Hahn, "Canon, Cult and Covenant," 227).

43. Turner, *Eros and Allegory*, 162.

44. Fagerberg, "Theologia Prima," 57. On the same page he writes, "In the liturgy we do what the angels do, namely, lose ourselves in a joy that erupts in praise."

45. Here I am echoing the call for such a liturgical hermeneutic voiced in Hahn,

mystagogical, moving from the visible signs to the invisible realities which the signs signify.[46]

The Second Vatican Council taught that the Eucharist is the "source and summit of the whole of Christian life" (*Lumen Gentium*, no. 11).[47] The Eucharistic liturgy is transformative and reconfigures the faithful so that they may live cruciform lives and be the presence of God's grace in creation. To paraphrase Abraham Heschel, our work, the labor of our lives, is oriented toward the Sabbath.[48] As Heschel explains, "The work on weekdays and the rest on the seventh day are correlated. The Sabbath is the inspirer, the other days the inspired."[49] Thus the ordinary work we perform during the

---

"Worship in the Word," 101–36; and Hahn, "Canon, Cult and Covenant," 207–35. In addition to mystagogy, Hahn emphasizes the importance of the divine economy and typology ("Worship in the Word," 130–35; and "Canon, Cult and Covenant," 226–29). On mystagogy in its relation to theology (including biblical exegesis), see especially Mazza, *La mistagogia*, an English translation of which is available as *Mystagogy*; and the difficult to find Golitzin, *Et Introibo*, which represents Bishop Golitzin's doctoral dissertation completed at the University of Oxford. See also the important work by Jean Corbon, who drafted the fourth section of the *Catechism of the Catholic Church* dealing with Christian prayer, *Liturgie de source*, an English translation of which is available as ibid., *Wellspring of Worship*. On the Christian mysteries, see especially Scheeben, *Die Mysterien des Christentums*, and English translation of which is available as *Mysteries of Christianity*. An early and much thinner volume of Scheeben's book originally appeared in 1865. Scheeben died before his revisions were complete, but the much more voluminous 1941 edition, which Josef Höfer edited, was made based upon Scheeben's own annotated two copies of the original.

46. See the very helpful discussion, which is an examination of Jesus' conversation with Nicodemus (John 3:1–21), in Hahn, "Temple, Sign, and Sacrament," 115–20. Hahn writes that, "This form of pedagogy from the 'earthly' to 'heavenly' may aptly be described by the Church's term 'mystagogy.' In particular, in the Nicodemus dialogue there is a mystagogy that leads from the *signs* that Jesus performs to the activity of the Spirit in the *sacraments*—in this case, the sacrament of baptism" (120).

47. "Totius vitae christianae fontem et culmen." Tanner, *Decrees of the Ecumenical Councils* 2. Indeed, *Dei Verbum* no. 23 even encourages the study of the sacred liturgies within the context of biblical interpretation and of the role of Scripture in the church's life.

48. Heschel, *Sabbath*. See also Heschel's comments about the importance of the eighth day (Sunday): "The famous Palestinian homilitician of the third century, Rabbi Levi . . . . explained why a boy is not circumcised until the eighth day: it is like a king who entered a province and issued a decree, saying: 'Let no visitors that are here see my face until they have first seen the face of my lady.' The lady is the Sabbath. Since there can be no seven continuous days without a Sabbath, the child is exposed to the covenant of the Sabbath before it is entered into the covenant of circumcision" (110n4). For more on Gen 1–3, Heschel, and implications for a theology of work, see Morrow, "Genesis 1–3."

49. Heschel, *Sabbath*, 22. Earlier he writes, "The Sabbath is not for the sake of the weekdays; the weekdays are for the sake of the Sabbath" (14).

week is sanctified by the worship/rest in which we participate on the Sabbath. In a Christian context, this takes on added meaning in the Eucharistic liturgy of the Lord's Day.[50] As Pope St. John Paul II quips in *Dies Domini*, his Apostolic Letter on the Lord's Day, " . . . Sunday in a way becomes the soul of the other days."[51] Thus, the relationship between the days of the workweek and Sunday becomes mystagogical, the ordinary pointing and moving toward the extraordinary; the natural labor itself becomes bound up with the divine labor of redemption and is sanctified by the Eucharistic celebration, the participation in the heavenly liturgical reality.[52]

Liturgical hermeneutics thus promise to be both "literary and historical, liturgical and sacramental," seamlessly integrating the findings of historical research, incorporating the full range of Scriptural senses, read in light of the Rule of Faith and the Church's Magisterium. This hermeneutical method underscores Scripture's "mystagogic purpose in bringing about, through the sacramental liturgy, the communion of believers with the God who has chosen to reveal himself in Scripture."[53] Just such a liturgical hermeneutic was at the forefront of Pope Benedict XVI's concerns.[54] Pope Benedict's 2010 Post-Synodal Apostolic Exhortation *Verbum Domini* highlights just how the sacred liturgy is Scripture's privileged setting.[55] Benedict goes so far as to write that, "*A faith-filled understanding of sacred Scripture must always refer back to the liturgy, in which the word of God is celebrated as a timely and living word.*"[56]

Thus, I believe that an explicit liturgical hermeneutic may be an important step in recovering an explicitly theological interpretation of

---

50. See John Paul II, *Dies Domini*. He explains, "When its significance and implications are understood in their entirety, Sunday in a way becomes a synthesis of the Christian life and a condition for living it well" (no. 81).

51. John Paul II, *Dies Domini*, no. 83. This is because, as he writes earlier in the same Apostolic Letter, "The grace flowing from this wellspring [the Eucharist] renews mankind, life and history" (no. 81).

52. See John Paul II, *Dies Domini*, no. 67, where he notes, "Through Sunday rest, daily concerns and tasks can find their proper perspective: the material things about which we worry give way to spiritual values."

53. Hahn, "Canon, Cult and Covenant," 229.

54. On Pope Benedict's exegesis, see Hahn, *Covenant and Communion*; Raurell, "Mètode d'aproximació," 435–58; Hahn, "At the School of Truth," 80–115; Hahn, "Hermeneutic of Faith," 415–40; and Hahn, "Authority of Mystery," 97–140.

55. Benedict XVI, *Verbum Domini*, nos. 52–72. Pope Benedict states that, "the liturgy is the privileged setting in which God speaks to us in the midst of our lives" (52).

56. Benedict XVI, *Verbum Domini*, no. 52.

Scripture that incorporates traditional and modern forms of exegesis.[57] Hahn enumerates the benefits of such a method:

> this new hermeneutic is at once literary and historical, liturgical and sacramental. It will be capable of integrating the contributions of historical and literary research while at the same time respecting the traditional meanings given to the Bible by the believing community in which the Bible continues to serve as the source and wellspring of faith and worship. A liturgical hermeneutic will recognize the liturgical content and "mission" of the Bible—its mystagogic purpose in bringing about, through the sacramental liturgy, the communion of believers with the God who has chosen to reveal himself in Scripture. It is, then, a hermeneutic that grasps the profound union of the divine Word incarnate in Christ, inspired in Scripture, and proclaimed in the church's sacramental liturgy.[58]

Where then should biblical theologians begin? We must begin in prayer, not ignoring historical and philological concerns, but rather integrating such concerns in a biblical theology done on bended knees.[59] One place to begin would be to study the Scriptures as they are juxtaposed within the liturgical cycle of readings. Wherever we begin, we should begin with prayer, for prayer and sacrifice are at the heart of Christian liturgy, the memorial of God's saving act and an entry into the sublime mystery of God's presence among us. Divine liturgy is the very wellspring of Christian worship.[60] It is in this context that we turn to a concrete example in the Feast of St. Joseph the Worker.

---

57. Fagerberg explains that, "It just may be that a particular scroll only blooms if it remains securely rooted in the whole of Scripture; and the whole of Scripture may only be intelligible if read as the marching orders for a liturgical procession; and the theology that comes from this liturgical life is about participation in the life of God" ("Theologia Prima," 57).

58. Hahn, "Canon, Cult and Covenant," 229.

59. The allusion here is to Hans Urs von Balthasar's contrast between "kneeling" and "sitting" theology, the prayerful and the academic, which comes from von Balthasar, "Theologie und Heiligkeit," 881–97 in *Wort und Wahrheit*. A more accessible version of this is von Balthasar, "Theologie und Heiligkeit," 195–224 in *Verbum Caro*. It is available in English as von Balthasar, "Theology and Sanctity," 181–86.

60. See Corbon, *Wellspring of Worship*.

## In the Carpenter's Workshop: Work as Worship

Although the most notable liturgical use of creation in Genesis is certainly the Easter Vigil, there is another liturgical celebration which also makes use of this passage. May 1 has been the Memorial of St. Joseph the Worker since Pope Pius XII inaugurated the feast in 1955.[61] The readings for that day make it an especially appropriate moment for investigation in light of this article's present concerns, since the first reading may be taken from the account of creation in Gen 1. The Genesis text, however, is not the only aspect of the liturgy that makes associations with the creation material covered in this article, rather the very structure of every Eucharistic liturgy links creation, the very fabric of our lives, and worship, in a way which provides a natural biblical hermeneutic, as Luke Timothy Johnson explains:

> The ordinary of the Mass is built upon the basis of biblical language, from the *kyrie* to the *agnus Dei*. Participation in the Eucharist meant an invitation to the world constructed by Scripture. The proper portions of the Mass included not only readings from Scripture ... and preaching on the basis of the readings, but also subtle interpretations of those readings through antiphons, responses, and prayers .... Catholics learned their Scripture through the practices of faith, and those practices also interpreted Scripture.[62]

The very structure and makeup of the Eucharistic liturgy itself creates biblical associations for the active participant. As Benedict XVI proclaims, "At the centre of everything the paschal mystery shines forth, and around it radiate all the mysteries of Christ and the history of salvation which becomes sacramentally present."[63] It is this mystery that imbues our labor with the qualities necessary to transform such labor into worship, which is part of what the very Feast of St. Joseph the Worker teaches.[64]

The first reading for the Memorial of St. Joseph the Worker may be taken from Gen 1:26—2:3.[65] This passage concerns the creation of humanity in the image of God on the sixth day of creation. The passage ends with

---

61. This memorial has been optional since 1969.
62. Johnson, "What's Catholic," 6.
63. Benedict XVI, *Verbum Domini*, no. 52.
64. John Paul II, *Redemptoris Custos*, no. 22: "In our own day, the Church has emphasized this by instituting the liturgical memorial of St. Joseph the Worker on May 1. Human work, especially manual labor, receive special prominence in the Gospel."
65. The first reading instead may be taken from Col 3:14–15, 17, 23–24.

God resting from work on the seventh day, the day which God makes holy. In this text, God's labor is ordered to the seventh day of rest. This parallels the actual liturgy itself, which moves from the liturgy of the word, celebrating Creation, to the liturgy of the Eucharist in which we anticipate and participate in the eternal heavenly rest, through entering into the very divine life of the Most Holy Triune God.

The responsorial psalm is taken from Ps 90 (2–4, 12–14, 16), where we hear sung the words: "Before the mountains were born, the earth and the world brought forth, from eternity to eternity you are God" (90:2).[66] Again, this Psalm hearkens back to creation in Genesis, to the work of God. Although not in the readings for the day, work was one of the tasks God gave in the Garden of Eden (Gen 2:15) well before the Fall. Such labor in the Garden is just one of the many forms of work we find in Scripture. Regarding this passage, Heschel emphasizes that, "Labor is not only the destiny of man; it is endowed with divine dignity."[67] John Paul II explains:

> Since work in its subjective aspect is always a personal action, an *actus personae*, it follows that *the whole person, body and spirit*, participates in it, whether it is manual or intellectual work . . . . an inner effort on the part of the human spirit, guided by faith, hope and charity, is needed in order that through these points the *work* of the individual human may *be given the meaning which it has in the eyes of God* and by means of which work enters into the salvation process on a par with the other ordinary yet particularly important components of its texture.[68]

In the life of St. Joseph, this labor takes on a special hue: at some point, St. Joseph performed his work with Jesus at his side.[69]

In the Gospel reading for the memorial from Matt 13:54–58 we find the crowd asking about Jesus, "Is he not the carpenter's son?" (55). We can imagine the kinds of things Jesus learned as the son of a carpenter. In his Apostolic Exhortation on St. Joseph, *Redemptoris Custos*, John Paul

---

66. The translation here is taken from the NAB.

67. Heschel, *Sabbath*, 27. See also the comments in Morrow, "Genesis 1–3"; and John Paul II, *Laborem Exercens*, "man's work is a participation in God's activity" (no. 25).

68. John Paul II, *Laborem Exercens*, no. 24. See also Morrow, "Genesis 1–3."

69. See John Paul II's comments regarding St. Joseph's role in being Jesus' father: "The growth of Jesus 'in wisdom and in stature, and in favor with God and man' (Lk 2:52) took place within the Holy Family under the eyes of Joseph, who had the important task of 'raising' Jesus, that is, feeding, clothing and educating him in the Law and in a trade, in keeping with the duties of a father" (ibid., *Redemptoris Custos*, no. 16).

II observes that, "The Gospel specifies the kind of work Joseph did in order to support his family: he was a carpenter. This simple word sums up Joseph's entire life."[70]

It is in connection with St. Joseph's work, and Jesus' hidden life as St. Joseph's apprentice, that we find labor transformed into worship, into divine work. In the words of John Paul II, "At the workbench where he plied his trade together with Jesus, Joseph brought human work closer to the mystery of the Redemption."[71]

Although Scripture does not record St. Joseph making a single sound, let alone uttering any words, his actions and his life speak volumes. In the words of one modern Saint, "A master of interior life, a worker deeply involved in his job, God's servant in continual contact with Jesus: that is Joseph.... With Saint Joseph, the Christian learns what it means to belong to God and fully to assume one's place among men, sanctifying the world."[72] St. Joseph is not one of the characters in the New Testament that stands out in a dramatic way, but rather, appears to us in a more hidden fashion.[73] John Paul II explains, "Work was the daily expression of love in the life of the Family of Nazareth.... If the Family of Nazareth is an example and a model for human families, in the order of salvation and holiness, so too, by analogy, is Jesus' work at the side of Joseph the carpenter."[74]

Writing elsewhere, John Paul II puts this in broader context, in light of Jesus' sanctification of human work. John Paul II notes that Jesus "*looks with love upon human work* and the different forms that it takes, seeing in each one of these forms a particular facet of man's likeness with God, the Creator and Father."[75] This work becomes redemptive also by uniting the suffering involved with work after the Fall with Christ's work of redemption on the cross:

---

70. John Paul II, *Redemptoris Custos*, no. 22.

71. John Paul II, *Redemptoris Custos*, no. 22. In the same section, he elaborates, "Along with the humanity of the Son of God, work too has been taken up in the mystery of the Incarnation, and has also been redeemed in a special way."

72. Escrivá, "In Joseph's Workshop," 88.

73. See the insightful comments in Suarez, *Joseph of Nazareth*, 13: St. Joseph "is more appropriately to be included in the long and less colorful list of men and women who, if by some accident they happen to be noticed at all, will hardly incline an observer to give them a second glance.... Joseph passes through the Gospel without our hearing him utter so much as a single word." See also Hahn, *Joy to the World*, 67–82.

74. John Paul II, *Redemptoris Custos*, no. 22.

75. John Paul II, *Laborem Exercens*, no. 26.

> By enduring the toil of work in union with Christ crucified for us, man in a way collaborates with the Son of God for the redemption of humanity. He shows himself a true disciple of Christ by carrying the cross in his turn every day in the activity that he is called upon to perform.... The Christian finds in human work a small part of the Cross of Christ and accepts it in the same spirit of redemption in which Christ accepted his Cross for us. In work, thanks to the light that penetrates us from the Resurrection of Christ, we always find a *glimmer* of new life, of the *new good*, as if it were an announcement of 'the new heavens and the new earth' in which man and the world participate precisely through the toil that goes with work.[76]

Joseph's own sanctification of ordinary work in the context of the Holy Family, and of his manual labor, serves as an important model for most of us. As the spiritual writer Federico Suarez points out, like St. Joseph, "It is not necessary for all of us to shine before men; they do not even need to know of our existence.... It is sufficient merely to carry out the little, commonplace, almost banal duties of each day with love and humility and with the intention of pleasing God."[77] This is the message of the Feast of St. Joseph the Worker, and it is a message driven home especially well in light of Gen 1–3. John Paul II, with his characteristically penetrating insight, summarizes the central point: "What is crucially important here is the sanctification of daily life, a sanctification which each person must acquire according to his or her own state, and one which can be promoted according to a model accessible to all people."[78]

Thus, we see one potentially fruitful means of employing a liturgical hermeneutic in the specific instance of the Feast of St. Joseph the Worker. Such a liturgical reading can help form Christian minds to think about the world in light of Scripture and the Sacraments. Wilken's comments about the liturgical context of early Christian thought and life are particularly apropos here, when he writes:

> Before there were treatises on the Trinity, before there were learned commentaries on the Bible, before there were disputes about the teaching on grace, or essays on the moral life, there was awe and adoration before the exalted Son of God alive and present in the church's offering of the Eucharist. This truth preceded every effort

---

76. John Paul II, *Laborem Exercens*, no. 27.
77. Suarez, *Joseph of Nazareth*, 19.
78. John Paul II, *Redemptoris Custos*, no. 24.

to understand and nourished every attempt to express in words and concepts what Christians believed.[79]

Our reading of Gen 1–3 underscores the message of the Feast of St. Joseph the Worker; that the world is created as one expansive sanctuary for us to dwell in and worship God with the ordinary work of our lives oriented toward sacramental worship. In addition to what we might call liturgical justification, the ecclesial juxtaposition of biblical passages together in the Mass, shows how reading and praying Scripture in light of the liturgy can be a fruitful means of encountering the living word of God, and of making biblical interpretation theological once again. We will explore another means of theologically reading Scripture, using typology, in the next chapter.

---

79. Wilken, *Spirit of Early Christian Thought*, 36.

# 4

# Heavenly Bread

A Mystagogical Reading
of 1 Kings 19

IN THE PREVIOUS CHAPTER we made an argument for the importance of a liturgical interpretation of Scripture, especially focused on the lectionary. The lectionary of the Roman Rite of the Catholic Church, as with all other lectionaries, has changed over time, sometimes including more passages from Scripture and sometimes including fewer passages from Scripture.[1] One need not limit such liturgical interpretations to passages that occur in the lectionary. As I mentioned in the last chapter, the liturgy helps form habits of interpretation that apply to Scripture even when those passages are read outside of the liturgy. Christians formed in, by, and through their participation in the Church's liturgical life carry with them the interpretive tools that make a liturgical hermeneutic natural.

In this chapter, I will attempt a theological reading of a very short passage, 1 Kgs 19:3–8. At one level the interpretation will be typological, focusing on how the text might point forward to Jesus and the Eucharist. At another level, it is mystagogical, because, as a typological reading that focuses on how the Old Testament points forward to the Sacraments—in this case, the Eucharist—it encourages the reader to move beyond the Old Testament signs to the reality of the Sacrament itself. I hope to ground this, however, in the literal sense. My arguments on the literal-level, are rather uncommon, as far as I can tell, and thus, I maintain them only very

---

1. For a marvelous introduction to the Old Testament that includes the references to all of the Old Testament passages found in the present Roman Catholic lectionary, see Bergsma and Pitre, *Catholic Introduction*.

tentatively. This is in sharp contrast to my reading of Gen 1–3 in the second chapter, where, as my copious sources attest, the arguments concerning creation and temple, Adam and priesthood, are as old as recorded Jewish and Christian biblical interpretation.

## The Elijah Narrative in 1 Kgs 19:3–8

The Elijah narratives in 1 and 2 Kgs are textually complex, and the compositional history of 1 Kgs 17–19, in particular, is hotly contested within historical critical scholarship.[2] Examining this textual history, which has some importance in discussions of the literal sense, is beyond the scope of what I will be covering in this chapter. In this chapter I focus exclusively on a few specific verses from within this broader Elijah cycle, namely 1 Kgs 19:3–8. In this passage we find Elijah fleeing into the wilderness, petitioning the Lord, begging for death, and then falling asleep. An angel appears to Elijah, touches him, and commands him to arise and eat the bread and drink the water which has mysteriously appeared. After the angel repeats the command, Elijah eats and drinks and continues on a forty-day journey to Horeb where he has an encounter with God.

I propose that this passage is suggestive of a death and resurrection scene, where Elijah's falling asleep may be a reference to death, and his arising akin to resurrection. If this is correct, that Elijah actually dies and is raised, then it points forward typologically to the death and resurrection of Jesus. After his apparent resurrection, Elijah is fed with the mystical angelic bread and drink, which I suggest points forward to the Eucharist Jesus institutes at the Last Supper, which Christians continue to celebrate today.[3]

The passage under discussion reads as follows:

> Frightened, [Elijah] fled at once for his life. He came to Beer-sheba, which is in Judah, and left his servant there; he himself went a day's journey into the wilderness. He came to a broom bush and sat down under it, and prayed that he might die. "Enough!" he cried. "Now, O Lord, take my life, for I am no better than my fathers." He lay down and fell asleep under a broom bush.

2. Flannery, "Go Back," 163; and Keinänen, *Traditions in Collision*, 1–12. See also Lawrie, "Telling Of(f)," 163–80; Herr, "Variations of a Pattern," 292–94; Cohn, "Literary Logic," 333–50; and Carlson, "Élie à L'Horeb," 416–39.

3. Throughout this chapter, I will be using the words "mystical" and "mysticism" in the ways April D. DeConick uses them in her programmatic essay, "What Is Early Jewish," 1–24.

> Suddenly an angel touched him and said to him, "Arise and eat." He looked about; and there, beside his head, was a cake baked on hot stones and a jar of water! He ate and drank, and lay down again. The angel of the Lord came a second time and touched him and said, "Arise and eat, or the journey will be too much for you." He arose and ate and drank; and with the strength from that meal he walked forty days and forty nights as far as the mountain of God at Horeb (1 Kgs 19:3–8).[4]

In the broader context of this passage Elijah has just killed the prophets of Ba'al (18:40). In response to his attack, Jezebel sends a messenger (*ml' k*) to give Elijah what amounts to a death threat. Elijah's response to this turn of events is to flee into the wilderness seeking refuge. There is a play on words between the messenger (*ml' k*) sent by Jezebel, and the angel/messenger (*ml' k*) sent by God.

The plain sense reading of this passage, and, indeed, the standard interpretations, is simply that Elijah is depicted falling asleep due to exhaustion. Then, strengthened miraculously by nourishment from an angel, Elijah proceeds to Horeb for his Moses-like theophanic encounter with God. In this chapter, however, I would like to entertain a slightly different reading of the text. I suggest that Elijah does not merely take a snooze due to his exhaustion, but rather that Elijah actually dies a physical death in the wilderness, and then is raised from the dead by the angel of the Lord, after which he is fed with mystical food, heavenly bread, which strengthens him for his journey to the Mountain of God. This reading also provides us with a different take on the conclusion of the Elijah narratives. When we read that the prophet is taken to heaven on a fiery chariot (2 Kgs 2:11), there is no need for Elijah's physical death. The prophet has already died and been raised, and now Elijah dramatically ascends to the heavenly abode of God.

## The Sleep of Death

Since this reading of the passage goes against the standard interpretations, we may ask ourselves what grounds we have for understanding Elijah's falling asleep as death, especially if we are focusing on the literal level of the text. Why even consider the possibility that this instance of "falling asleep" signifies death? Of course, it is evident that one of the Greek phrases the

---

4. All English translations in this chapter for the Hebrew Bible are taken from the NJPS unless otherwise mentioned.

Septuagint uses here for Elijah's falling asleep, *ekoimēthē*, is used later in the New Testament as a euphemism for dying. We see this, for example, in 1 Cor where those who have fallen asleep is a reference to those who have died. Thus, when we read *koimōntai* in 1 Cor 11:30, *ekoimēthēsan* in 15:6, *koimēthentes* in 15:18, and *kekoimēmenōn* in 15:20, all refer to those who have physically died. In and of itself, however, this New Testament use of the phrase is inadequate for making a case that death is implied in the Elijah passage presently under discussion. Both verbs for falling asleep/lying down (*ekoimēthē* and *hupnōsen*) employed in the Greek text of 1 Kgs have overlapping spheres of meaning.

In addition to the Greek euphemism of falling asleep for death, there are many places as well where the equivalent Hebrew phrase for falling asleep also refers to death. Unlike the common recognition of this Greek euphemism, however, this Hebrew usage is discussed less frequently in the literature. In our present passage, the Hebrew word the Septuagint translates as *hupnōsen* is *yiyšan*. We find forms of this same verb being used euphemistically for death in a number of places. Ps 13:4 makes it clear that death is indicated when it employs the phrase, '*išan hamāwet*, "sleep of death." But even in other passages, like *miyšēnê* ' *admat-* ' *āpār* "those who sleep in the dust of the earth" in Dan 12:2, *wěyāšěnû šěnat-* ' *ôlām* "and then sleep an endless sleep" in Jer 51:39, and *yāšanětî* "I would be asleep" in Job 3:13, are all instances where "sleep" unambiguously identifies death.

Hendrik Jagersma has made a persuasive case for reading sleep euphemistically as death in Elijah's sarcastic remark to the prophets of Ba'al in the chapter which precedes the one at hand. In 1 Kgs 18:27, we read Elijah's comment that perhaps Ba'al, their god, *yāšēn* "is asleep." Based on the ritual described in the passage, comparative Ugaritic literature, and the other Hebrew parallels I have just mentioned where sleep is a euphemism for death, Jagersma argues that Elijah is mocking the prophets with the insulting suggestion that perhaps their god is dead.[5] Interestingly, the Hebrew verb the Septuagint translates with *ekoimēthē* is *škb*, here *wayiškab*. One usage of *škb* is to refer, not only to lying down, but to dying. Thus, we see that even in Hebrew, falling asleep can be used to identify physical death and not merely natural sleep. But, again, this linguistic observation does not help us solve the interpretation of Elijah's falling asleep.

---

5. Jagersma, "*yšn*," 674–76. See also the comments in Hauser, "Yahweh Versus Death," 44. On the Ugaritic background to the idea of Ba'al's death (sleep of death) and the necessity to resurrect (awaken) Ba'al, as the background for understanding this passage, see, e.g., Keinänen, *Traditions in Collision*, 101–6; and Bronner, *Stories of Elijah*, 111–19.

## Death and Resurrection

In order to proceed, we must ask ourselves, why would Elijah die in this passage? Why might we consider that his falling asleep in fact indicates physical death? A preliminary answer might be that death is precisely what Elijah asked of God in his prayer. God allowing Elijah to die in the desert could be interpreted as a response to Elijah's prayer. 1 Kgs 19:4 tells us that Elijah "prayed that he might die. 'Enough!' he cried, 'Now, O Lord, take my life....'" It is then that Elijah lies down and falls asleep. When we follow the narrative, we see that the next action that takes place is that an angel appears and touches Elijah. Previously, a messenger (*ml' k*) had been sent by Jezebel to spell out Elijah's doom in the form of his impending death. Now we see another messenger (*ml' k*), this time from God. In my reading here, this divinely sent messenger brings the opposite message to Elijah—not death, but life—and Elijah is hence brought back to life.

Earlier, in the previous chapter, Elijah had told king Ahab, "Go up, eat and drink" (1 Kgs 18:41).[6] Now, the angel says to Elijah, "Arise and eat" (1 Kgs 19:5), and Elijah arises, and he eats and he drinks. If we take the opportunity to turn to the reception history of the Elijah narratives, we might note that Epiphanius links the verse from Eph, "Therefore it is said, 'Awake, O sleeper, and arise from the dead, and Christ shall give you light'" (Eph 5:14) with Elijah.[7]

Epiphanius furthermore makes a link between this arising from the dead with the raising of Lazarus in the Gospel of John, as well as with the raising of the synagogue ruler's daughter in Luke's Gospel, who Jesus identifies as asleep (*katheudei*).[8] Epiphanius certainly hit upon some interesting parallels with Luke and John. But it is also intriguing that in the Gospel of Mark, the synagogue ruler's daughter is not only described as asleep (*katheudei*), but Jesus' words to her include the Aramaic word *koum* (arise) left untranslated in the Greek with a simple explanatory gloss. In the Hebrew text of 1 Kgs 19:5 and 7, the word is the same, *qûm* in both.

---

6. In Hebrew, ' *alēh* ' *ĕkōl ûštēh*.

7. See the text and comments in *Books of Elijah*, 76–79.

8. For anyone reading the Syriac text, the fact that the Gospel of Mark includes the Aramaic phrase in the Greek text would be lost on the reader, since Syriac, a dialect of Aramaic, includes the phrase also in Luke, as a natural Syriac translation of the Greek. Thus, in 1 Kgs 19:5 and 7 we find the word: *qwm*. In Mark 5:41, we find the same word: *qwmy*. But we also have this word in Luke's account (8:54): *qwmy*.

Likewise, in the account of Lazarus's death and resurrection, in John 11, we again find the description of Lazarus as having fallen asleep, *kekoimētai* (11:11), and then Jesus says that Lazarus will arise or resurrect, *anastēsetai*. John's Gospel here uses the same verb the Septuagint employs to translate *qûm* when the angel commands Elijah: *anastēthi*, and then, *anasta*.[9] Of course, this is the verbal form the New Testament employs for resurrection, *anastasis*. None of this is conclusive, since these words, in both Hebrew and Greek, are common for natural arising, and not simply referring to supernatural resurrection. My arguments pertain to the entire context of the passage, and not merely to the translation of these Hebrew and Greek words.

## Elijah in the Wilderness

The narratives in 1 Kgs 17–19 are replete with verbs indicating dying and killing, and these words are contrasted with the sustaining of life.[10] God is depicted as the giver and sustainer of life. We see this particularly in the nourishment given to Elijah after he awakens. After he arises, he is fed with a cake and water provided by an angel. The emphasis that this is the angel of the Lord clarifies for the reader that this is no ordinary messenger, unlike the messenger Jezebel who was sent to Elijah. Such clarification might be necessary for the reader, since both the Hebrew and Greek words for angel and messenger are the same, and Elijah had just been visited by a human messenger sent with a message of impending death.

The cake of bread provided in the desert, and mysterious water, should call to mind when Moses and the Israelites were fed with Manna and water in their desert wandering after the exodus. Typologically these clearly refer to the Sacraments Jesus will institute. Paul alluded to something similar in his typological interpretation of the divine sustenance in the Wilderness period when he mentioned that, "our fathers were all under the cloud, and all passed through the sea, and all were baptized into Moses in the cloud and in the sea,

---

9. Peter Leithart sees this lying down and arising again as symbolic of death and resurrection. See Leithart, *1 and 2 Kings*, 141. That this passage is at least symbolic of death and resurrection was noticed over three decades ago in White, "Initiation Legend," 305, where White persuasively makes numerous links between the Elijah story and Genesis narratives concerning Hagar and Ishmael.

10. Lawrie, "Telling Of(f)," 175. On 176n27, Lawrie writes that, "The narrative itself [17–19] makes much use of *verbs* of killing and sustaining. The contrast between killing and sustaining is indeed a 'theme' that fits into the rhetoric of the narrative."

and all ate the same supernatural food and all drank the same supernatural drink. For they drank from the same supernatural Rock which followed them, and the Rock was Christ" (1 Cor 10:1–4, RSVCE).

The parallels between this passage in 1 Kgs and the wilderness narratives in the Pentateuch concerning Moses and the Israelites are striking.[11] As Moses and the Israelites travel forty years in the wilderness, so Elijah travels for forty days in the wilderness. Just as the Israelites drank water in the desert which the Lord provided through Moses, so Elijah drinks the water in the desert which the Lord provides through an angel. The Israelites fed on the manna in the wilderness, mystical bread which, in its rendering of Ps 77:25 the Septuagint renders as "bread of angels" (*arton angelōn*).[12]

Deut 18:15–19 points to a prophet like Moses which the Lord will raise up.[13] There is a sense in which Elijah is a prophet like Moses, as the many parallels between him and Moses (and the wilderness accounts in general) make clear.[14] Here is a very short list of some of the most significant parallels between Moses and Elijah:

1. Moses himself, in Exod 32:31, asks that his life be taken away from him, just as Elijah does here in 1 Kgs 19.[15]

2. As Moses parted the Red Sea (Exod 14:21), so Elijah parted the Jordan river (2 Kgs 2:8).

3. As Moses was responsible for feeding the hungry Israelites in the wilderness with water from the rock and calling down Manna from heaven (Exod 16:4–18), so Elijah was responsible with the provision and multiplication of food and drink when these staples were running out for the widow and her son (1 Kgs 17:10–16).

---

11. See the comments in Keinänen, *Traditions in Collision*, 149–55; and Gregory, "Irony and the Unmasking," 144–46.

12. This is Ps 78:25 following the Hebrew text. The Hebrew text reads, *leḥem ' abîrîm* "bread of mighty ones." NJPS translates this as "a hero's meal." I think the most important work on the manna, and especially on how it relates to Jesus' institution of the Eucharist, is Pitre, *Jesus and the Last Supper*, 148–250.

13. On situating Jesus within the context of Jewish expectations of a prophet like Moses, see especially Pitre, *Jesus and the Last Supper*, 53–147.

14. Of course these parallels were not lost on early Jewish interpreters, as evidenced in the ninth century *Pesikta Rabbati*.

15. Lawrie, "Telling Of(f)," 174.

4. Both Moses and Elijah survive for forty days without eating or drinking (Deut 9:9 and 1 Kgs 19:8).[16]
5. Finally, both Moses and Elijah encounter God at Horeb.[17]

Perhaps the expectation of a new Moses-like figure partly accounts for Second Temple and later Jewish expectation of new manna, new heavenly bread when the Messiah arrived.[18] Texts including *2 Baruch* (29:3-8), *Midrash Rabbah* on Eccl 1:9, and *Mekilta* on Exod 16:25, all point to a future manna in the eschatological messianic age. As just one example, consider *2 Baruch*:

> And it will happen that when all that which should come to pass in these parts is accomplished, *the Messiah will begin to be revealed.... And those who are hungry will enjoy themselves and they will, moreover, see marvels every day.... And it will happen that at that time that the treasury of manna will come down again from on high,* and they will eat of it in those years because these are they who will have arrived at the consummation of time (*2 Baruch* 29:3 and 6-8).[19]

In the words of *Genesis Rabbah* (82:8), this would be "bread of the age to come." Elijah's association with the messianic age in Jewish tradition is clear, not only from the reference to Elijah's return on the Day of the Lord in Mal 3:23, but also the cup of wine set aside for Elijah in some Jewish traditions of the Passover Seder. In all of these and other traditions, Elijah is seen as the herald of the Messiah.[20] The differences between Elijah and Moses, however,

---

16. See the comments in Kugel, *How to Read*, 532, where he brings up these parallels and adds: "Elijah is a classically northern (Israelite) sort of prophet. A Moses-like worker of miracles.... He can also make it rain or make it stop (1 Kings 17:1) and bring a dead boy back to life (17:17-24); he is fed by the ravens (17:6) or by angels (19:5)." On that page, and the following (532), Kugel claims that these sorts of miracles are trademarks of northern prophets. Thus, Elisha also performs some of them, as does Jesus, another northerner, a Galilean prophet.

17. Sweeney, *I and II Kings*, 231 claims that the depiction of Elijah's trek to the Mountain of God "draws heavily upon the wilderness traditions." On the many parallels between Moses and Elijah journeying to Horeb, see Coote, "Yahweh," 115-20.

18. See especially Pitre, *Jesus and the Last Supper*, 148-250.

19. As quoted in Pitre, *Jesus and the Last Supper*, 158 (italics in Pitre's quotation).

20. Mal 3:23 in the Hebrew Masoretic Text (3:22 in the Greek Septuagint) is 4:5 in the Latin Vulgate, which most Christian English translations of the Old Testament follow. Incidentally, another connection between Moses and Elijah is that both are mentioned together in the same context in this passage from Mal (3:22-23 in MT; 3:22 and 24 in

are sufficient to see how Elijah is not entirely a new Moses, but the bread he consumes does appear to resemble the Manna which Jewish mystical traditions associate with heavenly food, angelic bread.

## Bread from Heaven

The description of the bread in 1 Kgs 19:6 presents it as a "cake," (*enkruphias* in the Septuagint; *'ūgat* in the Masoretic Text) which is how the Manna is described as being eaten in Num 11:8 (*enkruphias* in the Septuagint; *'ūgôt* in the Masoretic Text). It is the eating of this Manna-like cake, and the drinking of this water, that empowers Elijah to make the forty day trek to Horeb, the Mountain of God, and encounter the Lord in the cave.[21] In 1 Kgs 19:6, the cake is described as *rĕṣāpîm* ("baked on live coals," or "baked on hot stones" as the NJPS renders it). It is interesting to note that the only other time we find this expression, "live coal," used in this form is in Isaiah's vision of the heavenly temple.[22] In both instances, it requires an angel to provide the object for the prophet. In 1 Kgs the angel of the Lord brings the cake on hot coals to Elijah, whereas in Isa 6 one of the seraphim brings the hot coal to purify Isaiah's mouth.

There is another more proximate parallel with these events. Earlier in the Elijah narratives, in 1 Kgs 17, God sends Elijah to the widow and her son. Elijah asks the widow for bread. She explains that she does not have sufficient flour to make him any bread. He instructs her to make a small cake (*enkruphian mikron* in the Septuagint; *'ūgāh qĕṭanāh* in the Masoretic Text). When she obediently does what Elijah asked her, the flour and oil are miraculously multiplied for the remainder of the drought. Immediately following this scene, we find a description of Elijah raising the dead son.

---

LXX; and 4:4–5 in the Vulgate). See Gilbert, "Why Moses," 218. On Elijah as herald of the Messiah in Jewish liturgical traditions, see, e.g., Wiener, *Prophet Elijah*, 132–35.

21. Douglas Lawrie seems to take this provision of food as natural food: "This time no superhuman power possesses Elijah to enable him to undertake the journey; ordinary food has to do the trick." See Lawrie, "Telling Of(f)," 173. I think the context makes clear that such food, as provided by the angel of the Lord, is not natural but mystical. See, e.g., Cogan, *1 Kings*, 452n6. Indeed, Jyrki Keinänen calls the food, "heavenly sustenance," in Keinänen, *Traditions in Collision*, 158n8. Marvin Sweeney links the cake Elijah eats with the unleavened bread the Israelites consume in the exodus. See, Sweeney, *I and II Kings*, 231.

22. *Riṣpāh*. See Leithart, *1 and 2 Kings*, 141n1. The Hebrew word employed here is simply a stone, one used for paving, used elsewhere (e.g., Ezek 40:17 and Esth 1:6). It is used for heated stone or coal only in Isa 6 and 1 Kgs 19. See the comments in Cogan, *1 Kings*, 451–52n6.

He prays to God, and God responds by returning life to the son (1 Kgs 17:17–24).[23] Here we have a context with death, resurrection, and feeding on miraculous bread. Unlike the Manna, which is clearly depicted as supernatural food, the flour Elijah multiples appears to remain ordinary flour; the miracle is simply in the multiplication of the flour.

As I conclude, I want to give a brief overview of the broader context to the Elijah narratives. When we begin the Elijah narratives, we see God feeding Elijah in the desert with bread from a raven and water from a stream. When the lack of sustenance threatens life, as with the widow and her son, God miraculously provides the food which is lacking, staving off death. From the provision of food, to Elijah's raising the dead son back to life, to the slaughter of the prophets of God, and Elijah's slaughter of the prophets of Ba'al, to Elijah's own petition to die, we see that life and death, and God's power over both, provide an overarching theme for these chapters. When we reach 1 Kgs 19:3–8, we are thus already prepared for a death and resurrection scene, as well as a miraculous feeding; we have already encountered such miracles earlier in the Elijah cycle.

If this reading is correct, then Elijah is prepared by his initial death and resurrection, and heavenly feeding, for his mystical experience at the Mountain of God. After arising, his mystical transformation begins by feeding on the bread of angels.[24] The forty day journey he undertakes is not simply a penitential fast which further prepares him for his encounter with God, but it is also a journey his heavenly sustenance prepared him to take. Eating the heavenly bread of the flaming coal, provided by the angel of the Lord, has prepared Elijah for his theophany. Elijah's later ascension is thus merely the mystical extension of his wilderness transformation.

23. I am aware that there is some debate as to whether or not the son is depicted as actually dying. See, e.g., Levenson, *Resurrection and the Restoration*, 256n20.

24. The idea of feeding on heavenly food is widespread in Jewish literature. Andrea Lieber has written a fascinating discussion of this motif within early Jewish and Christian traditions. See Lieber, "Jewish and Christian," 313–39. Significantly, on page 337 she points out that, "The eschatological banquet in rabbinic literature, where humans feast like angels, is consistently linked to exegesis of Exod 24:11." This is in itself interesting because in Exod 24, the Israelites are at the foot of the Mountain of God, Horeb/Sinai, just as Elijah is about to make a journey there. Moreover, Lieber cites rabbinic literature showing how, in such interpretive traditions (like *Genesis Rabbah* 2:2), angels, and eventually humans as well, feast upon the Shekhinah, a heavenly meal wherein they feast upon the divine presence itself: "It is indeed characteristic of the angelic beings that they are privileged to feast on the divine presence, and it is characteristic of the human condition to toil for food. Yet in the messianic age, the righteous too will enjoy a heavenly meal . . ." (338).

Typologically, such a reading clearly points forward to Jesus' own death and resurrection. Unlike Elijah, however, Jesus does not flee from torment, rather Jesus embraces such torment. Unlike Elijah, Jesus does not pray for death, but rather for life, all the while willing to lay down his life for the sake of those he loved, all of us. If Elijah is in some sense of type of Christ in these passages, he can also serve as a type of the Christian who seeks to follow Christ, wherein the bread from an angel which he consumes is a type of the Eucharist, the bread of angels which we consume. Like Elijah, Christians are nourished by the Sacraments and called to go out into the wilderness and do penance, seeking an encounter with God. For some this will be a flight into the desert, as in religious life, whereas for the majority, it will be living a hidden ascetical life seeking God in the most ordinary circumstances of everyday life. Thus, such a reading of the Elijah narratives becomes mystagogical, as it causes the reader to move beyond the literal sense of the text and beyond the typological way in which it might point forward to the Eucharist. Such a reading encourages Christians to reflect upon the very mystery of the Sacraments themselves and the implications they have for living the Christian life. In the next chapter, we will take this a step forward as we explore martyrological exegesis.

# 5

# St. Thomas More as Biblical Interpreter

## Martyrological Exegesis

IN THE LAST CHAPTER, we took a look at typological and mystagogical exegesis by focusing on one discrete set of verses from the Elijah narratives (1 Kgs 19:3–8). In this final chapter, I turn to what I am calling martyrological exegesis, which relates to the tropological or moral sense. As opposed to examining a specific biblical passage, I take St. Thomas More's exegesis as an example of martyrological exegesis. St. Thomas More presents us with a wonderful example of martyrological exegesis where his exegetical work was intended for inspiring its readers to live the virtues, to follow Christ, and provide consolation amidst tribulation. Such exegesis intended to aid the reader in living the martyrdom required in everyday ordinary life, and, also, if necessary, mental anguish, physical torture, and death on behalf of Christ. Before examining More's work here, in the first part I situate this discussion within the broader conversation concerning modern Catholic biblical interpretation, and particularly the notion of senses of Scripture, some of which we have already covered in the first chapter, therein explaining how I use terms like mystagogy and martyrdom for the purposes of this article. The second part of this chapter examines More's spiritual exegesis of Jesus' passion narratives, particularly regarding the agony in the garden of Gethsemane. In the third portion, I conclude with a look at this Saint's life, which provides the context for his interpretation of Scripture.

## Senses of Scripture and Making Sense of Scripture

In 1988 the then Joseph Ratzinger (Pope Emeritus Benedict XVI) delivered his famous Erasmus Lecture, "Biblical Interpretation in Conflict."[1] He noted the limitations, but also the dangers, of modern biblical interpretation. He called for a "criticism of criticism," wherein historical criticism applied its own methods to itself, examining its philosophical presuppositions to understand better its limits.[2] In the conversation which followed, Ratzinger spoke of the need for a biblical hermeneutic that combined the best of traditional Catholic exegesis, exemplified by the church fathers, but also the best of modern historical exegesis.[3]

More recently, the need for a liturgical or sacramental hermeneutic has been discussed, as this book addressed in chapter 3. As we noted there, the Bible began in the liturgy. Long before the Bible was a book, the texts of Scripture were proclaimed in liturgical celebrations centered on the Sacraments. Moreover, the Sacraments are where the truths of Scripture become actualized, where we encounter salvation history and are taken up into its living currents. Indeed, the very documents which became Scripture were canonized precisely for use in the Church's liturgy, and, furthermore, their use, already, in the liturgies of the major churches founded by the apostles, was one of the primary criteria the Church used in discerning their canonicity.[4] What is more, much of the content of Scripture, the very contours of salvation history, has a liturgical or sacramental focus, as we saw, for example, in our discussion of Gen 1–3 in chapter 2.[5] Finally, the point of Scripture is our sanctification, our divinization, and thus our future complete participation in the heavenly liturgy of eternity, which we already anticipate and participate in here and now at every celebration of the Mass.[6]

Within the framework of a liturgical or sacramental hermeneutic, we can move further, following the church fathers, and show how such

---

1. Benedict XVI, "Biblical Interpretation in Conflict," 91–126.

2. Benedict XVI, "Biblical Interpretation in Conflict," 100. On this see Waldstein, "Self-Critique," 732–47; and Hahn, *Covenant and Communion*, 25–40. For attempts to do this in the context of the history of historical criticism, see Hahn and Morrow, *Modern Biblical Criticism*; Morrow, *Pretensions*; Morrow, *Theology, Politics, and Exegesis*; Morrow, *Three Skeptics*; and Hahn and Wiker, *Politicizing the Bible*.

3. Stallsworth, "Story of an Encounter," 107–8.

4. Wilken, *First Thousand Years*, 43; and Hahn, "Canon, Cult and Covenant," 209–10.

5. Hahn, "Worship in the Word," 102 and 104–30.

6. Hahn, *Letter and Spirit*, 102 and 111.

exegesis, mystagogical by nature, must move beyond mystagogy to martyrdom.[7] This can be linked to the traditional *Quadruplex Sensus*, fourfold sense of Scripture, which is an elaboration on the standard two senses of Scripture.[8] The medieval tradition, as evidenced in a particularly helpful way by St. Thomas Aquinas, bequeathed these senses of Scripture to the Church.[9] These have been taken up by the Magisterium and are presented to us today as an essential part of Catholic biblical interpretation.[10]

In modern catechesis, we can see how this division is likewise exemplified in the *Roman Catechism*, and now the *Catechism of the Catholic Church*.[11] The literal sense pertains to the words of the text themselves, what those words would have meant for the sacred writer and original audience. Modern and ancient forms of rhetorical, grammatical, and historical exegesis would all be useful for establishing the literal sense. This first sense is the foundation for all that comes later, just as the first part of the *Catechism* deals with the Creed, the bedrock foundation of faith, from which comes all of the rest. The first spiritual sense, typology or allegory, focuses on a uniquely Christian reading of the Old Testament, wherein the Old is read in such a way as to see how it points forward to Christ, the Church, and the Sacraments. This level of exegesis corresponds to the theological virtue of faith, as it explores the basis of what we believe, and corresponds to the teachings on the Sacraments in the *Catechism*.[12] Mystagogy is, in a way, lived typology, but applied to our lived experience of the Sacramental life of the Church.[13] We understand the whole of Scripture typologically pointing to our lived Sacramental life. The second spiritual sense, tropology or moral, pertains to how we are to live, applying Scripture to our lives to better ourselves and assist us in our struggles to become saints. This level of exegesis corresponds to the theological virtue of charity, and we

---

7. Indeed, in her Père Marquette Lecture Robin Darling Young showed how in the early church martyrdom was viewed as a sort of lived Eucharist; it was a (super)natural extension of the sacred liturgy. See Young, *In Procession*.

8. See the marvelous treatment of this in *Catechism of the Catholic Church*, nos. 115–19.

9. Aquinas, *Summa Theologiae*, I, q. 1, a. 10. See Baglow, "Rediscovering St. Thomas Aquinas," 137–46.

10. Benedict XVI, *Verbum Domini*, nos. 37–38.

11. Benedict XVI, "Handing on the Faith," 32–34.

12. Benedict XVI, "Handing on the Faith," 33.

13. Huizenga, "Tradition of Christian Allegory," 92–95.

see this in the third part of the *Catechism* on the Decalogue.[14] Finally, the fourth sense, the third spiritual one, anagogy, elevates our interpretation to contemplate heavenly realities. This level of exegesis thus corresponds to the theological virtue of hope, and is mirrored in the section on prayer, and the Lord's Prayer in particular, in the fourth and final section of the *Catechism*.[15] If mystagogical exegesis is closely tied to typology, then martyrological exegesis is closely tied to tropology.

Martyrdom here should be understood more broadly than physical dying for the faith, which it would of course include, but encompasses as well, the daily dying to self and living as Christ for others. There is a parallel here between connecting mystagogy with martyrdom and Benedict XVI's discussions of *lectio divina*. Traditional treatments of *lectio divina* emphasize its four stages: *lectio* (reading); *meditatio* (meditation); *oratio* (prayer); and *contemplatio* (contemplation). When Pope Benedict wrote on *lectio divina*, however, he almost always included discussion of a fifth step: *actio* (action).[16] This fifth step corresponds to the martyrdom I describe here in the movement from mystagogical exegesis to martyrological exegesis. Such liturgical, sacramental, mystagogical exegesis, must find expression in the lived experience of Christians. Indeed, this is the very purpose of the tropological sense, to amend one's life such that it is formed in the life of Christ. Scripture's divine inspiration is ordered to sanctity. The very reason for divine inspiration is, in part, to make saints of Scripture's hearers and readers. In St. Paul's Second Letter to Timothy we read that, "All scripture is inspired by God and profitable for teaching, for reproof, for correction, and for training in righteousness," and the purpose St. Paul provides for these adjectival modifiers is so "that the man of God may be complete, equipped for every good work" (2 Tim 3:16, RSVCE). The upshot of all of this is, as Hahn writes:

> Our interpretation of Scripture has to be lived and prayed and preached, so that the meaning of the Holy Writ is writ large not only in the hearts and minds of Christians, but in the hearts and minds of their neighbors as well. Written text must become living Word,

---

14. Benedict XVI, "Handing on the Faith," 33.

15. Benedict XVI, "Handing on the Faith," 33.

16. See, for example, Benedict XVI, *Verbum Domini*, nos. 86–7. On the traditional stages of *lectio divina*, and its classic formulation, see Guigo II, "Ladder from Earth," 175–88.

creating new lives out of the shell of old, re-creating men and women in light of the mystery of Christ revealed in the Word of God.[17]

Mystagogy is a movement from the natural sensory signs to the deeper supernatural realities signified by the external signs. Precisely because the Sacraments involve both the signs and the divine realities which the signs signify and thereby communicate and impart, mystagogy is sacramental, and it facilitates and enables our deeper experience of the rich Christian sacramental life whereby we are divinized. Turning to Hahn again we read:

> The early Christians explained the sacraments by means of a method they called *mystagogy*, an initiation into the divine mysteries, the hidden plan of the saving work of Christ. Mystagogy moves a Christian's awareness from the visible to the invisible, from the temporal to the eternal, from the human to the divine, from the earthly to the heavenly, from the sacraments to the mysteries.[18]

All Catholic theological exegesis should in some way be oriented toward mystagogy, just as Scripture leads us to the Sacraments where we encounter Christ and are thereby transformed. But our reception of the Sacraments is not intended to remain there; we need the Sacraments, not only to be in contact with Christ, to commune with God and deepen our relationship with our Divine Father in Heaven, but rather so that we become Christ and make the gift of ourselves here and now in the concrete situations of our daily life.[19] This is in part what *Gaudium et Spes* means by, "the human creature, the only creature on earth whom God willed for its own sake, can attain its full identity only in sincere self-giving."[20] Jesus' crucifixion was the ultimate gift of himself to us, renewed with every celebration of the Eucharist. But, from the cross, in making the complete gift of himself, Jesus was only doing in time, in history, in the world, what he has always been doing from all eternity within the family life of the Most Holy Trinity.[21] Thus imitating Christ through the little martyrdoms we have the opportunity to live each day, we can move from mystagogy to martyrdom. In this context the lectionary of the Easter season is particularly helpful in expressing that mystagogy

---

17. Hahn, *Consuming the Word*, 114.
18. Hahn, *Consuming the Word*, 117. See CCC 1075.
19. Connor, "One Truth," 367–71; and John Paul II, *Man and Woman*, 189, 196–97, 259–60, and 340.
20. *Gaudium et Spes* no. 24. All citations from the Second Vatican Council in this chapter are taken from Tanner, *Decrees of the Ecumenical Councils*.
21. Hahn, *Evangelizing Catholics*, 137.

because it includes as the first readings for Mass passages from the Book of Acts where we encounter the first Christians giving witness (martyrdom) in their daily lives throughout the Roman Empire.

As we continue in the third millennium, we need to live our Christian lives in this way of mystagogical martyrdom. We need to live our lives in such a way that, in the words of that twentieth century saint of ordinary life, St. Josemaría Escrivá, our "bearing and conversation [become] such that everyone who sees [us] or hears [us] speak could say: This man reads the life of Jesus Christ."[22] In his recent discussion on the new evangelization, which he calls "the great work of our age,"[23] Hahn writes the following:

> The culture has turned toxic, and the gap between how the Church calls us to live and how the culture tells us to live has grown so wide, we can no longer bridge it . . . . [The New Evangelization] calls us to transform not just individuals but the entire culture, recognizing that just as the de-Christianization of culture led countless men and women away from the Church, so can the re-Christianization of culture lead men and women back to the Church . . . . [In the New Evangelization we are] transforming the culture by introducing the individuals within it to a Person who will transform the very fabric of their lives.[24]

Here I examine the exegesis of St. Thomas More, contextualizing his work in the broader matrix of his saintly life. More may have been canonized because of his martyrdom, but, I would argue, he was prepared to receive the graces necessary for martyrdom by struggling to live a holy life in conformity to Christ.[25] As Hahn has written about St. Maximilian Kolbe's martyrdom, so too of More's, "it was merely the final moment in a masterwork. Such sanctity is not built in a day. That moment was the fruit of a lifetime of love."[26] More is significant on many levels, but he can relate to the many married faithful in the Church, not simply because he died a martyr at the hands of the state—few of us will follow in his footsteps—but rather,

---

22. Escrivá, *The Way*, no. 2. I have changed the second person to first person in this quotation.

23. Hahn, *Evangelizing Catholics*, 26.

24. Hahn, *Evangelizing Catholics*, 44.

25. See Aquinas, *Summa Theologiae* IIa IIae q. 123, a. 5, as well as IIa IIae q. 124, which is entirely devoted to the topic of martyrdom, which he understands as the principal action of the virtue of fortitude, and finally IIa IIae q. 139 on the role of the virtue of fortitude as a gift of the Holy Spirit.

26. Hahn, *Angels and Saints*, 164.

as the revised edition of the *Roman Martyrology* underscores, "also as a family man of the most upright life."[27] Intellectual knowledge of Scripture, as important as it is, means little if it does not facilitate an encounter with Christ and a transformed life. Scripture should lead us to the sacraments, just as the sacraments should lead us to Scripture, and both must lead us to God, spiritually nourishing us and enabling us to continually die to self and live for the others. This is what St. Thomas More did, and, his struggles, like our own—struggles in family life, struggles at work, struggles in deepening the interior life, and even struggles with the state—provide a good model for us, making More a saint for our times.

## *The Sadness of Christ*: More's Mystagogical and Martyrological Exegesis

More wrote a number of texts from his prison cell in the Tower of London. Here in this chapter I will primarily examine one of these texts, the last one he wrote: *The Sadness of Christ*.[28] This text is an interesting example of More's exegesis, and it particularly relates to what I am calling martyrological exegesis as it is basically a commentary on the Gospel accounts of Jesus' agony in the Garden of Gethsemane. More's hope is to provide "comfort against tribulation," and he believes this is precisely what Jesus intended to do through his agony in the garden.

Before turning to More's important work to bring "comfort against tribulation," namely his *Sadness of Christ*, we would also benefit from briefly examining his earlier book *A Dialogue of Comfort against Tribulation*, a much longer work that deals with the same theme in more detail.[29] The entire volume of the *Dialogue* has to do with the virtue of fortitude, particularly courage, but also about the Christian value and meaning of human suffering. The main dialogue is between two fictional characters, Anthony and his nephew Vincent. Anthony and Vincent are in Hungary and are beset by the clear and present danger of ruthless Muslim Turkish invasion. The frightened Vincent approaches his uncle, bedridden with illness, who had already had to face the violent Turks before, and Vincent thus hoped to gain some wise advice. The bulk of More's volume depicts how Anthony encourages Vincent through their conversation; it is not so much that Vincent's fears have been

---

27. Kelly et al., "Preface," xii.
28. All references to *Sadness of Christ* will be taken from More, *Sadness of Christ*.
29. All references to *Dialogue* will be taken from More, *Dialogue*.

eliminated, but rather that Vincent's courage has increased. The parallels with More's England and the violence Catholics were facing during his time from the state are patently clear in the *Dialogue* when it is read in light of the context of More's writing location in prison.

At one point, very much in line with what More will later write in his *Sadness of Christ*, Anthony's response to Vincent describes Christ's prayers in agony in the garden: "his heart, so heavy with fear of the painful, cruel death that he well knew was at hand, made such a feverish commotion in his blessed body that the bloody sweat of his holy flesh dropped down on the ground."[30] Graphic as Anthony's description is, it is intended to bring comfort. Here, More, via his character Anthony, who really does represent More himself, seeks to emphasize how suffering does not lessen the effect of prayer, but if anything, can make it more effective. Again, Anthony encourages Vincent in like manner, explaining that, "these prayers of our Savior in his bitter Passion, and those of the holy martyrs in the heat of their torment, should enable us to see that no prayer made in a pleasurable situation is so strong and effectual as prayer made in tribulation."[31]

We find the spiritual and ascetical background to this linked in More's focus on prayer and the interior life. More's earlier work, *Life of Pico*, clarifies the ascetical context for what More later wrote directly on the matter of suffering and the sadness of Christ.[32] Gerard Wegemer calls the concluding half, Pico's (and More's) poetic compositions, "More's spiritual compendium."[33] And indeed these compositions are rich in spiritual insight, and would be profitable for modern Christians in their pilgrimages toward heaven. In his *Life of Pico*, More exhorts his reader to remember Christ's passion, "as you taste your cup of bitter pain, think then upon how Christ drank vinegar and gall for you."[34] Writing further, More explains how contemplating the passion of Christ can help us in our struggles against temptation:

> If you hold back your hands and do refrain from greedy snatching at some thing, think you how to the cross nails fixed His innocent hands. If pride be your temptation, think how He, though in the very form of God, yet for you came a humble servant, suffering

---

30. More, *Dialogue*, 75.
31. More, *Dialogue*, 75.
32. All references to *Life of Pico* are taken from More, *Life of Pico*.
33. Wegemer, "Introduction," ix.
34. More, *Life of Pico*, 55.

death most hateful and most vile upon a tree. When moved to wrath, recall to memory that He Who both was God and best of men, when treated basely with contempt, and scourged and thrust as if a thief between two thieves with much rebuke and shame, still did not speak the slightest word of anger or of scorn but all the pain did patiently endure.[35]

More's *The Sadness of Christ*, with the full, original title of *On the Sadness, Weariness, and Fear of Christ*, was the last book More ever wrote. His basic argument in that work was that the rebellion of Christ's human flesh, his sadness, weariness, and fear, was permitted in order to become a model for the rest of us, to teach us how to live courage when we face trials and tribulations, sufferings of any kind. The key to this, More emphasized, was prayer. More underscored how Christ's life, actions, and words, were an example for us to follow. Like Christ, "we must lift up our minds from the bustling confusion of human concerns to the contemplation of heavenly things."[36] In More's exegesis, he paid careful attention to all details, since he believed that, "not a single syllable can be thought inconsequential in a composition which was dictated by the Holy Spirit as the apostles wrote it."[37] And, moreover, "no factual account in all of Scripture is so gross and corporeal (so to speak) that it does not have life and breath from some spiritual mystery."[38] (93).

In a lengthy passage, More explains the reasons he believes Christ submitted to so much suffering and mental anguish in the Garden of Gethsemane:

> Moreover, because He came into the world to earn joy for us by His own sorrow, and since that future joy of ours was to be fulfilled in our souls as well as our bodies, so too He chose to experience not only the pain of torture in His body but also the most bitter feelings of sadness, fear, and weariness in His mind, partly in order to bind us to Him all the more by reason of His greater sufferings for us, partly in order to admonish us how wrong it is for us either to refuse to suffer grief for His sake (since He freely bore so many and such immense griefs for us) or to tolerate grudgingly the punishment due to our sins, since we see our holy Savior Himself endured by His own free choice such numerous and bitter kinds of torment, both

---

35. More, *Life of Pico*, 55–56.
36. More, *Sadness of Christ*, 2.
37. More, *Sadness of Christ*, 3.
38. More, *Sadness of Christ*, 93.

> bodily and mental.... Finally.... since He foresaw that there would be many people of such a delicate constitution that they would be convulsed with terror at any danger of being tortured, He chose to enhearten them by the example of His own sorrow, His own sadness, His own weariness and unequaled fear, lest they should be so disheartened as they compare their own fearful state of mind with the boldness of the bravest martyrs that they would yield freely what they fear will be won from them by force.[39]

More continues:

> To such a person as this, Christ wanted His own deed to speak out (as it were) with His own living voice: "O faint of heart, take courage and do not despair. You are afraid, you are sad, you are stricken with weariness and dread of the torment with which you have been cruelly threatened. Trust me. I conquered the world, and yet I suffered immeasurably more from fear, I was sadder, more afflicted with weariness, more horrified at the prospect of such cruel suffering drawing eagerly nearer and nearer. Let the brave man have his high-spirited martyrs, let him rejoice in imitating a thousand of them. But you, my timorous and feeble little sheep, be content to have me alone as your shepherd, follow my leadership; if you do not trust yourself, place your trust in me."[40]

More makes a personal invitation to his reader: "Reader, let us pause for a little at this point and contemplate with a devout mind our commander lying on the ground in humble supplication."[41] He berates the reader, and includes himself, "our actions too, in how many ways do they betray that our minds are wandering miles away? We scratch our heads, clean our fingernails with a pocketknife, pick our noses with our fingers, meanwhile making all the wrong responses. Having no idea what we have already said and what we have not said, we make a wild guess as to what remains to be said."[42]

He provides a thought experiment to drive the point home:

> Imagine, if you will, that you have committed a crime of high treason against some mortal prince or other who has your life in his hands but who is so merciful that he is prepared to temper his wrath because of your repentance and humble supplication, and to commute the death sentence into a monetary fine or even to

---

39. More, *Sadness of Christ*, 15–16.
40. More, *Sadness of Christ*, 16.
41. More, *Sadness of Christ*, 18.
42. More, *Sadness of Christ*, 20.

suspend it completely if you give convincing signs of great shame and sorrow. Now when you have been brought into the presence of the prince, go ahead and speak to him carelessly, casually, without the least concern. While he stays in one place and listens attentively, stroll around here and there as you run through your plea. Then when you have had enough of walking up and down, sit down on a chair, or if courtesy seems to require that you condescend to kneel down, first command someone to come and place a cushion beneath your knees, or better yet, to bring a prie-dieu with another cushion to lean your elbows on. Then yawn, stretch, sneeze, spit without giving it a thought, and belch up the fumes of your gluttony. In short, conduct yourself in such a way that he can clearly see from your face, your voice, your gestures, and your whole bodily deportment that while you are addressing him you are thinking about something else. Tell me now, what success could you hope for from such a plea as this?[43]

More contrasts this with how our life of prayer should be, and could be if we contemplated Christ's prayer in Gethsemane as our model: "I wish that whatever our bodies may be doing, we would at the same time constantly lift up our minds to God."[44] This is because, "nothing is more profitable than prayer."[45] When Christ implores his disciples to watch and pray, More explains that, "Here we are enjoined to be constant in prayer, and we are informed that prayer is not only useful but also extremely necessary."[46] For, "prayer is the only safeguard against temptation and . . . if someone refuses it entrance into the castle of his soul and shuts it out by yielding to sleep, through such negligence he permits the besieging troops of the devil . . . to break in."[47] He explains further, "Therefore, to those whose hearts are troubled, meditation on this agony provides great consolation, and rightly so, since it was for this very purpose—to console the afflicted—that our

---

43. More, *Sadness of Christ*, 20–21. He writes further, "Certainly we would consider it quite mad to defend ourselves in this way before a mortal prince against a charge that carries the death penalty. And yet such a prince, once he had destroyed our bodies, could do nothing further. And do we think it is reasonable, when we have been caught committing a whole series of far more serious crimes, to beg pardon so contemptuously from the king of all kings, God Himself, who when He has destroyed our bodies has the power to send both body and soul together to hell?" (21).
44. More, *Sadness of Christ*, 21.
45. More, *Sadness of Christ*, 23.
46. More, *Sadness of Christ*, 27.
47. More, *Sadness of Christ*, 55.

Savior in His kindness made known His own affliction, which no one else knew or could have known."[48]

These pieces of sage advice aimed at the consolation of Christians during times of tribulation, are not merely theoretical for More, but emerge out of his lived experience of suffering, and indeed awaiting death by torture and humiliation. Although More was simply beheaded, and that lasting a fraction of a moment, this was not the death he awaited though it was the death he received. He was not made aware of the king's decision to commute his sentence to beheading, like Bishop St. John Fisher, until the day he was lead to the gallows. What More awaited in his prison cell was the same fate that befell his Carthusian friends, who had been led past his cell on their way to be tortured to death publicly.

## More as Saint and Martyr

More's works on Scripture cannot be understood apart from the context of his life.[49] In his Post-Synodal Apostolic Exhortation on Scripture, *Verbum Domini*, Benedict XVI wrote, "The interpretation of sacred Scripture would remain incomplete were it not to include listening to *those who have truly lived the word of God: namely, the saints* .... The most profound interpretation of Scripture comes precisely from those who let themselves be shaped by the word of God through listening, reading and assiduous meditation."[50] This is certainly the case with More. More struggled to live the virtues in his daily life; his Christian faith was implicated in all that he thought, said, and did. This can be seen from his daily working life, as well as from his daily family life. Moreover, More's life of prayer and piety was not some extraneous add-on to his normal quotidian routine, but rather was naturally integrated imbuing his smallest actions with the love of God and neighbor.

More's father was a lawyer, and he secured a fine education for his son. Already by age twelve More served Archbishop John Morton, England's Lord Chancellor, as a page in Lambeth Palace, a position held for two years. In his

---

48. More, *Sadness of Christ*, 32.

49. For the biographical material that follows on More I am relying upon Kelly et al., *Thomas More's Trial*; the essays in Logan, *Cambridge Companion*, especially Barron, "Making," 3–21, McConica, "Thomas More," 22–45, Curtis, "More's Public Life," 69–92, and Marshall, "Last Years," 116–38; Vázquez de Prada, *Sir Tomás Moro*; Berglar, *Thomas More*; Ackroyd, *Life of Thomas More*; and Wegemer, *Thomas More*.

50. Benedict XVI, *Verbum Domini*, no. 48.

role as Morton's page, and throughout their decade-long friendship, More received an early first-hand education in the court and ecclesiastical politics of the England of his age. More proceeded to classical studies at Oxford, and then legal training at one of the best schools in London, afterwards studying classics more intensely in the best northern humanist tradition.[51] Eventually, More was elected to parliament, was a celebrated lawyer, became undersheriff of London which involved serving as a judge, and his career culminated with his becoming one of King Henry VIII's royal counselors and finally the first layman Lord Chancellor of England.[52] More loved God from a very early age, and he wrestled with his vocation. He even spent four years living with the Carthusians, immersing himself in their daily prayer routine.[53] As his close friend Erasmus would write of him, More chose rather to become "a chaste husband rather than a licentious priest."[54]

Although More is a prime example of how the laity can achieve holiness through their ordinary work and family lives, he probably did not have a concept of the universal call to holiness quite like that outlined in *Lumen Gentium*, since, as comments in his *Dialogue Concerning Heresies* seem to indicate, he did not appear to have thought it possible that laity could achieve quite the level of sanctity that was achievable as a priest or religious.[55] More's sanctity, his struggle to live the virtues, was evidenced in all aspects of his life, especially at home and at work.[56] More was not instantly the perfect husband for his first wife, Jane, but rather, his marriage took much effort. Their love for one another steadily grew, as they welcomed four children into their family within their first five-and-a-half

---

51. McConica, "Thomas More," 22–45; McCutcheon, "More's Rhetoric," 46–68; Curtis, "More's Public Life," 70–72; Vázquez de Prada, *Sir Tomás Moro*, 48–54; Berglar, *Thomas More*, 6–7, 12–15, and 113–32; Ackroyd, *Life of Thomas More*, 29–37 and 71–86; and Wegemer, *Thomas More*, 5–8, 13–14, and 48–49.

52. Wegemer, *Thomas More*, 50–51, 54–56, 70, 72–77, and 134–37.

53. Barron, "Making," 13–14; Vázquez de Prada, *Sir Tomás Moro*, 70–90; Berglar, *Thomas More*, 7–11; Ackroyd, *Life of Thomas More*, 96–111; and Wegemer, *Thomas More*, 3, 10, and 15.

54. Erasmus, *Epistles 3*, 394, quoted in Wegemer, *Thomas More*, 11.

55. More, *Complete Works 6*, 107 and 298; Berglar, *Thomas More*, 215; and Wegemer, *Thomas More*, 12–13. For *Lumen Gentium* on the universal call to holiness, see nos. 39–42, but also see nos. 30–38 on the role of the laity. For example, *Lumen Gentium* states that, "all the faithful, whatever their condition or rank, are called to the fullness of the Christian life and the perfection of charity" (no. 40).

56. For examples of his virtuous reputation in his work, particularly honesty, integrity, prudence, and fortitude, see Wegemer, *Thomas More*, 51–60.

years of marriage. Wegemer writes that, "The strong love that was 'born and confirmed' between Thomas and Jane stemmed in large part from their mutual commitment to grow in virtue."[57]

Suffering and difficulty entered More's life far beyond the normal busyness and challenges of raising a young family; his wife Jane died the same year she gave birth to their fourth child. With so many pressing matters at work, coupled with the needs of his family, and particularly the raising of four young children, none of which had yet reached six years of age, More decided to get married again as quickly as possible, and to the most virtuous woman he could find. This time he married a widow, Alice Middleton, who was six years older than he was. He had known her late husband well through work. Alice's educational background was rather poor, whereas More was one of Europe's finest man of letters, and, as with his prior marriage, More and Alice had their struggles. And yet, More's friend Erasmus marveled at how intimate a true friendship they had in their marriage.

In part, their love-filled marriage was without a doubt strengthened by More's tireless, and even sacrificial, devotion to his family. Wegemer remarks that, "Placing such an emphasis on his family duties was a distinguishing characteristic of More as husband and father.... More was absolutely clear that his family was his first responsibility. So important to him were his family duties that he was willing to change his career rather than neglect them."[58] One of the many sacrifices he made for his family was the sacrifice of his literary output, which was a longstanding passion of his, and for which he was especially gifted. As a lawyer, he took pains to arrange his work schedule so as to spend enough time with his family. One of the most courageous, and creative, actions he took in this regard is described in a story Roper reports. When working for the king, More had to change his personality slowly, almost imperceptibly. This was because the king so much enjoyed his presence, that he kept More from being at home each night so that he could dine with the king and be the life of the party. Eventually, and ever so subtly, his manner changed so much that the king no longer called for him as often, thus allowing More to spend more time with his family. And this had been the result of a conscious and concerted effort on More's part.

More saw the education of his children as one of the key duties of his role as a father. Indeed, for More, education was nothing other than

57. Wegemer, *Thomas More*, 30.
58. Wegemer, *Thomas More*, 34.

"cultivating the garden of the soul."[59] He sought to instill the virtues in his children, and he attempted to do this by befriending them, and of course attempting to the best of his abilities, and with the grace of God, to model the virtues as by living them in his own daily life. He brought rich culture into their family lives, and strove to make their hope steeped in Christian joy. More's home, moreover, was the frequent meeting place of a host of people from all over, as More's circle of friends expanded, and Christian hospitality was an important part of their regular family life. The virtues he lived in family life More also lived in his work life, as a lawyer and judge, and also as a counselor for the king. More was famous for his integrity and courage. His exercise of prudence and fortitude can be glimpsed in his knowing how and when to correct the king in the advice he gave him as friend and counselor; this was also demonstrated in More's discernment as to when his official role at court could no longer be to anyone's benefit, precipitating his decision to resign his post as Lord Chancellor of England.

We can see from his prison letters More's supernatural vision, as well as his faith, hope, and charity.[60] In a letter to his daughter, Margaret, More wrote, "Our Lord be thanked, I am in good health of body, and in good quiet of mind; and of worldly things I no more desire than I have. I beseech him make you all merry in the hope of heaven."[61] And again, "mine own death (for the fear thereof, I thank our Lord, the fear of hell, the hope of heaven and the passion of Christ daily more and more assuage)."[62] In another letter written to give someone else comfort, More penned the following, "but I put my trust in God and in the merits of his bitter passion, and I beseech him give me and keep me the mind to long to be out of this world and to be with him."[63] We can see in these letters the same sage Christian advice More wrote about in his other works, including especially those like *The Sadness of Christ* and his *Dialogue* which he wrote from prison. These letters serve as windows into More's soul at the time of their writing. He was living out the Christian mysteries he had celebrated his whole life, now in his flesh, in the sufferings he endured as a prisoner. We can see the Lord at work in More through his letters, especially in this lengthy excerpt from a letter to his daughter near the end of his life:

59. Wegemer, *Thomas More*, 79.
60. All references to More's letters are taken from More, *For All Seasons*.
61. More, *For All Seasons*, 229.
62. More, *For All Seasons*, 231.
63. More, *For All Seasons*, 267.

> In devising whereupon, albeit (mine own good daughter) that I found myself (I cry God mercy) very sensual and my flesh much more shrinking from pain and from death than me thought it the part of a faithful Christian man, in such a case as my conscience gave me, that in the saving of my body should stand the loss of my soul, yet I thank our Lord, that in that conflict the Spirit had in conclusion the mastery. . . . though a man lose of his years in this world, it is more than manifold recompensed by coming the sooner to heaven. . . . And therefore mine own good daughter I assure you—thanks be to God—the thinking of any such thing, albeit it has grieved me ere this, yet as this day grieves me nothing. And yet I know well for all this mine own frailty, and that Saint Peter which feared it much less than I, fell in such fear soon after that at the word of a simple girl he forsook and forswore our Savior. And therefore am I not, Meg, so mad as to warrant myself to stand. But I shall pray, and I pray thee mine own good daughter to pray with me, that it may please God that has given me this mind, to give me the grace to keep it.[64]

More's trial and execution are a study in Christian and legal wit as well as Christian fortitude, charity, and joy. Indeed, More was even able to joke on his way to the scaffold where he was to be beheaded. Wegemer remarks that, "his good humor was not simply a matter of temperament; it was deeply theological, rooted in the cultivated virtues of a faith lived in the present moment, a hope that did not depend on appearances, and a charity rooted in eternity."[65] His fortitude, however, was evident throughout these events. This can be seen in that his initial death sentence was the same as the Carthusians who had been marched to their deaths outside his prison cell. They were hanged (but not to death), castrated and emasculated, stretched out and eviscerated, followed immediately by decapitation and quartering. This was to be More's fate, as far as he was aware, when he made his courageous response before the court. His execution was only commuted to simple beheading the day of his martyrdom.

---

64. More, *For All Seasons*, 274–75.
65. Wegemer, *Thomas More*, 222.

## The Movement from Mystagogical Exegesis to Martyrological Exegesis

More lived a life of prayer from his earliest years, but his intense spiritual plan of life that would last until his execution, although aspects of it were curtailed during his imprisonment, began while he lived among the Carthusians. This included a daily routine of Holy Mass, mental prayer and more liturgical prayers (especially the Psalms), the rosary, spiritual reading of the Bible (in particular the Gospels) as well as of the writings of Saints, frequent confession, and a rigorous plan of mortifications that included wearing a hair shirt underneath his clothing, fasting, and taming his tongue to speak charitably.[66] More's "hair shirt and his fasting served as prayers of the senses, physical reminders he employed to stay united to God."[67] We catch a glimpse of his interior life in the advice he puts in his *Life of Pico*, particularly in the poetic compositions at the end, but also in the biographical narrative with which the work begins.

More emphasizes how, "Over and above all this he [Pico] often . . . 'gave alms' in his own body."[68] More refers here to the Christian practice of mortification, dying to self through what St. Josemaría would call, "prayer of the senses."[69] Christians historically have lived a spirit of mortification in big things—fasting, use of a discipline or whip, wearing a hair shirt (like More) or the more modern chain cilice (apparently inspired by St. Catherine of Siena),[70] cold showers, sleeping on the floor, standing on a pole, sleep deprivation, etc.—and little things like taking less of something one prefers at mealtime, taking more of something someone does not like at meal time, omitting use of one condiment or another, making the effort to smile, refraining from uncharitable comments, etc. St. Josemaría provides a useful list:

> That witty remark, the joke held on the tip of your tongue; the cheerful smile for someone who annoys you; that silence when

---

66. Wegemer, *Thomas More*, 15; and Wegemer, introduction to More, *Sadness*, xxi.

67. Wegemer, *Thomas More*, 23.

68. More, *Life of Pico*, 16. Writing further on the same page, he clarifies what he means: "But many days—and specifically those days that recall Christ's passion and death for our sakes—Pico beat and scourged his flesh in remembrance of that great act of generosity and in reparation for his former offenses."

69. Escrivá, *Christ is Passing*, 19 and 180.

70. On St. Catherine of Siena's role here, see Capua, *Life of Saint Catherine*, 44 and 68–69.

you're unjustly accused; your friendly conversation with people you find boring and tactless; the daily effort to overlook one irritating or impertinent detail after another in the persons who live with you . . . This, with perseverance, is indeed solid interior mortification.[71]

These are all ways of "giving alms with one's body." Indeed, some of these "little" things, can be quite difficult, like smiling charitably with someone we do not get along with or who annoys us, as St. Josemaría again writes, "Sometimes a smile can be the best proof of a spirit of penance."[72]

The spiritual advice More includes coming from (More's revised version) *Life of Pico*, all concerns prayer, in some way or another, and these are points More struggled to live himself, throughout his life. The following are a brief list of examples More provides:

1. "If we kept steadily before our eyes the painful death that Christ suffered for love of us, and then turned our thoughts to our own death, we would surely have a horror of sin."[73]

2. "I pass over what a great source of peace and felicity it is to the mind when a man has nothing troubling on his conscience and is not pricked by the secret goad of hidden evil-doing. This unquestionably is a pleasure that far exceeds all other pleasures that can be obtained or desired in this life."[74]

---

71. Escrivá, *Way*, no. 173.

72. Escrivá, *Forge*, no. 149. Indeed, Escrivá confides, "I assure you that a smile is sometimes more difficult than an hour's worth of cilice." See Escrivá, *Friends of God*, 210. For Escrivá, this advice about smiling was not merely theoretical, but came from his own experience as his private journal notes from a retreat in 1941 reveal: "It's hard for me to smile . . . . What a good mortification—one ready at hand, and unnoticed! If my spiritual director approves, I'll do my particular exam on cheerfulness. It's no small thing! Resolution: To smile, smile always, for love of Jesus Christ." See Vázquez de Prada, *Founder of Opus Dei II*, 384. By "particular exam," that is, "particular examination of conscience," Escrivá is referring to one small point to work on, examined briefly midday and then again at the beginning of a general examination of conscience at night before going to bed, where "you ought to go straight towards acquiring a definite virtue or uprooting the defect which is dominating you" (*Way*, no. 241). He always viewed the general exam as "like defense," and the particular exam as "like attack.—The first is one's armor. The second, a sword of Toledo steel" (*Way*, no. 238). The particular exam was a "weapon of attack" to "get at" the "root" of one's faults discovered from fruitful general exams (*Way*, no. 240).

73. More, *Life of Pico*, 20.

74. More, *Life of Pico*, 29.

3. "Against the world and the devil you have two particularly effective remedies with which, as if by two wings, you shall be lifted out of the vale of tears into heaven: almsgiving and prayer."[75]

4. "When I stir you to pray, I do not mean prayer of many words but that prayer which speaks honestly to God in the secret chamber of the mind and the privy closet of the soul. This is the prayer by which one not only makes oneself present in mind to the Father through the glowing darkness of contemplation but joins one's mind to him in an ineffable manner known only to those who have experienced it."[76]

5. "If you are concerned for your well-being, if you wish to be safe from the snares of the devil, the storms of this world, the ambush of your enemies; if you long to be acceptable to God, if you crave to be happy at last—then let no day pass without at least once making yourself present to God in prayer."[77]

6. "you shall also find matter enough for prayer in the reading of Holy Scripture, which I heartily urge you now to keep constantly at hand . . . . You can do nothing more pleasing to God or more profitable to yourself than constantly, day and night, take up and read the books of Holy Scripture. Provided one turns to them with an honest and humble heart, there lies hidden in these pages a certain heavenly strength, lively and effective, with marvelous power to transform the reader's mind and turn it to the love of God."[78]

At the end of the volume, More includes two useful lists of rules for the spiritual life, not only coming from Pico (as More revised them), but also coming from More's own ascetical struggle to grow in love for God and for neighbor. The first is More's "Twelve Rules of Pico," which are a veritable treasury of spiritual insights which More followed throughout his life:

Rule 1, "we must engage in constant war against the world, the flesh, the devil."[79]

Rule 2 is an admonition to avoid hell.[80]

---

75. More, *Life of Pico*, 32.
76. More, *Life of Pico*, 32–33.
77. More, *Life of Pico*, 33.
78. More, *Life of Pico*, 33.
79. More, *Life of Pico*, 54.
80. More, *Life of Pico*, 54.

Rule 3 is a reminder that we should not expect comfort if we seek heaven, since Christ had to suffer, so shall we.[81]

Rule 4, "we ought not merely not resent this strife but should be glad and joyful of it— indeed should crave it."[82]

Rule 5, we must solely place our trust in Christ and not in ourselves, thus, "let us with all diligence beseech Him with prayers, with tears, with heartfelt groans for help of grace and of His holy saints."[83]

Rule 6, "In constant watch upon your tower, then, stand with the prophet vigilant, on guard."[84]

Rule 7, "Compel yourself . . . not just to stand unvanquished by the devil's power but . . . most valiantly to strive to vanquish him and drive him from the field."[85]

Rule 8, "Conduct yourself with valor in the fight. . . . when once you've won a triumph, prepare yourself and gird for war anew, as if to sally forth to fight again."[86]

Rule 9, be humble and modest.[87]

Rule 10, Fight at the first sign of temptation; "Dash out their brains upon a rock."[88]

Rule 11, "conscience draws more inner joy from virtue than does the body draw from any sin."[89]

---

81. More, *Life of Pico*, 55.
82. More, *Life of Pico*, 55.
83. More, *Life of Pico*, 56.
84. More, *Life of Pico*, 57.
85. More, *Life of Pico*, 57.
86. More, *Life of Pico*, 57–58.
87. More, *Life of Pico*, 58.
88. More, *Life of Pico*, 58.
89. More, *Life of Pico*, 58–59, quotation at 59.

Rule 12, "Though you be tempted, have no thought of quitting."[90]

Similar to these rules are More's "The Twelve Weapons of Spiritual Battle."[91] At the outset, he lists all twelve in bullet point format for easy memorization, so they can aide one in the time of trial, tribulation, and temptation:

> The pleasure scant and brief
>
> Its companions: grief and weariness
>
> The loss of something better
>
> This life itself a dream, a shadow
>
> Death near at hand and unannounced
>
> The fear of going forth impenitent
>
> Eternal joy, eternal pain
>
> The nature and the dignity of man
>
> The peace of a good mind
>
> The great benefits that come from God
>
> The painful cross of Christ
>
> The witness of martyrs and example of saints[92]

For the remainder of the little guide More simply elaborates each point, by just a few sentences. For example, under the eleventh point, "The painful cross of Christ," More write, "When temptation blazes in you like flame, think then upon the dolorous pain of Christ. Think of the Man of Sorrows, His piteous cross, the blood so freely flowing from His veins, think of His precious heart now carved in two. Think how all this He suffered to redeem you. Let Him not lose you whom He's bought so dear."[93] Finally, in More's, "The Twelve Properties of Conditions of a Lover," More underscores, "See here a model also for God's lover: to keep God constantly in mind, to meditate on Him and ever pray, while others play and revel, sing and dance. No earthly joy, pastime, or foolish sport should coax or turn aside his ardent mind from dwelling upon God, his heavenly love."[94]

---

90. More, *Life of Pico*, 59.

91. More, *Life of Pico*, 61–65. In the quotations from this guide, I have removed the stanzas and poetic structure, while leaving the translation the same.

92. More, *Life of Pico*, 61.

93. More, *Life of Pico*, 64.

94. More, *Life of Pico*, 71. Here I have removed the stanzas and poetic structure, while

## LITURGY AND SACRAMENT, MYSTAGOGY AND MARTYRDOM

The reason I began this section with More's interior life and advice about the interior life is because this is fundamental in both mystagogical and martyrological exegesis. Without interior life, there can be no mystagogical or martyrological exegesis. More's exegesis combined with a study of More's life, such as especially Wegemer's provides, gives us a number of lessons, but the most important is that, "these world crises are crises of saints."[95] Indeed, commenting on this very quotation, John Paul II exclaimed, "What power this doctrine has regarding the arduous, and at the same time, appealing work of the new evangelization, to which the entire Church has been called!"[96] We must struggle to become saints if we wish to engage fruitfully in mystagogical and martyrological exegesis, and such exegesis is desperately needed in our times. By so striving for sanctity in all of the little concrete realities of our daily life, we will learn docility to the Holy Spirit, so that, we too, like More, will have the prudence needed to know when and how we must live Christian martyrdom. By the cardinal virtue of prudence, More knew when and how he needed to correct the king in the guidance he was called upon to provide. More knew when he had to resign from his job.[97] More knew how and when to keep silent.[98] Finally, More knew when it was time to accept punishment and tribulation, and ultimately, the martyrdom of physical death for Christ.

So how can we move from mystagogical exegesis to martyrological? As mystagogical exegesis is the fulfillment of typology, so too martyrological exegesis is the fulfillment of tropology. Mystagogical exegesis moves us to a deeper experience of the Mysteries of God, of the Sacraments, as well as to

---

leaving the translation the same.

95. Escrivá, *Way*, no. 301. The full point clarifies what he means here: "A secret.—An open secret: these world crises are crises of saints.—God wants a handful of men 'of his own' in each human activity.—And then . . . *pax Christi in regno Christi*—the peace of Christ in the kingdom of Christ."

96. John Paul II, "Address," 480n3.

97. Wegemer, *Thomas More*, 134–56.

98. More's "silence," is often misunderstood. More remained "silent" in that he did not openly oppose the content of the oath he was eventually asked to swear—nor did he take the oath. But he was not completely silent, as Wegemer explains, ". . . Thomas More was a statesman of rare ability and perception, and he was fully aware of the potential consequences of Henry's caesaropapist designs. He knew that the revolutionary move Henry was making was sure to destroy the unity of Christendom . . . . More was not one to sit back quietly while such dangerous conditions developed . . . . he devised a courageous and highly effective plan of opposition to Henry's despotic designs" (*Thomas More*,149).

a deeper understanding of them. So too, martryological exegesis leads us to a deeper lived witness (martyrdom). It is the movement from tropological exegesis (how should we live in light of this passage from Scripture), to the struggle to live out those virtues. Inextricably bound up with such exegesis is the Sacrament of Confession and the guidance we receive in spiritual direction, as it was for More. Study of the ancient languages, history, archaeology, culture, rhetorical devices, of the Bible and of its surrounding milieu, is beneficial for literal exegesis. Studying the Old Testament in light of the New, and the New in light of the Old, as well as the rich history of patristic and medieval biblical interpretation, not to mention the ways in which texts from the Old and New are juxtaposed in the liturgy we attend each day or week, is essential for typological exegesis. Examining the Scriptures in light of our lived experience, in light of the current challenges we face, at work, in family life, in the broader society in which we live at the local, national, and global levels, is necessary for tropological exegesis. Examining the Sacred Page in light of the truths of faith concerning heaven is the only way forward for anagogical exegesis.

For mystagogical exegesis, we need both to read Scripture in light of the Sacraments and the liturgy, but also to frequent the Sacraments ever better disposed in light of such interpretation. Such interpretation is performative, as the words of Scripture are performative. Martyrological exegesis, likewise, is performative. The insights we come to through the work of tropology, must be concretized to fit the specifics of our life situation, with all of its many challenges (big and small). Such interpretation must be performative; it must become real in our lives through struggle. This might involve the struggle to speak out, to endure financial and legal persecution on account of our faith, or even physical and mortal tribulation perhaps leading to physical death. For most of us, most of the time, it will mean struggling to make the place we live bright and cheerful, not only by our devotion to our home lives, but also in struggling to make the gift of ourselves by loving the others we interact with each day in the little things and big things, both of which involve sacrifice. More's commentary on Christ's agony in the garden reminds us that we have a pioneer who walked down this road, blazing a trail for us to follow, encouraging us by the example he gave, and empowering us by his life-giving sacrifice which we receive in the Sacraments.

If there has been one lamentable fact of modern biblical interpretation it is that it has made it become more difficult to read Scripture as a life-giving and spiritually nourishing text, there for our sanctification, for our deification. Instead, we are left with the bones of some decayed organism from a long time ago. As Benedict XVI wrote, "The dismemberment of the Bible has led to a new variety of allegorism: One no longer reads the text but the supposed experience of supposed communities. The result is often highly fanciful allegorical interpretation . . . ."[99] We need a faithful Catholic biblical hermeneutic that will assist us in our own fidelity to God.

One part of why Christians have been martyred likely has to do with the truth of what More wrote when he explained, "the person whose conscience is full of guilty sores is so sensitive that he views even the face of his victim as a reproach and shrinks from it with dread."[100] Such responses can sometimes lead to violence. Christians who are present to the world as leaven may have to face this possibility, as did More, even if more likely such confrontations will not often lead to the physical death as a martyr. We have to keep in mind, as Hahn reminds us, "conflict between earthly states has an unseen dimension in the heavens. Our troubles and our struggles in this world are not simply anxieties over material discomforts. They're also—and primarily—spiritual struggles. Spiritual combat. Spiritual warfare."[101]

In an interview regarding his canonization of St. Thomas More, Pope Pius XI exhorted his audience, explaining that, "There is a martyrdom which occurs in the continual persevering fidelity in little things, in those demands for diligence in the divine service, in the daily duty which becomes a daily cross."[102] This is the martyrdom we are all called to live. Left on our own, we would not be able to live such a life, certainly not in such a way that we would live it out heroically, as the great Saints of our Church. But we are not left alone; God has given us all the means we need. What remains for us is to take up the challenge of martyrdom, the smiling martyrdom of each day. This is the martyrdom all are called to live.

---

99. Benedict XVI, *Nature and Mission*, 65. For the history of such "secular allegorism," see Morrow, *Three Skeptics*, 104–38.

100. More, *Sadness of Christ*, 83.

101. Hahn, *Angels and Saints*, 84–85.

102. Pius XI, "Holy Father," 338, quoted in Wegemer, *Thomas More*, 226.

# Conclusion

THIS BOOK WAS AN attempt at pointing the way forward to a theological biblical interpretation, building both on the insights of the great Christian biblical interpreters of the early centuries and the medieval period, as well as on cutting edge modern biblical and ancient Near Eastern scholarship of more recent times. My hope is to echo the call for a liturgical and sacramental hermeneutic for which some recent theologians have called, showing the rich fruits such a hermeneutic might bring forth.[1]

I began in the first chapter with an overview of the history of Catholic biblical interpretation from the patristic period to the present. Then, in the second chapter, I examined Gen 1–3, situating the passage in its ancient Near Eastern context, in its canonical biblical context, as well as in the context of early Jewish and Christian biblical interpretation. Understood from these vantage points, Gen 1–3 depicts God creating the world as one large temple where he can be worshipped, preparing the worshipers for eternity in heaven, and that humanity was created with a priestly vocation, called by God to mediate God to the world, and consecrate the world to God.

In the third chapter, I made the case for why a liturgical hermeneutic is so important. The Bible was canonized for liturgy. When the earliest Christians were attempting to discern which texts were inspired by God, they did so because they understood that such inspired texts were the appropriate readings which prepared for the Sacraments. They were trying to discover what would be best to read at the sacred liturgy. The lectionary and other liturgical biblical readings (Divine Office, etc.), juxtapose various portions of the Bible together, thus creating a natural canonical hermeneutic, which is Christological at heart. Thus, Scripture heard read at

1. E.g., Hahn, "Worship in the Word," 101–36; Hahn, *Letter and Spirit*; and Hahn, "Canon, Cult and Covenant," 207–35.

the liturgy, or read in light of these liturgical juxtapositions, helps teach and reinforce to Christians that Jesus Christ is the key to Scripture. I then applied this hermeneutic to Gen 1 in the context of its reading at the Feast of St. Joseph the Worker.

The fourth chapter attempted a mystagogical reading of 1 Kgs 19:3–8. I tentatively argued that the literal sense of the text indicated that Elijah actually died and was raised from the dead. Understood this way, I moved to a typological reading where his death and resurrection pointed forward to Jesus' own death and resurrection as recorded in the New Testament. In light of the bread and water that an angel provided to Elijah after raising him, I argued for a mystagogical interpretation linking this bread with the Eucharist in which Christians participate.

The final chapter explored the idea of martyrological exegesis. I used the example of St. Thomas More to illustrate what such martyrological exegesis might look like. More proves to be an important example because he combined three characteristics that supported each other in his martyrological exegesis. First of all, he interpreted Scripture in a way that was meant to make the Scripture alive and present in the life of Christians. Secondly, he himself strove to live a holy life, fruit of profound tropological exegesis lived out in the ordinary circumstances of his everyday life. Finally, he died a martyr's death, bringing his life's work of fidelity to the Lord to completion. He thus serves as a model biblical interpreter, who lived what he read and interpreted in the pages of Scripture.

Such a theological exercise as that found in this book is important because too often in modern biblical studies, the Bible is read in two problematic ways. Sometimes it is read as a collection of ancient historical texts from a long gone era, written by those now dead, with no claim on the lives of believers. On the other hand, and also problematic, the Bible is read in one of many postmodern ways where the history is arbitrary and unimportant, and, although it might be applied to a believer's life now, it is done so in a somewhat arbitrary way. In other words, the Bible is used to defend or justify one's favorite ideological positions. Neither of these ways of reading the Bible makes sense of what those Christians who played a role in determining the biblical canon were intending, nor of the lives of those sacred human authors of Scripture. Nor does it take into account the long-standing Christian doctrine and conviction that Scripture has God, the Almighty Creator of heaven and earth, as its primary author. These interpretations ignore that the same God who created all of reality, with its natural and physical laws, is the same God who inspired Scripture.

The importance of this teaching should not be underestimated, for it implies that Scripture must have a claim on my life. It means that I need to allow myself to be challenged by what I read in Scripture. It means that I might have to change my life, in fact, it means that I do have to change my life, continually, for as long as I live. For the great Christian tradition bequeaths to us, not only the notion of Scripture's inspiration, but a profoundly disturbing and comforting notion about God, the Almighty Creator and source of all existence. God is not a mere notion. Nor is he only the Creator. Rather, the God who created everything, is a person, which, if it means anything at all, means that he is a person in relationship. This is part of the profoundity of Christian teaching on the Trinity. God revealed himself to us in Jesus, and that changed everything.

God reveals himself to us as a person and thus a relationship. As Catholics read the Scriptures and the tradition, it is in the Sacraments where Jesus established that he most clearly communicates his very life to us. Hahn puts it well when he explains, "Jesus Christ is what the Church has to offer our society, and in the sacraments His life breaks into our world in a way that is perfectly suited to our embodied nature. The sacraments, therefore, are the central feature of Christian life so long as our bodies occupy space and time."[2] The Scriptures and the Sacraments thus go hand-in-hand. The Scriptures are intended to teach us, but also, they are an encounter with God. Even more, they prepare us for the two most intimate encounters we will have with God in this life: meeting God in that intimate union we experience with each reception of the Sacraments; and our death.

When Scripture serves one's ideological purposes, it no longer can correct the person's course. As opposed to leading someone to God, it leads one only to oneself; he becomes curved in on self, which is nothing other than sin, a rupture in the relationship with God and with others. When Scripture remains a mere ancient historical document, a dead letter, it no longer has relevance for the reader, beyond intellectual curiosity. But Scripture is nothing other than God's loving communication to humankind. Yes, it is a record of a spiritual family, a family history. Yes, it is autobiographical; the readers can see themselves in its pages, and they can recognize Scripture in their lives. In this sense, Scripture really is about me. I find my life repeating various episodes from Scriptures pages, and I find relevance to

2. Hahn, *First Society*, 160.

my life in most of the passages I read from Scripture each day. But Scripture is far more than that. It is far more than even the Church's document, safeguarded and interpreted properly throughout the ages, for clarifying doctrine, settling theological disputes, etc. It is far more than that, because it is for me, and not just for the generic "us." It is for me, and for you. It is God's love letter to his beloved.

This is where the ultimate importance of Scripture comes in. We do not sufficiently realize who we are or who God is. Put more precisely, I (and you), do not realize—at least most of the time—who I am (and who you are). Ephesians 1:4 gives us a clue: "he chose us in him before the foundation of the world, that we should be holy and blameless before him" (RSVCE). God chose me before the very foundation of the world. He loved me into existence. Knowing all the silly and sinful mistakes I would make, God still loved me into being deciding that the world he made would not be complete without me. Thus, through all the tortuous paths of this life, God is ever at my side, guiding me, even when all appears lost, in my darkest moments. In Jesus, God reveals himself as father, friend, and lover. Compared to God all human loves fall short. God alone, in Jesus, loved perfectly in a human way with the fullness of divine love. Thus it is a profound truth, that God loves me more than anyone else does, but perhaps more poignantly, God loves me more than I love anyone else. Thus, the Bible exists for me. It is one among many examples of God pursuing me, his beloved. And as much as this is true of me, it is true of you. God loves each of us—me and you—with an individual love. Like a parent who loves each child completely, equally, individually, even more so does God love me as if I was the only one. And the same is true of you.

When we close ourselves off to this loving encounter with God, in Sacraments and in Scripture, we lose sight of who we are and of who God is, and we risk making a mess of our lives, and of the lives of others. The importance of reading Scripture theologically, but also liturgically, sacramentally, mystagogically, and martyrologically, lies in our continually becoming increasingly open to the love of God which seeks to transform us into true lovers of God and lovers of others for love of God. Scripture exists so that we might become Saints. But this goal must not be left in the abstract, it has to be concretized in the diverse circumstances of our lives: in bearing patiently and joyfully with my annoying coworker or neighbor; in continuing to court my spouse decades into my marriage; in teaching my children the virtues through my good example; in extending mercy to someone who hurt me; in putting love in the thousands of little ordinary details of my daily life. Scripture can facilitate such growth in charity, in love, only when we trust it, as we trust God, and only when we allow ourselves to experience the love God has for us in Scripture even by means of correction.

Thus, the debate about the relationship between theology and biblical exegesis is practical and the stakes are high. The good news is that the Bible is not the reserve of scholars and linguists, of specialists, but is intended for all. The most challenging part, I would maintain, is not that meticulous study of ancient history and languages is beneficial, but so difficult and really only accessible to the few—it is, this is true—but rather that when we read Scripture with the requisite childlike trust, and allow it to have a claim on our lives, it will not leave us unchanged. This can be difficult and even painful.

Such openness to the Word of God, however, will bear abundant fruit in our lives. Only then can we really appreciate that the Word of God is also a word from God to me. Scripture is a love letter written for me personally. It is written with care and with great sacrifice by the lover of my soul, the one with whom I will be united for eternity at the moment of my death, at which point my restless heart will find its repose, as St. Augustine so wisely understood. If we want to prepare ourselves for that moment—and, the fact of the matter is, all of life is really one great preparation for that final moment—we would do well to immerse ourselves in the prayerful reading and studying of the Sacred Page. Such attention to Scripture is a central means, although not the only one, of making our loving response to the one who loves us with an incomprehensible madness. It is only in the light of God's mad love for us that we can make sense of our lives, with all the suffering we encounter. We benefit in recalling that, as Jesus explained to the disciples whom he loved, "In the world you have tribulation; but be of good cheer, I have overcome the world" (John 16:33, RSVCE).

# Bibliography

Ackroyd, Peter. *The Life of Thomas More*. London: Chatto & Windus, 1998.
Amsler, Frédéric. "Les sources des évangiles synoptiques de Loisy à la recherche actuelle." In *Alfred Loisy cent ans après: Autour d'un petit livre: Actes du colloque international tenu à Paris, les 23-24 mai 2003*, edited by François Laplanche et al., 93-105. Turnhout: Brepols, 2007.
Anderson, Gary A. *The Genesis of Perfection: Adam and Eve in Jewish and Christian Imagination*. Louisville: Westminster John Knox, 2001.
Aquinas, St. Thomas. *Summa Theologiae*. Latin text available online. https://www.corpusthomisticum.org/.
Arnaldez, Roger. "Spinoza et la pensée arabe." *Revue de synthèse* 89-91 (1978) 151-74.
Arnold, Claus. "'Lamentabili sane exitu' (1907). Das Römische Lehramt und die Exegese Alfred Loisy." *Zeitschrift für Neuere Theologiegeschichte* 11 (2004) 24-51.
———. "The Roman Magisterium and Anti-Modernism." In *Religious Modernism in the Low Countries*, edited by Leo Kenis and Ernestine van der Wall, 159-69. Leuven: Peeters, 2013.
Arnold, Claus, and Giacomo Losito, eds. *La censure d'Alfred Loisy (1903): Les documents des Congrégations de l'Index et du Saint Office*. Vatican City: Libreria Editrice Vaticana, 2009.
———, ed. *"Lamentabili sane exitu" (1907). Les documents préparatoires du Saint Office*. Rome: Libreria Editrice Vaticana, 2011.
Asad, Talal. *Formations of the Secular: Christianity, Islam, Modernity*. Stanford: Stanford University Press, 2003.
———. *Genealogies of Religion: Discipline and Reasons of Power in Christianity and Islam*. Baltimore: Johns Hopkins University Press, 1993.
Astruc, Jean. *Conjectures sur la Genèse*. Edited by Pierre Gibert. Paris: Éditions Noêsis, 1999.
———. *Conjectures sur les mémoires originaux dont il paroît que Moyse s'est servi pour composer le Livre de la Genèse*. Brussels: Chez Fricx, 1753.
Augustine, Saint. *De doctrina christiana*. http://www.augustinus.it/latino/dottrina_cristiana/index2.htm.
Auvray, Paul. "Richard Simon et Spinoza." In *Religion, érudition et critique à la fin du XVIIe siècle et début du XVIIIe*, edited by Baudouin de Gaiffier et al., 201-14. Paris: Presses universitaires de France, 1968.

# BIBLIOGRAPHY

Averbeck, Richard E. "A Preliminary Study of Ritual and Structure in the Cylinders of Gudea." PhD diss., Annenberg Research Institute, 1987.

———. "Ritual Formula, Textual Frame, and Thematic Echo in the Cylinders of Gudea." In *Crossing Boundaries and Linking Horizons: Studies in Honor of Michael C. Astour on His 80th Birthday*, edited by Gordon D. Young et al., 37–93. Bethesda: CDL, 1997.

———. "Sumer, the Bible, and Comparative Method: Historiography and Temple Building." In *Mesopotamia and the Bible: Comparative Explorations*, edited by Mark W. Chavalas and K. Lawson Younger Jr., 88–125. Grand Rapids: Baker Academic, 2002.

Baglow, Christopher. *"Modus et forma": A New Approach to the Exegesis of Saint Thomas Aquinas with an Application to the Lectura super Epistolam ad Ephesios*. Rome: Pontifical Biblical Institute, 2002.

———. "The Principle(s) of Ecclesial Nature: The Church in the Ephesians Commentary of St. Thomas Aquinas." In *Reading Sacred Scripture with Thomas Aquinas: Hermeneutical Tools, Theological Questions and New Perspectives*, edited by Piotr Roszak and Jörgen Vijgen, 531–54. Madrid: Fédération Internationale des Instituts d'Études Médiévales, 2015.

———. "Rediscovering St. Thomas Aquinas as Biblical Theologian." *Letter and Spirit* 1 (2005) 137–46.

———. "Sacred Scripture and Sacred Doctrine in Saint Thomas Aquinas." In *Aquinas on Doctrine: A Critical Introduction*, edited by Thomas Weinandy et al., 1–26. London: T. & T. Clark, 2004.

Baldovin, John F., SJ. *The Urban Character of Christian Worship: The Origins, Development, and Meaning of Stational Liturgy*. Rome: Pontificia Institutum Studiorum Orientalium, 1987.

Balentine, Samuel E. *The Torah's Vision of Worship*. Minneapolis: Fortress, 1999.

*Baltimore Catechism*. Baltimore: Third Plenary Council of Baltimore, 1885.

Barber, Michael. *Coming Soon: Unlocking the Book of Revelation and Applying Its Lessons Today*. Steubenville: Emmaus Road, 2006.

———. "The Historical Jesus and Cultic Restoration Eschatology: The New Temple, the New Priesthood and the New Cult." PhD diss., Fuller Theological Seminary, 2010.

———. *Salvation: What Every Catholic Should Know*. Greenwood Village: Augustine Institute, 2019.

———. *Singing in the Reign: The Psalms and the Liturgy of God's Kingdom*. Steubenville: Emmaus Road, 2001.

Barron, Caroline M. "The Making of a London Citizen." In *Cambridge Companion to Thomas More*, edited by George M. Logan, 3–21. Cambridge: Cambridge University Press, 2011.

Barthélemy, Dominique. *Studies in the Text of the Old Testament: An Introduction to the Hebrew Old Testament Project: English Translation of the Introductions to Volumes 1, 2, and 3 Critique textuelle de l'Ancien Testament*. Winona Lake, IN: Eisenbrauns, 2012.

Bataillon, Louis-Jacques, et al., eds. *Étienne Langton. Prédicateur, bibliste, théologien*. Turnhout: Brepols, 2010.

Bauks, Michaela. "Genesis 1 als Programmschrift der Priesterschrift (Pg)." In *Studies in the Book of Genesis: Literature, Redaction and History*, edited by A. Wénin, 333–45. Leuven: Leuven University Press, 2001.

# BIBLIOGRAPHY

Bea, Augustin. *Die Geschichtlichkeit der Evangelien.* Trans. Josef Hosse. Paderborn: Schöningh, 1966.

———. *L'historicité des évangiles.* N.d.: n.d., 1964.

———. *La Parola di Dio e l'Umanità: la doctrina del Concilio sulla rivelazione.* Assisi: Città della Editrice, 1967.

———. *De Pentateucho.* Rome: Pontifical Biblical Institute, 1933.

———. *La Storicità Dei Vangeli.* Brescia: Morcelliana, 1964.

———. *The Study of the Synoptic Gospels: New Approaches and Outlooks.* Edited by Joseph A. Fitzmyer, SJ. New York: Harper & Row, 1964.

Beale, G. K. *The Temple and the Church's Mission: A Biblical Theology of the Dwelling Place of God.* Downers Grove, IL: Apollos, 2004.

Béchard, Dean P., SJ, ed. and trans. *The Scripture Documents: An Anthology of Official Catholic Teachings.* With a foreword by Joseph A. Fitzmyer, SJ. Collegeville, MN: Liturgical, 2002.

Bellamah, Timothy. "The Interpretation of a Contemplative: Thomas' Commentary *Super Iohannem*." In *Reading Sacred Scripture with Thomas Aquinas: Hermeneutical Tools, Theological Questions and New Perspectives,* edited by Piotr Roszak and Jörgen Vijgen, 229–56. Madrid: Fédération Internationale des Instituts d'Études Médiévales, 2015.

———. "The Lament of a Preacher: Stephen Langton's Commentary *Super Threnos*." In *Étienne Langton. Prédicateur, bibliste, théologien,* edited by Louis-Jacques Bataillon, et al., 327–52. Turnhout: Brepols, 2010.

Ben-Dov, Jonathan. *Head of All Years: Astronomy and Calendars at Qumran in their Ancient Context.* Leiden: Brill, 2008.

Benedict XVI, Pope (Joseph Ratzinger). "Biblical Interpretation in Conflict." In *God's Word: Scripture—Tradition—Office,* by Joseph Ratzinger, edited by Peter Hünermann and Thomas Söding, translated by by Henry Taylor, 91–126. San Francisco: Ignatius, 2008.

———. *Church, Ecumenism and Politics: New Essays in Ecclesiology.* New York: Crossroad, 1988.

———. "Dogmatic Constitution on Divine Revelation: Origin and Background." In *Commentary on the Documents of Vatican II Volume III: Declaration on the Relationship of the Church to Non-Christian Religions, Dogmatic Constitution on Divine Revelation, and Decree on the Apostolate of the Laity,* edited by Herbert Vorgrimler, 155–66. New York: Herder & Herder, 1969.

———. "The End of Time." In *The End of Time? The Provocation of Talking about God: Proceedings of a Meeting of Joseph Cardinal Ratzinger, Johann Baptist Metz, Jürgen Moltmann, and Eveline Goodman-Thau in Ahaus,* edited by Tiemo Rainer Peters and Claus Urban, 4–25. English edition translated and edited by J. Matthew Ashley. New York: Paulist, 2004.

———. *God and the World: Believing and Living in Our Time: A Conversation with Peter Seewald.* Translated by Henry Taylor. San Francisco: Ignatius, 2002.

———. "Handing on the Faith and the Sources of the Faith." In *Handing on the Faith in an Age of Disbelief: Lectures Given at the Church of Notre-Dame de Fourvière in Lyons, France and at Notre-Dame Cathedral in Paris,* by Joseph Cardinal Ratzinger with Archbishop Dermot J. Ryan et al., 13–40. San Francisco: Ignatius, 2006.

———. "Introduction." In *The Lord,* by Romano Guardini, xi–xiv. Washington, DC: Regnery, 1982.

———. *Jesus of Nazareth I: From the Baptism in the Jordan to the Transfiguration*. New York: Doubleday, 2007.

———. *Jesus of Nazareth II: Holy Week: From the Entrance into Jerusalem to the Resurrection*. San Francisco: Ignatius, 2011.

———. *Jesus of Nazareth III: The Infancy Narratives*. New York: Image, 2012.

———. "Kirchliches Lehramt und Exegese. Reflexionen aus Anlass des 100-jährigen Bestehens der Päpstlichen Bibelkommission." *Internationale Kathlische Zeitschrift: Communio* 32 (2003) 522–29.

———. *The Nature and Mission of Theology: Essays to Orient Theology in Today's Debates*. Trans. Adrian Walker. San Francisco: Ignatius, 1995.

———. "Sacred Scripture in the Life of the Church." In *Commentary on the Documents of Vatican II Volume III: Declaration on the Relationship of the Church to Non-Christian Religions, Dogmatic Constitution on Divine Revelation, and Decree on the Apostolate of the Laity*, edited by Herbert Vorgrimler, 262–72. New York: Herder & Herder, 1969.

———. *The Spirit of the Liturgy*. Trans. John Saward. San Francisco: Ignatius, 2000.

———. *Verbum Domini*. 2010. http://www.vatican.va/content/benedict-xvi/en/apost_exhortations/documents/hf_ben-xvi_exh_20100930_verbum-domini.html.

Benin, Stephen D. *The Footprints of God: Divine Accommodation in Jewish and Christian Thought*. Albany: State University of New York, 1993.

Berglar, Peter. *Thomas More: A Lonely Voice Against the Power of the State*. New York: Scepter, 1999.

Bergsma, John. "Cultic Kingdoms in Conflict in the Book of Daniel." *Letter and Spirit* 5 (2009) 51–76.

———. *Jesus and the Dead Sea Scrolls: Revealing the Jewish Roots of Christianity*. New York: Image, 2019.

———. "The Jubilee: A Post-Exilic Priestly Attempt to Reclaim Lands?" *Biblica* 84 (2003) 225–46.

Bergsma, John, and Brant Pitre. *A Catholic Introduction to the Bible Volume 1: The Old Testament*. San Francisco: Ignatius, 2018.

Berman, Joshua. "CTH 133 and the Hittite Provenance of Deuteronomy 13." *Journal of Biblical Literature* 130 (2011) 25–46.

Berndt, Rainer, ed. *Bibel und Exegese in der Abtei Saint-Victor zu Paris: Form und Funktion eines Grundtextes im europäischen Rahmen*. Münster: Aschendorff Verlag, 2009.

———. "Étienne Langton et les victorins, ou l'embarras des lacunes." In *Étienne Langton. Prédicateur, bibliste, théologien*, edited by Louis-Jacques Bataillon et al., 125–63. Turnhout: Brepols, 2010.

———. "Exegese des Alten Testaments: die Grundstruktur christlicher Theologie bei den Viktorinern." In *Bibel und Exegese in der Abtei Saint-Victor zu Paris: Form und Funktion eines Grundtextes im europäischen Rahmen*, edited by Rainer Berndt, 423–41. Münster: Aschendorff, 2009.

———. "The School of St. Victor in Paris." In *Hebrew Bible/Old Testament: The History of Its Interpretation Volume I: From the Beginnings to the Middle Ages (Until 1300) Part 2: The Middle Ages*, edited by Magne Sæbø, 467–95. Göttingen: Vandenhoeck & Ruprecht, 2000.

Bernier, Jean. *La critique du Pentateuque de Hobbes à Calmet*. Paris: Champion, 2010.

Betz, John R. "Glory(ing) in the Humility of the Word: The Kenotic Form of Revelation in J.G. Hamann." *Letter and Spirit* 6 (2010) 141–79.

# BIBLIOGRAPHY

Bieringer, Reimund. "Biblical Revelation and Exegetical Interpretation According to *Dei Verbum* 12." In *Vatican II and Its Legacy*, edited by M. Lamberigts and L. Kenis, 25–58. Leuven: Leuven University Press, 2002.

Binder, Susanne. "Joseph's Rewarding and Investiture (Genesis 41:41–43) and the Gold of Honour in New Kingdom Egypt." In *Egypt, Canaan and Israel: History, Imperialism, Ideology and Literature*, edited by S. Bar et al., 44–64. Leiden: Brill, 2011.

Blank, Reiner. *Analyse und Kritik der formgeschichtlichen Arbeiten von Martin Dibelius und Rudolf Bultmann*. Basel: Reinhardt, 1981.

Blenkinsopp, Joseph. *Prophecy and Canon: A Contribution to the Study of Jewish Origins*. Notre Dame: University of Notre Dame Press, 1977.

———. "Structure of P." *Catholic Biblical Quarterly* 38 (1976) 275–92.

Bloch-Smith, Elizabeth. "Solomon's Temple: The Politics of Ritual Space." In *Sacred Time, Sacred Place: Archaeology and the Religion of Israel*, edited by Barry M. Gittlen, 83–94. Winona Lake, IN: Eisenbrauns, 2002.

———. "'Who Is the King of Glory?' Solomon's Temple and Its Symbolism." In *Scripture and Other Artifacts: Essays on the Bible and Archaeology in Honor of Philip J. King*, edited by Michael D. Coogan et al., 18–31. Louisville: Westminster/John Knox, 1994.

*The Books of Elijah Parts 1–2*. Collected and translated by Michael E. Stone and John Strugnell. Missoula, MT: Scholars, 1979.

Boyle, John F. "Authorial Intention and the *Divisio textus*." In *Reading John with St. Thomas Aquinas: Theological Exegesis and Speculative Theology*, edited by Michael Dauphinais and Matthew Levering, 3–8. Washington, DC: The Catholic University of America Press, 2005.

———. "On the Relation of St. Thomas's Commentary on Romans to the *Summa theologiae*." In *Reading Romans with St. Thomas Aquinas*, edited by Matthew Levering and Michael Dauphinais, 75–82. Washington, DC: The Catholic University of America Press, 2012.

———. "The Theological Character of the Scholastic 'Division of the Text' with Particular Reference to the Commentaries of Saint Thomas Aquinas." In *With Reverence for the Word: Medieval Scriptural Exegesis in Judaism, Christianity, and Islam*, edited by Jane Dammen McAuliffe, Barry D. Walfish, and Joseph W. Goering, 276–83. Oxford: Oxford University Press, 2003.

———. "Thomas Aquinas and Sacred Scripture." *Pro Ecclesia* 4 (1995) 92–104.

Bright, Pamela. *The Book of Rules of Tyconius: Its Purpose and Inner Logic*. Notre Dame: University of Notre Dame Press, 1985.

Bronner, Leah. *The Stories of Elijah and Elisha: As Polemics Against Baal Worship*. Leiden: Brill, 1968.

Brown, Raymond E., SS. *The Gospel According to John*. 2 vols. Anchor Yale Bible Commentary. New Haven, CT: Yale University Press, 1966.

———. *The Sensus Plenior of Sacred Scripture*. Baltimore: St. Mary's University Press, 1955.

Brown, Stephen. "The Intellectual Context of Later Medieval Philosophy: Universities, Aristotle, Arts, Theology." In *Routledge History of Philosophy Volume III: Medieval Philosophy*, edited by John Marenbon, 188–203. London: Routledge, 1998.

———. "The Theological Role of the Fathers in Aquinas's *Super Evangelium S. Ioannis Lectura*." In *Reading John with St. Thomas Aquinas: Theological Exegesis and Speculative Theology*, edited by Michael Dauphinais and Matthew Levering, 9–22. Washington, DC: The Catholic University of America Press, 2005.

# BIBLIOGRAPHY

Bunta, Silviu. "The Likeness of the Image: Adamic Motifs and צלם Anthropology in Rabbinic Traditions about Jacob's Image Enthroned in Heaven." *Journal for the Study of Judaism* 37 (2006) 55–84.

———. "Yhwh's Cultic Statue after 597/586 B.C.E.: A Linguistic and Theological Reinterpretation of Ezekiel 28:12." *Catholic Biblical Quarterly* 69 (2007) 222–41.

Burigana, Riccardo. *La Bibbia nel Concilio: La redazione della constituzione "Dei Verbum" del Vaticano II*. Bologna: Società Editrice il Mulino, 1998.

———. "La commissione 'De divina Revelatione.'" In *Les commissions conciliaires à Vatican II*, edited by M. Lamberigts-Cl. and Soetens-J. Grootaers, 27–61. Leuven: Leuven University Press, 1996.

Burns, J. Patout. "Delighting the Spirit: Augustine's Practice of Figurative Interpretation." In *De Doctrina Christiana: A Classic of Western Culture*, edited by Duane W. H. Arnold and Pamela Bright, 182–94. Notre Dame: University of Notre Dame Press, 1995.

Burtchaell, James Tunstead, CSC. *Catholic Theories of Biblical Inspiration Since 1810: A Review and Critique*. Cambridge: Cambridge University Press, 1969.

Callender, Dexter E., Jr. *Adam in Myth and History: Ancient Israelite Perspectives on the Primal Human*. Winona Lake, IN: Eisenbrauns, 2000.

Candler, Peter M., Jr. "Liturgically Trained Memory: A Reading of *Summa Theologiae* III.83." *Modern Theology* 20 (2004) 423–45.

———. *Theology, Rhetoric, Manuduction, Or Reading Scripture Together on the Path to God*. Grand Rapids: Eerdmans, 2006.

Carl, Fr. Scott, ed. *Verbum Domini and the Complementarity of Exegesis and Theology*. Grand Rapids: Eerdmans, 2015.

Carlson, R. A. "Élie à L'Horeb." *Vetus Testamentum* 19 (1969) 416–39.

Carruthers, Mary. *The Craft of Thought: Meditation, Rhetoric, and the Making of Images, 400–1200*. Cambridge: Cambridge University Press, 1998.

Cassuto, Umberto. *A Commentary on the Book of Exodus*. Trans. Israel Abrahams. Jerusalem: Magnes, 1967.

———. *A Commentary on the Book of Genesis Part I: From Adam to Noah: Genesis I–VI*. Translated by Israel Abrahams. Jerusalem: Magnes, 1961.

———. *The Documentary Hypothesis and the Composition of the Pentateuch: Eight Lectures*. Jerusalem: Shalem, 2006.

———. "La creazione del mondo nella Genesi." *Annuario di studi ebraici* 1 (1934) 9–47.

———. *La Questione della Genesi*. Florence: Le Monnier, 1934.

*Catechism of the Catholic Church*. 2nd ed. Vatican City: Libreria Editrice Vaticana, 1997.

Catry, Patrick. *Paroles de Dieu, amour et Esprit-Saint chez saint Grégoire le Grand*. Bellefontaine: Abbaye de Bellefontaine, 1984.

Catto, Jeremy. "The Philosophical Context of the Renaissance Interpretation of the Bible." In *Hebrew Bible/Old Testament: The History of Its Interpretation II: From the Renaissance to the Enlightenment*, edited by Magne Sæbø, 106–22. Göttingen: Vandenhoeck & Ruprecht, 2008.

Cavalletti, Sofia. "Memorial and Typology in Jewish and Christian Liturgy." *Letter and Spirit* 1 (2005) 69–86.

Cavanaugh, William T. "Eucharistic Sacrifice and Social Imagination in Early Modern Europe." *Journal of Medieval and Early Modern Studies* 31 (2001) 585–605.

———. "'A Fire Strong Enough to Consume the House': The Wars of Religion and the Rise of the State." *Modern Theology* 11 (1995) 397–420.

———. *The Myth of Religious Violence: Secular Ideology and the Roots of Modern Conflict*. Oxford: Oxford University Press, 2009.

———. *Torture and Eucharist: Theology, Politics, and the Body of Christ*. Oxford: Blackwell, 1998.

Childs, Brevard S. "The Canon in Recent Biblical Studies: Reflections on an Era." In *Canon and Biblical Interpretation*, edited by Craig G. Bartholomew et al., 33–57. Grand Rapids: Zondervan, 2006.

———. *The New Testament as Canon: An Introduction*. Philadelphia: Fortress, 1984.

———. *Old Testament Theology in a Canonical Context*. Philadelphia: Fortress, 1985.

Clark, Mark J. "The Commentaries on Peter Comestor's *Historia scholastica* of Stephen Langton, Pseudo-Langton, and Hugh of St. Cher." *Sacris Erudiri* 44 (2005) 301–446.

———. "The Commentaries of Stephen Langton on the *Historia scholastica* of Peter Comestor." In *Étienne Langton, prédicateur, bibliste, théologien: Études réunies*, edited by Louis-Jacques Bataillon et al., 373–93. Turnhout: Brepols, 2010.

———. "Le cours d'Étienne Langton sur l'*Histoire scolastique* de Pierre le Mangeur: le fruit d'une tradition unifiée." In *Pierre le Mangeur ou Pierre de Troyes: maître du XIIe siècle: Études réunies*, edited by Gilbert Dahan, 243–66. Turnhout: Brepols, 2013.

———. *The Making of the Historia Scholastica, 1150–1200*. Toronto: Pontifical Mediaeval Institute, 2015.

———. "Peter Comestor and Peter Lombard: Brothers in Deed." *Traditio* 60 (2005) 85–142.

Cogan, Mordechai. *1 Kings: A New Translation with Introduction and Commentary*. Anchor Bible. New York: Doubleday, 2001.

Cohn, Robert L. "The Literary Logic of 1 Kings 17–19." *Journal of Biblical Literature* 101 (1982) 333–50.

Colin, Pierre. *L'audace et le soupçon: La crise moderniste dans le catholicisme française (1893–1914)*. Paris: De Brouwer, 1997.

Connor, Robert A. "The One Truth of Freedom: Gift of Self." *Communio* 21 (1994) 367–71.

Cook, Johann. "The Septuagint of Genesis: Text and/or Interpretation?" In *Studies in the Book of Genesis: Literature, Redaction and History*, edited by A. Wénin, 315–29. Leuven: Leuven University Press, 2001.

Coote, Robert E. "Yahweh Recalls Elijah." In *Traditions in Transformation: Turning Points in Biblical Faith*, edited by Baruch Halpern and Jon D. Levenson, 115–20. Winona Lake, IN: Eisenbrauns, 1981.

Corbon, Jean. *Liturgie de source*. Paris: Editions du Cerf, 1980.

———. *The Wellspring of Worship*. Translated by Matthew J. O'Connell. San Francisco: Ignatius, 2005.

Currid, John D. *Ancient Egypt and the Old Testament*. With a foreword by Kenneth A. Kitchen. Grand Rapids: Baker, 1997.

———. "An Examination of the Egyptian Background of the Genesis Cosmogony." *Biblische Zeitschrift* 35 (1991) 18–40.

Curtis, Cathy. "More's Public Life." In *Cambridge Companion to Thomas More*, edited by George M. Logan, 69–92. Cambridge: Cambridge University Press, 2011.

Dahan, Gilbert. "Les commentaires bibliques d'Étienne Langton: exégèse et herméneutique." In *Étienne Langton. Prédicateur, bibliste, théologien*, edited by Louis-Jacques Bataillon et al., 201–39. Turnhout: Brepols, 2010.

———. *L'Exégèse chrétienne de la Bible en Occident médiéval: XIIe–XIVe siècles*. Paris: Cerf, 1999.

# BIBLIOGRAPHY

———. "Les exégèses des Pierre le Mangeur." In *Pierre le Mangeur ou Pierre de Troyes: maître du XIIe siècle: Études réunies*, edited by Gilbert Dahan, 49–87. Turnhout: Brepols, 2013.

———. *Lire la Bible au moyen-âge: Essais d'herméneutique médiévale*. Geneva: Librairie Droz, 2009.

———. "Thomas Aquinas: Exegesis and Hermeneutics." In *Reading Sacred Scripture with Thomas Aquinas: Hermeneutical Tools, Theological Questions and New Perspectives*, edited by Piotr Roszak and Jörgen Vijgen, 45–70. Madrid: Fédération Internationale des Instituts d'Études Médiévales, 2015.

Daly, Gabriel, OSA. "Theological and Philosophical Modernism." In *Catholicism Contending with Modernity: Roman Catholic Modernism and Anti-Modernism in Historical Context*, edited by Darrell Jodock, 88–112. Cambridge: Cambridge University Press, 2000.

Dauphinais, Michael, and Matthew Levering, eds. *Reading John with St. Thomas Aquinas: Theological Exegesis and Speculative Theology*. Washington, DC: The Catholic University of America Press, 2005.

D'Costa, Gavin. *Theology in the Public Square: Church, Academy, and Nation*. Oxford: Blackwell, 2005.

de Lubac, Henri. *Exégèse médiévale: les quatre sens de l'Écriture I*. Paris: Aubier, 1959.

———. *Exégèse médiévale: les quatre sens de l'Écriture II*. Paris: Aubier, 1959.

———. *Exégèse médiévale: les quatre sens de l'Écriture III*. Paris: Aubier, 1961.

———. *Exégèse médiévale: les quatre sens de l'Écriture IV*. Paris: Aubier, 1964.

———. *Medieval Exegesis Volume 1: The Four Senses of Scripture*. Translated by Mark Sebanc. With a foreword by Robert Louis Wilken. Grand Rapids: Eerdmans, 1998.

———. *Medieval Exegesis Volume 2: The Four Senses of Scripture*. Trans. E. M. Macierowski. Grand Rapids: Eerdmans, 2000.

———. *Medieval Exegesis Volume 3: The Four Senses of Scripture*. Trans. E. M. Macierowski. Grand Rapids: Eerdmans, 2009.

de Wette, Wilhelm Martin Leberecht. *Beiträge zur Einleitung in das Alte Testament I. Kritischer Versuch über die Glaubwürdigkeit der Bücher und Gesetzgebung*. Halle: Schimmelpfenning, 1806.

DeConick, April D. "What Is Early Jewish and Christian Mysticism?" In *Paradise Now: Essays on Early Jewish and Christian Mysticism*, edited by April D. DeConick, 1–24. Atlanta: Society of Biblical Literature, 2006.

Delmas, Sophie. "Le réception de l'*Historia scholastica* chez quelques maîtres en théologie du XIIIe siècle." In *Pierre le Mangeur ou Pierre de Troyes: maître du XIIe siècle: Études réunies*, edited by Gilbert Dahan, 267–87. Turnhout: Brepols, 2013.

Donahue, John R., SJ. "Joseph A. Fitzmyer, S.J.: Scholar and Teacher of the Word of God." *U.S. Catholic Historian* 31 (2013) 63–83.

Duffy, Eamon. *The Stripping of the Altars: Traditional Religion in England c. 1400–c. 1580*. New Haven, CT: Yale University Press, 1992.

Duffy, Kevin. "The Ecclesial Hermeneutic of Raymond E. Brown." *Heythrop Journal* 39 (1998) 37–56.

Dulaey, Martine. "La sixième Règle de Tyconius et son résumé dans le 'De doctrina christiana." *Revue des Études Augustiniennes et Patristiques* 35 (1989) 83–103.

Dulles, Avery, SJ. "Vatican II on the Interpretation of Scripture." *Letter and Spirit* 2 (2006) 17–26.

# BIBLIOGRAPHY

Dunn, Matthew W. I. "Raymond Brown and the *Sensus Plenior* Interpretation of the Bible." *Studies in Religion/Sciences religieuses* 36 (2007) 531–51.

Egger, Christoph. "Viktorinische Exegese in Süddeutschland und Österreich im 12. und 13. Jahrhundert." In *Bibel und Exegese in der Abtei Saint-Victor zu Paris: Form und Funktion eines Grundtextes im europäischen Rahmen*, edited by Rainer Berndt, 539–55. Münster: Aschendorff, 2009.

Emery, Gilles, OP. "Biblical Exegesis and the Speculative Doctrine of the Trinity in St. Thomas Aquinas's *Commentary on St. John*." In *Reading John with St. Thomas Aquinas: Theological Exegesis and Speculative Theology*, edited by Michael Dauphinais and Matthew Levering, 23–61. Washington, DC: The Catholic University of America Press, 2005.

Erasmus, Desiderius. *Epistles of Erasmus*. Vol. 3. Translated by Francis Nichols. New York: Russell & Russell, 1962.

Escrivá, St. Josemaría. *Christ Is Passing By*. Princeton: Scepter, 2002.

———. *The Forge*. New York: Scepter, 2011.

———. *Friends of God*. New York: Scepter, 1981.

———. "In Joseph's Workshop" (homily 19 March 1963). In *Christ Is Passing By*, 72–88. Princeton: Scepter, 2002.

———. *The Way: A Critical-Historical Edition Prepared by Pedro Rodríguez*. New York: Scepter, 2009 (2002).

Eubank, Nathan. *First and Second Thessalonians*. Grand Rapids: Baker Academic, 2019.

Fagerberg, David W. "Divine Liturgy, Divine Love: Toward a New Understanding of Sacrifice in Christian Worship." *Letter and Spirit* 3 (2007) 95–111.

———. "Liturgical Asceticism: Enlarging our Grammar of Liturgy." *Pro Ecclesia* 13 (2004) 202–14.

———. "Theologia Prima: The Liturgical Mystery and the Mystery of God." *Letter and Spirit* 2 (2006) 55–67.

———. *Theologia Prima: What Is Liturgical Theology?* 2nd ed. Chicago: Hillenbrand, 2004.

Farkasfalvy, Denis, OCist. "Inspiration and Interpretation." In *Vatican II: Renewal within Tradition*, edited by Matthew L. Lamb and Matthew Levering, 77–100. Oxford: Oxford University Press, 2008.

———. *Inspiration and Interpretation: A Theological Introduction to Sacred Scripture*. Washington, DC: The Catholic University of America Press, 2010.

Farmer, William R. "State *Interesse* and Markan Primacy: 1870–1914." In *Biblical Studies and the Shifting of Paradigms, 1850–1914*, edited by Henning Graf Reventlow and William Farmer, 15–49. Sheffield: Sheffield Academic, 1995.

Feil, Ernst. "From the Classical *Religio* to the Modern *Religion*: Elements of a Transformation between 1550 and 1650." In *Religion in History: The Word, the Idea, the Reality*, edited by Michel Despland and Gérard Vallée, 31–43. Waterloo: Wilfrid Laurier University Press, 1992.

———. *Religio: Die Geschichte eines neuzeitlichen Grundbegriffs vom Frühchristentum bis zur Reformation*. Göttingen: Vandenhoeck & Ruprecht, 1986.

———. *Religio: Dritter Band: Die Geschichte eines neuzeitlichen Grundbegriffs im 17. und frühen 18. Jahrhundert*. Göttingen: Vandenhoeck & Ruprecht, 2001.

———. *Religio: Vierter Band: Die Geschichte eines neuzeitlichen Grundbegriffs im 18. und 19. Jahrhundert*. Göttingen: Vandenhoeck & Ruprecht, 2007.

## BIBLIOGRAPHY

———. *Religio Zweiter Band: Die Geschichte eines neuzeitlichen Grundbegriffs zwischen Reformation und Rationalismus (ca. 1540–1620)*. Göttingen: Vandenhoeck & Ruprecht, 1997.

Fishbane, Michael. *Biblical Interpretation in Ancient Israel*. Oxford: Clarendon, 1985.

———. *Text and Texture: Close Readings of Selected Biblical Texts*. New York: Schocken, 1979.

Fisher, Loren R. "Temple Quarter." *Journal of Semitic Studies* 8 (1963) 34–41.

Fitzmyer, Joseph A., SJ. *The Biblical Commission's Document "The Interpretation of the Bible in the Church": Text and Commentary*. Rome: Editrice Pontificio Istituto Biblico, 1995.

Flannery, Frances. "'Go Back by the Way You Came': An Internal Textual Critique of Elijah's Violence in 1 Kings 18–19." In *Writing and Reading War: Rhetoric, Gender, and Ethics in Biblical and Modern Contexts*, edited by Brad E. Kelle and Frank Ritchel Ames, 161–73. Atlanta: Society of Biblical Literature, 2008.

Fletcher-Louis, Crispin H. T. *All the Glory of Adam: Liturgical Anthropology in the Dead Sea Scrolls*. Leiden: Brill, 2002.

———. "God's Image, His Cosmic Temple and the High Priest: Towards an Historical and Theological Account of the Incarnation." In *Heaven on Earth: The Temple in Biblical Theology*, edited by T. Desmond Alexander and Simon Gathercole, 81–99. Carlisle: Paternoster, 2004.

———. "Jesus as the High Priestly Messiah: Part 1." *Journal for the Study of the Historical Jesus* 4 (2006) 155–75.

———. "Jesus as the High Priestly Messiah: Part 2." *Journal for the Study of the Historical Jesus* 5 (2007) 57–79.

———. "The Temple Cosmology of P and Theological Anthropology in the Wisdom of Jesus ben Sira." In *Of Scribes and Sages: Early Jewish Interpretation and Transmission of Scripture*, edited by Craig A. Evans, 69–113. London: T. & T. Clark, 2004.

———. "The Worship of Divine Humanity as God's Image and the Worship of Jesus." In *The Jewish Roots of Christological Monotheism: Papers from the St. Andrews Conference on the Historical Origins of the Worship of Jesus*, edited by Carey C. Newman et al., 112–28. Leiden: Brill, 1999.

Fogarty, Gerald P., SJ. *American Catholic Biblical Scholarship: A History from the Early Republic to Vatican II*. San Francisco: Harper & Row, 1989.

Frampton, Travis L. *Spinoza and the Rise of Historical Criticism of the Bible*. New York: T. & T. Clark, 2006.

Freedman, R. David. "The Father of Modern Biblical Scholarship." *Journal of the Ancient Near Eastern Society* 19 (1989) 31–38.

Gadenz, Pablo T. *The Gospel of Luke*. Grand Rapids: Baker Academic, 2018.

———. "Jesus the New Temple in the Thought of Pope Benedict XVI." *Nova et Vetera* 11 (2013) 211–30.

———. "Magisterial Teaching on the Inspiration and Truth of Scripture: Precedents and Prospects." *Letter and Spirit* 6 (2010) 67–91.

———. "Overcoming the Hiatus between Exegesis and Theology: Guidance and Examples from Pope Benedict XVI." In *Verbum Domini and the Complementarity of Exegesis and Theology*, edited by Fr. Scott Carl, 41–62. Grand Rapids: Eerdmans, 2015.

Gaeta, Giancarlo. "Le *Regole* per l'interpretazione della Scrittura da Ticonio ad Agostino." *Annali di storia dell'esegesi* 4 (1987) 109–18.

# BIBLIOGRAPHY

Gage, Warren Austin. *The Gospel of Genesis: Studies in Protology and Eschatology.* Winona Lake, IN: Carpenter, 1984.

García de Haro, Ramón. *Historia teológica del modernismo.* Pamplona: Ediciones Universidad de Navarra, 1972.

Gese, Hartmut. *Essays on Biblical Theology.* Translated by Keith Crim. Minneapolis: Augsburg, 1981.

———. "Wisdom, Son of Man, and the Origins of Christology: The Consistent Development of Biblical Theology." *Horizons in Biblical Theology* 3 (1981) 23–57.

Gibert, Pierre. *L'invention critique de la Bible: XVe–XVIIIe siècle.* Paris: Gallimard, 2010.

Gilbert, Maurice, SJ. *The Pontifical Biblical Institute: A Century of History (1909–2009).* Rome: Gregorian University Press, 2009.

———. "Why Moses and Elijah at the Transfiguration?" *Rivista Biblica* 57 (2009) 217–22.

Golitzin, Hieromonk Alexander. *Et Introibo Ad Altare Dei: The Mystagogy of Dionysius Areopagita, with Special Reference to Its Predecessors in the Eastern Tradition.* Thessaloniki: Patriachikon Idryma Paterikōn Meletōn, 1994.

Gordon, Cyrus H. "Higher Critics and Forbidden Fruit." *Christianity Today* 4 (1959) 3–6.

Goshen-Gottstein, M.H. "The Textual Criticism of the Old Testament: Rise, Decline, Rebirth." *Journal of Biblical Literature* 102 (1983) 365–99.

Gosse, Bernard. "Les traditions sur Abraham et sur le jardin d'Éden en rapport avec Is 51, 2–3 et avec le livre d'Ézéchiel." In *Studies in the Book of Genesis: Literature, Redaction and History*, edited by A. Wénin, 421–27. Leuven: Leuven University Press, 2001.

Gregory the Great, Pope. *Moralia in Job.* Patrologia Latina online database. http://pld.chadwyck.co.uk/.

Gregory, Russell. "Irony and the Unmasking of Elijah." In *From Carmel to Horeb: Elijah in Crisis*, edited by Alan J. Hauser and Russell Gregory, 91–170. Sheffield: Sheffield Academic, 1990.

Grelot, Pierre. "Commentaire du chapitre III." In *La Révélation Divine Tome II: Constitution dogmatique 'Dei verbum'*, edited by B.-D. Dupuy, 345–80. Paris: Cerf, 1968.

Greschat, Katharina. *Die Moralia in Job Gregors des Großen: Ein christologisch-ekklesiologischer Kommentar.* Tübingen: Mohr Siebeck, 2005.

Grillmeier, Alois. "The Divine Inspiration and the Interpretation of Sacred Scripture." In *Commentary on the Documents of Vatican II Volume III: Declaration on the Relationship of the Church to Non-Christian Religions, Dogmatic Constitution on Divine Revelation, and Decree on the Apostolate of the Laity*, edited by Herbert Vorgrimler, 199–246. New York: Herder & Herder, 1969.

Grisez, Germain. "The Inspiration and Inerrancy of Scripture." *Letter and Spirit* 6 (2010) 181–90.

Gross, Michael B. *The War Against Catholicism: Liberalism and the Anti-Catholic Imagination in Nineteenth-Century Germany.* Ann Arbor: University of Michigan Press, 2004.

Guigo II. "The Ladder from Earth to Heaven." *Letter and Spirit* 2 (2006) 175–88.

Hahn, Scott. *Angels and Saints: A Biblical Guide to Friendship with God's Holy Ones.* New York: Image, 2014.

———. "At the School of Truth: The Ecclesial Character of Theology and Exegesis in the Thought of Benedict XVI." In *The Bible and the University*, edited by David Lyle Jeffrey and C. Stephen Evans, 80–115. Grand Rapids: Zondervan, 2007.

———. "The Authority of Mystery: The Biblical Theology of Benedict XVI." *Letter and Spirit* 2 (2006) 97–140.

———. "Canon, Cult and Covenant: The Promise of Liturgical Hermeneutics." In *Canon and Biblical Interpretation*, edited by Craig G. Bartholomew et al., 207–35. Grand Rapids: Zondervan, 2006.

———. "Christ, Kingdom, and Creation: Davidic Christology and Ecclesiology in Luke-Acts." *Letter and Spirit* 3 (2007) 113–38.

———. *Consuming the Word: The New Testament and the Eucharist in the Early Church*. New York: Image, 2013.

———. *Covenant and Communion: The Biblical Theology of Pope Benedict XVI*. Grand Rapids: Brazos, 2009.

———. "Covenant, Cult, and the Curse-of-Death: Διαθήκη in Heb 9:15–22." In *Hebrews: Contemporary Methods—New Insights*, edited by Gabriella Gelardini, 65–88. Leiden: Brill, 2005.

———. *Evangelizing Catholics: A Mission Manual for the New Evangelization*. Huntington: Our Sunday Visitor, 2014.

———. *A Father Who Keeps His Promises: God's Covenant Love in Scripture*. Cincinnati: Charis, 1998.

———. *First Comes Love: Finding Your Family in the Church and the Trinity*. New York: Doubleday, 2002.

———. *First Society: The Sacrament of Matrimony and the Restoration of the Social Order*. Steubenville: Emmaus Road, 2018.

———. "For the Sake of Our Salvation: The Truth and Humility of God's Word." *Letter and Spirit* 6 (2010) 21–45.

———. "The Hermeneutic of Faith: Pope Benedict XVI on Scripture, Liturgy, and Church." *The Incarnate Word* 1 (2007) 415–40.

———. "Introduction." *Letter and Spirit* 7 (2011) 7–12.

———. *Joy to the World: How Christ's Coming Changed Everything (and Still Does)*. New York: Image, 2014.

———. "Kingdom and Church in Luke-Acts: From Davidic Christology to Kingdom Ecclesiology." In *Reading Luke: Interpretation, Reflection, Formation*, edited by Craig G. Bartholomew et al., 294–326. Grand Rapids: Zondervan, 2005.

———. *The Kingdom of God as Liturgical Empire: A Theological Commentary on 1–2 Chronicles*. Grand Rapids: Baker Academic, 2012.

———. *Kinship By Covenant: A Canonical Approach to the Fulfillment of God's Saving Promises*. New Haven, CT: Yale University Press, 2009.

———. *Letter and Spirit: From Written Text to Living Word in the Liturgy*. New York: Doubleday, 2005.

———. "Liturgy and Empire: Prophetic Historiography and Faith in Exile in 1–2 Chronicles." *Letter and Spirit* 5 (2009) 13–50.

———. "Scripture and the Liturgy: Inseparably United." *Origins* 35 (2006) 648–53.

———. "Temple, Sign, and Sacrament: Towards a New Perspective on the Gospel of John." *Letter and Spirit* 4 (2008) 107–43.

———. "Worship in the Word: Toward a Liturgical Hermeneutic." *Letter and Spirit* 1 (2005) 101–36.

Hahn, Scott W., and Benjamin Wiker. *Politicizing the Bible: The Roots of Historical Criticism and the Secularization of Scripture 1300–1700*. New York: Herder & Herder, 2013.

Hahn, Scott W., and Jeffrey L. Morrow. *Modern Biblical Criticism as a Tool of Statecraft (1700–1900)*. Steubenville: Emmaus Academic, 2020.

## BIBLIOGRAPHY

Hahn, Scott W., and John Kincaid. "The Multiple Literal Sense in Thomas Aquinas's Commentary on Romans and Modern Pauline Hermeneutics." In *Reading Romans with St. Thomas Aquinas*, edited by Matthew Levering and Michael Dauphinais, 163–82. Washington, DC: The Catholic University of America Press, 2012.

Hallo, William W., and K. Lawson Younger Jr., eds. *The Context of Scripture Volume I: Canonical Compositions from the Biblical World.* Leiden: Brill, 2003.

———, ed. *The Context of Scripture Volume II: Monumental Inscriptions from the Biblical World.* Leiden: Brill, 2003.

Haran, Menahem. "The Priestly Image of the Tabernacle." *Hebrew Union College Annual* 36 (1965) 191–222.

Hauser, Alan J. "Yahweh Versus Death—The Real Struggle in 1 Kings 17–19." In *From Carmel to Horeb: Elijah in Crisis*, edited by Alan J. Hauser, 9–89. Sheffield: Sheffield Academic, 1990.

Healy, Mary. "Aquinas's Use of the Old Testament in His Commentary on Romans." In *Reading Romans with St. Thomas Aquinas*, edited by Matthew Levering and Michael Dauphinais, 183–95. Washington, DC: The Catholic University of America Press, 2012.

Heitz, Carol. "Architecture et liturgie processionelle à l'époque préromane." *Revue de l'Art* 24 (1974) 30–47.

Herr, Denise Dick. "Variations of a Pattern: 1 Kings 19." *Journal of Biblical Literature* 104 (1985) 292–94.

Heschel, Abraham Joshua. *The Sabbath: Its Meaning for Modern Man.* New York: Farrar, Straus and Giroux, 2005.

Hess, Richard S., and David Toshio Tsumura, eds. *"I Studied Inscriptions from before the Flood": Ancient Near Eastern, Literary, and Linguistic Approaches to Genesis 1–11.* Winona Lake, IN: Eisenbrauns, 1994.

Hill, Harvey. "French Politics and Alfred Loisy's Modernism." *Church History* 67 (1998) 521–36.

———. "Leo XIII, Loisy, and the 'Broad School': An Early Round of the Modernist Crisis." *Catholic Historical Review* 89 (2003) 39–59.

———. "Loisy's *L'Évangile et l'Église* in Light of the 'Essais.'" *Theological Studies* 67 (2006) 73–98.

———. "Loisy's 'Mystical Faith': Loisy, Leo XIII, and Sabatier on Moral Education and the Church." *Theological Studies* 65 (2004) 73–94.

———. "The Politics of Loisy's Modernist Theology." In *Catholicism Contending with Modernity: Roman Catholic Modernism and Anti-Modernism in Historical Context*, edited by Darrell Jodock, 169–90. Cambridge: Cambridge University Press, 2000.

———. *The Politics of Modernism: Alfred Loisy and the Scientific Study of Religion.* Washington, DC: The Catholic University of America Press, 2002.

Hill, William F., SS. "Edward Philip Arbez, S.S., M.A., S.T.D.—1881–1967." *Catholic Biblical Quarterly* 31 (1969) 72–75.

———. "Reverend Edward P. Arbez, S.S." *Catholic Biblical Quarterly* 23 (1961) 113–24.

Himmelfarb, Martha. "The Temple and the Garden of Eden in Ezekiel, the Book of Watchers, and the Wisdom of ben Sira." In *Sacred Places and Profane Spaces: Essays in the Geographics of Judaism, Christianity, and Islam*, edited by Jamie Scott and Paul Simpson-Housley, 63–78. New York: Greenwood, 1991.

Hoffmeier, James K. *Ancient Israel in Sinai: The Evidence for the Authenticity of the Wilderness Tradition.* Oxford: Oxford University Press, 2005.

———. *Israel in Egypt: The Evidence for the Authenticity of the Exodus Tradition*. Oxford: Oxford University Press, 1996.

———. *"Sacred" in the Vocabulary of Ancient Egypt*. Freiburg: Universitäts and Vandenhoeck & Ruprecht, 1985.

———. "Some Thoughts on Genesis 1 and 2 and Egyptian Cosmology." *Journal of the Ancient Near Eastern Society* 15 (1983) 39–49.

———. "The Structure of Joshua 1–11 and the Annals of Thutmose III." In *Faith, Tradition, and History: Old Testament Historiography in Its Near Eastern Context*, edited by A. R. Millad et al., 165–79. Winona Lake, IN: Eisenbrauns, 1994.

Holmes, Jeremy. "Participation and the Meaning of Scripture." In *Reading Sacred Scripture with Thomas Aquinas: Hermeneutical Tools, Theological Questions and New Perspectives*, edited by Piotr Roszak and Jörgen Vijgen, 91–114. Madrid: Fédération Internationale des Instituts d'Études Médiévales, 2015.

Huizenga, Leroy A. *Behold the Christ: Proclaiming the Gospel of Matthew*. Steubenville: Emmaus Road, 2019.

———. "The Tradition of Christian Allegory Yesterday and Today." *Letter and Spirit* 8 (2013) 77–99.

Huizinga, Johan. *The Autumn of the Middle Ages*. Translated by Rodney J. Payton and Ulrich Mammitzsch. Chicago: University of Chicago Press, 1996.

Hultgren, Stephen. *From the Damascus Covenant to the Covenant of the Community: Literary, Historical, and Theological Studies in the Dead Sea Scrolls*. Leiden: Brill, 2007.

Hupfeld, Hermann W. *Die Quellen der Genesis und die Art ihrer Zusammensetzung von neuem untersucht*. Berlin: Wiegandt und Grieben, 1853.

Hurowitz, Victor (Avigdor). *I Have Built You an Exalted House: Temple Building in the Bible in Light of Mesopotamian and Northwest Semitic Writings*. Sheffield: Journal for the Study of the Old Testament, 1992.

———. "The Priestly Account of Building the Tabernacle." *Journal of the American Oriental Society* 105 (1985) 21–30.

Illich, Ivan. *In the Vineyard of the Text: A Commentary to Hugh's Didascalicon*. Chicago: University of Chicago Press, 1993.

Iversen, Gunilla. "'Lex est umbra futurorum': exégèse biblique poésie liturgique à Saint-Victor." In *Bibel und Exegese in der Abtei Saint-Victor zu Paris: Form und Funktion eines Grundtextes im europäischen Rahmen*, edited by Rainer Berndt, 83–103. Münster: Aschendorff, 2009.

Izquierdo, César. "Cómo se ha entendido el «modernismo teológico»: Discusión historiográfica." *Anuario de Historia de la Iglesia* 16 (2007) 35–75.

Jagersma, H. "*yšn* in 1. Könige xviii 27." *Vetus Testamentum* 25 (1975) 674–76.

Janowski, Bernd. *Gottes Gegenwart in Israel: Beiträge zur Theologie des Alten Testaments*. Neukirchen-Vluyn: Neukirchener, 1993.

Jodock, Darrell, ed. *Catholicism Contending with Modernity: Roman Catholic Modernism and Anti-Modernism in Historical Context*. Cambridge: Cambridge University Press, 2000.

———. "Introduction I: The Modernist Crisis." In *Catholicism Contending with Modernity: Roman Catholic Modernism and Anti-Modernism in Historical Context*, edited by Darrell Jodock, 1–19. Cambridge: Cambridge University Press, 2000.

———. "Introduction II: The Modernists and the Anti-Modernists." In *Catholicism Contending with Modernity: Roman Catholic Modernism and Anti-Modernism in Historical Context*, edited by Darrell Jodock, 20–28. Cambridge: Cambridge University Press, 2000.

John Paul II, Pope. "Address." October 14, 1993. As cited in St. Josemaría Escrivá, *The Way: A Critical-Historical Edition Prepared by Pedro Rodríguez*, 480n3. New York: Scepter, 2009.

———. "Address Commemorating the Twenty-Fifth Anniversary of *Dei Verbum* (1990)." In *The Scripture Documents: An Anthology of Official Catholic Teachings*, edited and translated by Dean P. Béchard, SJ, with a foreword by Joseph A. Fitzmyer, SJ. Collegeville, MN: Liturgical, 2002.

———. *Dies Domini*. 1998. http://www.vatican.va/holy_father/john_paul_ii/apost_letters/documents/hf_jp-ii_apl_05071998_dies-domini_en.html.

———. *Laborem Exercens*. 1981. http://www.vatican.va/holy_father/john_paul_ii/encyclicals/documents/hf_jp-ii_enc_14091981_laborem-exercens_en.html.

———. *Man and Woman He Created Them: A Theology of the Body*. Translated with an introduction and index by Michael Waldstein. Boston: Pauline, 2006.

———. *Redemptoris Custos*. 1989. http://www.vatican.va/holy_father/john_paul_ii/apost_exhortations/documents/hf_jp-ii_exh_15081989_redemptoris-custos_en.html.

———. *Scripturarum Thesaurus* (1979). In *The Scripture Documents: An Anthology of Official Catholic Teachings*, edited and translated by Dean P. Béchard, SJ, with a foreword by Joseph A. Fitzmyer, SJ. Collegeville, MN: Liturgical, 2002.

Johnson, Luke Timothy. "The Crisis in Biblical Scholarship." *Commonweal* 120 (1993) 18–21.

———. "The Glass is Half Full/Empty." *Commonweal* (1998) 30.

———. "How Not to Read the Bible." *Commonweal* 126 (1999) 22–26.

———. "Imagining the World Scripture Imagines." *Modern Theology* 14 (1998) 165–80.

———. "An Inexhaustible Text." *Commonweal* (1998) 26–29.

———. "So What's Catholic About It?: The State of Catholic Biblical Scholarship." *Commonweal* 125 (1998) 12–16.

———. "What's Catholic About Catholic Biblical Scholarship?" In *The Future of Catholic Biblical Scholarship: A Constructive Conversation*, by Luke Timothy Johnson and William S. Kurz, SJ, 3–34. Grand Rapids: Eerdmans, 2002.

Jones, Andrew Willard. *Before Church and State: A Study of Social Order in the Sacramental Kingdom of St. Louis IX*. Steubenville: Emmaus Academic, 2017.

Jones, Lindsay. *The Hermeneutics of Sacred Architecture: Experience, Interpretation, Comparison: Volume One: Monumental Occasions: Reflections on the Eventfulness of Religious Architecture*. Cambridge: Harvard University Press, 2000.

Kauffman, Christopher J. *Tradition and Transformation in Catholic Culture: The Priests of Saint Sulpice in the United States from 1791 to the Present*. New York: Macmillan, 1988.

Kaufmann, Yehezkel. "Probleme der israelitisch-jüdischen Religionsgeschichte." *Zeitschrift für die alttestamentliche Wissenschaft* 51 (1933) 35–47.

———. *The Religion of Israel*. Abridged and translated by Moshe Greenberg. Chicago: University of Chicago Press, 1960.

Kearney, Peter J. "Creation and Liturgy: The P Redaction of Ex 25–40." *Zeitschrift für die alttestamentliche Wissenschaft* 89 (1977) 375–87.

Keating, Daniel. "Exegesis and Christology in Thomas Aquinas." In *Reading Sacred Scripture with Thomas Aquinas: Hermeneutical Tools, Theological Questions and New Perspectives*, ed. Piotr Roszak and Jörgen Vijgen, 507-30. Madrid: Fédération Internationale des Instituts d'Études Médiévales, 2015.

Keinänen, Jyrki. *Traditions in Collision: A Literary and Redaction-Critical Study on the Elijah Narratives 1 Kings 17-19*. Göttingen: Vandenhoeck & Ruprecht, 2001.

Kelly, Henry Ansgar, et al. "Preface." In *Thomas More's Trial by Jury: A Procedural and Legal Review with a Collection of Documents*, edited by Henry Ansgar Kelly et al., xi-xvii. Rochester: Boydell, 2011.

Kikawada, Isaac M. "The Double Creation of Mankind in 'Enki and Ninmah,' 'Atrahasis,' I 1-351, and 'Genesis' 1-2." *Iraq* 45 (1983) 43-45.

Kikawada, Isaac M., and Arthur Quinn. *Before Abraham Was: The Unity of Genesis 1-11*. Nashville: Abingdon, 1985.

Kitchen, Kenneth A. *Pentateuchal Criticism and Interpretation* (Lecture Notes). Derbyshire: Theological Students' Fellowship, 1965.

Kleinhans, Arduin. "De nova Enchiridii Biblici editione." *Antonianem* 30 (1955) 63-65.

Kline, Meredith G. *Images of the Spirit*. Grand Rapids: Baker, 1980.

———. *Kingdom Prologue*. S. Hamilton, MA: Meredith G. Kline, 1993.

Knoch, Wendelin. "Exegese und Dogmatik: Theologische Implikationen der Trennung von systematischer und biblischer Theologie in der Frühscholastik." *Theologie und Glaube* 97 (2007) 1-11.

Kruggel, James C. "Scripture, Tradition, and the Magisterium in the Teaching of Vatican II." PhD diss., The Catholic University of America Press, 2013.

Kugel, James L. *How to Read the Bible: A Guide to Scripture, Then and Now*. New York: Free Press, 2007.

———. "One Hundred Years of the Pontifical Biblical Commission." In *Parole del Centenario: 1909-2009*, 79-87. Rome: Gregorian and Biblical, 2010.

———. "One Hundred Years of the Pontifical Biblical Institute." Presentation at the Society of Biblical Literature 2009 International Meeting, Celebrating the Centenary of the Pontifical Biblical Institute, Opening Session, Aula Magna Pontificia Università Gregoriana (20 giugno 2009-h. 17.00). http://www.biblico.it/Centenario/sbl_luglio09.html. Also available online at the Society of Biblical Literature website: https://www.sbl-site.org/publications/article.aspx?articleId=835.

Kurtz, Paul Michael. "The Way of War: Wellhausen, Israel, and Bellicose *Reiche*." *Zeitschrift für die alttestamentliche Wissenschaft* 127 (2015) 1-19.

Lawrie, Douglas. "Telling Of(f) Prophets: Narrative Strategy in 1 Kings 18:1—19:18." *Journal of Northwest Semitic Languages* 23 (1997) 163-80.

Lazarus-Yafeh, Hava. *Intertwined Worlds: Medieval Islam and Bible Criticism*. Princeton: Princeton University Press, 1992.

Lease, Gary. "Vatican Foreign Policy and the Origins of Modernism." In *Catholicism Contending with Modernity: Roman Catholic Modernism and Anti-Modernism in Historical Context*, edited by Darrell Jodock, 31-55. Cambridge: Cambridge University Press, 2000.

Leclercq, Jean. *L'Amour des lettres et le désir de Dieu: Initiation aux auteurs monastiques du moyen âge*. Paris: Cerf, 1957.

———. *The Love of Learning and the Desire for God: A Study of Monastic Culture*. Translated by Catharine Misrahi. New York: Fordham University Press, 1982.

Legaspi, Michael C. *The Death of Scripture and the Rise of Biblical Studies*. Oxford: Oxford University Press, 2010.
Leithart, Peter J. *1 and 2 Kings*. Grand Rapids: Brazos, 2006.
Levenson, Jon D. *Creation and the Persistence of Evil: The Jewish Drama of Divine Omnipotence*. San Francisco: Harper & Row, 1988.
———. *The Hebrew Bible, the Old Testament, and Historical Criticism: Jews and Christians in Biblical Studies*. Louisville: Westminster/John Knox, 1993.
———. "The Paronomasia of Solomon's Seventh Petition." *Hebrew Annual Review* 6 (1982) 135–38.
———. *Resurrection and the Restoration of Israel: The Ultimate Victory of the God of Life*. New Haven, CT: Yale University Press, 2006.
———. *Sinai and Zion: An Entry into the Jewish Bible*. Minneapolis: Winston, 1985.
———. "The Temple and the World." *Journal of Religion* 64 (1984) 275–98.
———. *Theology of the Program of Restoration of Ezekiel 40–48*. Cambridge: Scholars Press for the Harvard Semitics Museum, 1976.
Levering, Matthew. "Aquinas on Romans 8: Predestination in Context." In *Reading Romans with St. Thomas Aquinas*, edited by Matthew Levering and Michael Dauphinais, 196–215. Washington, DC: The Catholic University of America Press, 2012.
———. "Does the Paschal Mystery Reveal the Trinity?" In *Reading John with St. Thomas Aquinas: Theological Exegesis and Speculative Theology*, edited by Michael Dauphinais and Matthew Levering, 78–91. Washington, DC: The Catholic University of America Press, 2005.
———. *Engaging the Doctrine of Revelation: The Mediation of the Gospel through Church and Scripture*. Grand Rapids: Baker Academic, 2014.
———. "The Old Testament in Aquinas' Moral Theology." In *Reading Sacred Scripture with Thomas Aquinas: Hermeneutical Tools, Theological Questions and New Perspectives*, edited by Piotr Roszak and Jörgen Vijgen, 349–74. Madrid: Fédération Internationale des Instituts d'Études Médiévales, 2015.
———. *Sacrifice and Community: Jewish Offering and Christian Eucharist*. Oxford: Blackwell, 2005.
Levering, Matthew, and Michael Dauphinais, eds. *Reading Romans with St. Thomas Aquinas*. Washington, DC: The Catholic University of America Press, 2012.
Lieber, Andrea. "Jewish and Christian Heavenly Meal Traditions." In *Paradise Now: Essays on Early Jewish and Christian Mysticism*, edited by April DeConick, 313–39. Leiden: Brill, 2007.
Lobrichon, Guy. "Le Mangeur au festin. L'*Historia scholastica* aux mains de ses lecteurs: Glose, Bible en images, Bibles historiales (fin XIIIe–XIVe siècle)." In *Pierre le Mangeur ou Pierre de Troyes: maître du XIIe siècle: Études réunies*, edited by Gilbert Dahan, 289–312. Turnhout: Brepols, 2013.
Logan, George M., ed. *Cambridge Companion to Thomas More*. Cambridge: Cambridge University Press, 2011.
Lorberbaum, Menachem. "Spinoza's Theological–Political Problem." In *Political Hebraism: Judaic Sources in Early Modern Political Thought*, edited by Gordon Schochet, Fania Oz-Salzberger, and Meirav Jones, 167–90. Jerusalem: Shalem, 2008.
Luscombe, David. "Peter Comestor and Biblical Chronology." *Irish Theological Quarterly* 80 (2015) 136–48.

———. "The Place of Peter Comestor in the History of Medieval Theology." In *Pierre le Mangeur ou Pierre de Troyes: maître du XIIe siècle: Études réunies*, edited by Gilbert Dahan, 27–45. Turnhout: Brepols, 2013.

Machinist, Peter. "The Road Not Taken: Wellhausen and Assyriology." In *Homeland and Exile: Biblical and Ancient Near Eastern Studies in Honour of Bustenay Oded*, edited by Gershon Galil et al., 469–531. Leiden: Brill, 2009.

Malcolm, Noel. *Aspects of Hobbes*. Oxford: Oxford University Press, 2002.

———, ed. *Thomas Hobbes: Leviathan Volume 1: Editorial Introduction*. Oxford: Oxford University Press, 2012.

———, ed. *Thomas Hobbes: Leviathan Volume 2: The English and Latin Texts (i)*. Oxford: Oxford University Press, 2012.

———, ed. *Thomas Hobbes: Leviathan Volume 3: The English and Latin Texts (ii)*. Oxford: Oxford University Press, 2012.

Mâle, Emile. *The Gothic Image: Religious Art in France of the Thirteenth Century*. Translated by Dora Nussey. New York: Harper & Row, 1972.

Maly, Eugene H. "Israel—God's Liturgical People." In *Liturgy for the People: Essays in Honor of Gerald Ellard, S.J., 1894–1963*, ed. William J. Leonard, SJ, 10–20. Milwaukee: Bruce, 1963.

Marshall, Peter. "The Last Years." In *Cambridge Companion to Thomas More*, edited by George M. Logan, 116–38. Cambridge: Cambridge University Press, 2011.

Martens, Peter W. "Origen Against History? Reconsidering the Critique of Allegory." *Modern Theology* 28 (2012) 635–56.

———. *Origen and Scripture: The Contours of the Exegetical Life*. Oxford: Oxford University Press, 2012.

Martin, Francis. "Election, Covenant, and Law." *Nova et Vetera* 4 (2006) 865–71.

———. "Revelation and Its Transmission." In *Vatican II: Renewal within Tradition*, edited by Matthew L. Lamb and Matthew Levering, 55–75. Oxford: Oxford University Press, 2008.

Mazza, Enrico. *La mistagogia: una teologia della liturgia in epoca patristica*. Rome: C.L.V.- Edizioni liturgiche, 1988.

———. *Mystagogy*. Translated by Matthew J. O'Connell. New York: Pueblo, 1989.

McConica, James. "Thomas More as Humanist." In *Cambridge Companion to Thomas More*, edited by George M. Logan, 22–45. Cambridge: Cambridge University Press, 2011.

McCutcheon, Elizabeth. "More's Rhetoric." In *Cambridge Companion to Thomas More*, edited by George M. Logan, 46–68. Cambridge: Cambridge University Press, 2011.

McDermott, Ryan. "Henri de Lubac's Genealogy of Modern Exegesis and Nicholas of Lyra's Literal Sense of Scripture." *Modern Theology* 29 (2013) 124–56.

McDonald, Lee M. *The Formation of the Christian Biblical Canon*. Rev. ed. Peabody, MA: Hendrickson, 1995.

———. "Identifying Scripture and Canon in the Early Church: The Criteria Question." In *The Canon Debate*, edited by Lee Martin McDonald and James A. Sanders, 416–39. Peabody, MA: Hendrickson, 2002.

McGovern, Thomas James. "The Divine Origin and the Interpretation of the Bible in Chapter III of the Dogmatic Constitution 'Dei Verbum.'" *Cuadernos Doctorales. Excerpta e dissertationibus in Sacra Theologia* 17 (1990) 98–179.

# BIBLIOGRAPHY

Mégier, Elisabeth. "Zur Artikulation von Bibel und Geschichte in der 'Chronica' alias 'Liber de tribus maximis circumstantiis gestorum' Hugo von Sankt Viktor." In *Bibel und Exegese in der Abtei Saint-Victor zu Paris: Form und Funktion eines Grundtextes im europäischen Rahmen*, edited by Rainer Berndt, 335–61. Münster: Aschendorff, 2009.

Mesguich, Sophie Kessler. "Early Christian Hebraists." In *Hebrew Bible/Old Testament: The History of Its Interpretation II: From the Renaissance to the Enlightenment*, edited by Magne Sæbø, 254–75. Göttingen: Vandenhoeck & Ruprecht, 2008.

Meyers, Carol L. *The Tabernacle Menorah: A Synthetic Study of a Symbol from the Biblical Cult*. Missoula, MT: Scholars, 1976.

Michaelis, Johann David. *Einleitung in die göttlichen Schriften des Alten Bundes*. Hamburg: Bohnsche Buchhandlung, 1787.

Miller, Athanasius. "Das neue biblische Handbuch." *Benediktinische Monatschrift* 31 (1955) 49–50.

Minnis, Alastair. *Medieval Theory of Authorship: Scholastic Literary Attitudes in the Later Middle Ages*. 2nd ed. With a new preface by the author. Philadelphia: University of Pennsylvania, 2010.

Mirri, F. Saverio. *Richard Simon e il metodo storico-critico di B. Spinoza. Storia di un libro e di una polemica sulla sfondo delle lotte politico-religiose della Francia di Luigi XIV*. Florence: Le Monnier, 1972.

Misner, Paul. "Catholic Anti-Modernism: The Ecclesial Setting." In *Catholicism Contending with Modernity: Roman Catholic Modernism and Anti-Modernism in Historical Context*, edited by Darrell Jodock, 56–87. Cambridge: Cambridge University Press, 2000.

Momigliano, Arnaldo. "Religious History without Frontiers: J. Wellhausen, U. Wilamowitz, and E. Schwarz." *History and Theory* 21 (1982) 49–64.

Monson, John M. "The Temple of Solomon: Heart of Jerusalem." In *Zion, City of Our God*, edited by Richard S. Hess and Gordon J. Wenham, 1–22. Grand Rapids: Eerdmans, 1999.

More, Thomas, Saint. *The Complete Works of St. Thomas More Volume 6: A Dialogue Concerning Heresies*. Edited by Thomas Lawler et al. New Haven, CT: Yale University Press, 1981.

———. *A Dialogue of Comfort against Tribulation*. Princeton: Scepter, 1998.

———. *For All Seasons: Selected Letters of Thomas More*. Edited by Stephen Smith. New York: Scepter, 2012.

———. *The Life of Pico Della Mirandola: 'A Very Spectacle To All'*. New York: Scepter, 2010.

———. *The Sadness of Christ: And Final Prayers and Benedictions*. New York: Scepter, 1993.

Morey, James H. "Peter Comestor, Biblical Paraphrase, and the Medieval Popular Bible." *Speculum* 68 (1993) 6–35.

Morrow, Jeffrey L. "The Acid of History: La Peyrère, Hobbes, Spinoza, and the Separation of Faith and Reason in Modern Biblical Studies." *Heythrop Journal* 58 (2017) 169–80.

———. *Alfred Loisy and Modern Biblical Studies*. Washington, DC: The Catholic University of America Press, 2019.

———. "Alfred Loisy and les Mythes Babyloniens: Loisy's Discourse on Myth in the Context of Modernism." *Journal for the History of Modern Theology/Zeitschrift für Neuere Theologiegeschichte* 21 (2014) 87–103.

———. "Alfred Loisy's Developmental Approach to Scripture: Reading the 'Firmin' Articles in the Context of Nineteenth- and Twentieth-Century Historical Biblical Criticism." *International Journal of Systematic Theology* 15 (2013) 324–44.

———. "'Arise and Eat': 1 Kings 19:3–8 and Elijah's Death, Resurrection and Bread from Heaven." *Journal of the Orthodox Center for the Advancement of Biblical Studies* 3 (2010) 1–7.

———. "Averroism, Nominalism, and Mechanization: Hahn and Wiker's Unmasking of Historical Criticism's Political Agenda by Laying Bare its Philosophical Roots." *Nova et Vetera* 14 (2016) 1293–1340.

———. "Babylon in Paris: Alfred Loisy as Assyriologist." *Journal of Religious History* 40 (2016) 261–76.

———. "Babylonian Myths and the Bible: The Historical and Religious Context to Loisy's Application of 'Myth' as a Concept." *Papers of the Nineteenth Century Theology Group* 44 (2013) 43–62.

———. "Creation as Temple-Building and Work as Liturgy in Genesis 1–3." *Journal of the Orthodox Center for the Advancement of Biblical Studies* 2 (2009) 1–13.

———. "Cut Off from Its Wellspring: The Politics Behind the Divorce of Scripture from Catholic Moral Theology." *Heythrop Journal* 56 (2015) 547–58.

———. "*Dei verbum* in Light of the History of Catholic Biblical Interpretation." *Josephinum Journal of Theology* 23 (2016) 227–49.

———. "The Early Modern Political Context to Spinoza's Bible Criticism." *Revista de Filosofía* 66 (2010) 7–24.

———. "The Enlightenment University and the Creation of the Academic Bible: Michael Legaspi's *The Death of Scripture and the Rise of Biblical Studies*." *Nova et Vetera* 11 (2013) 897–922.

———. "*Études Assyriologie* and 19th and 20th Century French Historical-Biblical Criticism." *Near Eastern Archaeological Society Bulletin* 59 (2014) 3–20.

———. "Études Bibliques: The Early Biblical Work of Alfred Loisy." *Modernism* 4 (2018) 12–32.

———. "Evangelical Catholics and Catholic Biblical Scholarship: An Examination of Scott Hahn's Canonical, Liturgical, and Covenantal Biblical Exegesis." PhD diss., University of Dayton, 2007.

———. "Faith, Reason and History in Early Modern Catholic Biblical Interpretation: Fr. Richard Simon and St. Thomas More." *New Blackfriars* 96 (2015) 658–73.

———. "The Fate of Catholic Biblical Interpretation in America." In *Weaving the American Catholic Tapestry: Essays in Honor of William L. Portier*, edited by Derek C. Hatch and Timothy R. Gabrielli, 41–59. Eugene, OR: Pickwick, 2017.

———. "French Apocalyptic Messianism: Isaac La Peyrère and Political Biblical Criticism in the Seventeenth Century." *Toronto Journal of Theology* 27 (2011) 203–13.

———. "Genesis 1–3 in Modern Jewish and Catholic Traditions: Towards a Theology of Work." In *Reading and Living Scripture: Essays in Honor of William S. Kurz, S.J.*, ed. Jeremy Holmes and Kent Lasnoski. Steubenville: Emmaus Academic, forthcoming.

———. "Historical Criticism as Secular Allegorism: The Case of Spinoza." *Letter and Spirit* 8 (2013) 189–221.

———. "*Leviathan* and the Swallowing of Scripture: The Politics behind Thomas Hobbes' Early Modern Biblical Criticism." *Christianity and Literature* 61 (2011) 33–54.

———. "Lives of Jesus and Historico-Critical Scepticism." In *The Cambridge History of Atheism*, edited by Michael Ruse and Stephen Bullivant. Cambridge: Cambridge University Press, forthcoming.

———. "Loisy, Alfred Firmin." In *Encyclopedia of the Bible and Its Reception 16: Lectionary–Lots*, edited by Christine Helmer et al., 1039–41. Berlin: Walter de Gruyter, 2018.

———. "Methods of Interpreting Scripture and Nature: The Influence of the Baconian Method on Spinoza's Bible Criticism." Annual of the History of Biblical Interpretation/ Jahrbuch für Auslegungsgeschichte der Bibel 1 (forthcoming).

———. "Newman, the Scholars, and the Jews: Newman's Use of the Old Testament in *Grammar of Assent* in Contrast with 19th Century Biblical Criticism." *Center for Catholic Studies, Seton Hall University, Summer Seminar Proceedings: "John Henry Newman"* 8 (2011) 20–22.

———. "The Politics of Biblical Interpretation: A 'Criticism of Criticism.'" *New Blackfriars* 91 (2010) 528–45.

———. "Pre-Adamites, Politics and Criticism: Isaac La Peyrère's Contribution to Modern Biblical Studies." *Journal of the Orthodox Center for the Advancement of Biblical Studies* 4 (2011) 1–23.

———. *Pretensions of Objectivity: Toward a Criticism of Biblical Criticism*. Eugene, OR: Pickwick, 2019.

———. "Religion and the Secular State: Loisy's Use of 'Religion' Prior to his Excommunication." In *Constructing Nineteenth-Century Religion: Literary, Historical, and Religious Studies in Dialogue*, edited by Joshua King and Winter Jade Werner, 25–45. Columbus: Ohio State University Press, 2019.

———. "Secularization, Objectivity, and Enlightenment Scholarship: The Theological and Political Origins of Modern Biblical Studies." *Logos* 18 (2015) 14–32.

———. "Spinoza and the Theo-Political Implications of his Freedom to Philosophize." *New Blackfriars* 99 (2018) 374–87.

———. "Spinoza's Use of the Psalms in the Context of His Political Project." *Interdisciplinary Journal of Research on Religion* 11 (2015) 1–18.

———. "Studies in Scripture for Moral Theologians." *Journal of Moral Theology* 7 (2018) 36–56.

———. *Theology, Politics, and Exegesis: Essays on the History of Modern Biblical Criticism*. Eugene, OR: Pickwick, 2017.

———. "Thomas More on the Sadness of Christ: From Mystagogy to Martyrdom." *Heythrop Journal* 58 (2017) 365–73.

———. *Three Skeptics and the Bible: La Peyrère, Hobbes, Spinoza, and the Reception of Modern Biblical Criticism*. Eugene, OR: Pickwick, 2016.

———. "Thy Kingdom Come: The Church and the Kingdom of God in Loisy's *L'Évangile et l'Église*." *Downside Review* 137 (2019) 3–13.

———. "The Untold History of Modern Biblical Scholarship's Pre-Enlightenment Secular Origins." *Journal of Theological Interpretation* 8 (2014) 145–55.

———. "Work as Worship in the Garden and the Workshop: Genesis 1–3, the Feast of St. Joseph the Worker, and Liturgical Hermeneutics." *Logos* 15 (2012) 159–78.

Müller, Sascha. *Richard Simon (1638–1712): Exeget, Theologe, Philosoph und Historiker*. Bamberg: Echter, 2006.

Munro, J. Iverach. *The Samaritan Pentateuch and Modern Criticism*. London: James Nisbet, 1911.

Murphy, Roland E. "Historical Criticism." *Commonweal* (February 27, 1998) 4 and 29.
———. "What Is Catholic About Catholic Biblical Scholarship?—Revisited." *Biblical Theology Bulletin* 28 (1998) 112–19.
Nahkola, Aulikki. *Double Narratives in the Old Testament: The Foundations of Method in Biblical Criticism*. Berlin: Walter de Gruyter, 2001.
———. "The *Memoires* of Moses and the Genesis of Method in Biblical Criticism: Astruc's Contribution." In *Sacred Conjectures: The Context and Legacy of Robert Lowth and Jean Astruc*, edited by John Jarick, 204–19. London: T. & T. Clark, 2007.
Nakamura, Hideki. "Schriftauslegung und Theologie bei Richard von Sankt Viktor." In *Bibel und Exegese in der Abtei Saint-Victor zu Paris: Form und Funktion eines Grundtextes im europäischen Rahmen*, edited by Rainer Berndt, 363–89. Münster: Aschendorff, 2009.
Narváez, Mauricio. "Intention, *probabiles rationes* and Truth: The Exegetical Practice in Thomas Aquinas: The Case of the *Expositio super Iob ad litteram*." In *Reading Sacred Scripture with Thomas Aquinas: Hermeneutical Tools, Theological Questions and New Perspectives*, edited by Piotr Roszak and Jörgen Vijgen, 141–70. Madrid: Fédération Internationale des Instituts d'Études Médiévales, 2015.
Nelson, Eric. *The Hebrew Republic: Jewish Sources and the Transformation of European Political Thought*. Cambridge: Harvard University Press, 2010.
Neuman, Kalman. "Political Hebraism and the Early Modern 'Respublica Hebraeorum': On Defining the Field." In *Political Hebraism: Judaic Sources in Early Modern Political Thought*, edited by Gordon Schochet et al., 57–71. Jerusalem: Shalem, 2008.
Nielsen, Lauge O. "Langton's Questions on the Ten Commandments: Biblical Scholarship and the Art of Disputation." In *Étienne Langton. Prédicateur, bibliste, théologien*, edited by Louis-Jacques Bataillon et al., 623–44. Turnhout: Brepols, 2010.
Ocker, Christopher. *Biblical Poetics Before Humanism and Reformation*. Cambridge: Cambridge University Press, 2002.
Ocker, Christopher, and Kevin Madigan. "After Beryl Smalley: Thirty Years of Medieval Exegesis, 1984–2013." *Journal of the Bible and Its Reception* 2 (2015) 87–130.
Ockham, William of. *Dialogus*. http://www.britac.ac.uk/pubs/dialogus/t31d3new.html.
O'Connell, Marvin R. "The Bishopric of Monaco, 1902: A Revision." *Catholic Historical Review* 71 (1985) 26–51.
———. *Critics on Trial: An Introduction to the Catholic Modernist Crisis*. Washington, DC: The Catholic University of America Press, 1994.
Olsen, Derek A. *Reading Matthew with Monks: Liturgical Interpretation in Anglo-Saxon England*. Collegeville, MN: Michael Glazier, 2015.
O'Malley, John W. *What Happened at Vatican II*. Cambridge: Harvard University Press, 2008.
Ong, Walter J., SJ. *The Presence of the Word: Some Prolegomena for Cultural and Religious History*. New Haven, CT: Yale University Press, 1967.
Osiek, Carolyn. "Catholic or catholic? Biblical Scholarship at the Center." *Journal of Biblical Literature* 125 (2006) 5–22.
Ossandón Widow, Juan Carlos. "Raymond E. Brown y el sentido literal de la Sagrada Escritura." *Annales theologici* 20 (2006) 337–56.
Ouellet, Cardinal Marc. *The Relevance and Future of Vatican II: Interviews with Father Geoffroy de la Tousche*. San Francisco: Ignatius, 2013 (2012).
*Parole del Centenario: 1909–2009*. Rome: Gregorian and Biblical, 2010.

Pasto, James. "When the End is the Beginning? Or When the Biblical Past is the Political Present: Some Thoughts on Ancient Israel, 'Post-Exilic Judaism,' and the Politics of Biblical Scholarship." *Scandinavian Journal of the Old Testament* 12 (1998) 157–202.

Pelikan, Jaroslav. *The Christian Tradition: A History of the Development of Doctrine 4: Reformation of Church and Dogma (1300–1700).* Chicago: University of Chicago Press, 1984.

Penco, Gregorio. "La dottrina dei sensi spirituali in S. Gregorio." *Benedictina* 17 (1970) 170–201.

Perreau-Saussine, Emile. "Why Draw a Politics from Scripture? Bossuet and the Divine Right of Kings." In *Political Hebraism: Judaic Sources in Early Modern Political Thought*, edited by Gordon Schochet et al., 90–106. Jerusalem: Shalem, 2008.

Persidok, Andrzej. "¿Revolucionario o 'genio simplificador'?: Santo Tomás de Aquino en la *Exégèse médiévale* de Henri de Lubac." *Biblica et Patristica Thoruniensia* 8 (2015) 67–80.

Pickstock, Catherine. *After Writing: On the Liturgical Consummation of Philosophy.* Oxford: Blackwell, 1998.

Pietsch, Andreas Nikolaus. *Isaac La Peyrère: Bibelkritik, Philosemitismus und Patronage in der Gelehrtenrepublik des 17. Jahrhunderts.* Berlin: Walter de Gruyter, 2012.

Pitre, Brant. *Jesus and the Jewish Roots of the Eucharist: Unlocking the Secrets of the Last Supper.* New York: Doubleday, 2011.

———. *Jesus and the Last Supper.* Grand Rapids: Eerdmans, 2015.

———. "Jesus, the New Temple, and the New Priesthood." *Letter and Spirit* 4 (2008) 56–63.

———. "The Mystery of God's Word: Inspiration, Inerrancy, and the Interpretation of Scripture." *Letter and Spirit* 6 (2010) 47–66.

———. "*Verbum Domini* and Historical-Critical Exegesis." In *Verbum Domini and the Complementarity of Exegesis and Theology*, edited by Fr. Scott Carl, 26–40. Grand Rapids: Eerdmans, 2015.

Pitre, Brant, et al. *Paul, a New Covenant Jew: Rethinking Pauline Theology.* Grand Rapids: Eerdmans, 2019.

Pius XI, Pope. "The Holy Father and the English Martyrs." *The Tablet* (March 16, 1935) 338.

Pontifical Biblical Commission. "The Interpretation of the Bible in the Church (1993)." In *The Scripture Documents: An Anthology of Official Catholic Teachings*, edited and translated by Dean P. Béchard, SJ, with a foreword by Joseph A. Fitzmyer, SJ, 244–317. Collegeville, MN: Liturgical, 2002.

Popkin, R.H. "Millenarianism and Nationalism—A Case Study: Isaac La Peyrère." In *Millenarianism and Messianism in Early Modern European Culture Volume IV: Continental Millenarians: Protestants, Catholics, Heretics*, edited by John Christian Laursen and Richard H. Popkin, 74–84. Dordrecht: Kluwer Academic, 2001.

Portier, William L. "Church Unity and National Traditions: The Challenge to the Modern Papacy, 1682–1870." In *The Papacy and the Church in the United States*, edited by Bernard Cooke, 25–54. New York: Paulist, 1989.

———. *Divided Friends: Portraits of the Roman Catholic Modernist Crisis in the United States.* Washington, DC: The Catholic University of America Press, 2013.

Poulat, Émile. *Histoire, dogme et critique dans la crise moderniste.* 3rd ed. Paris: Albin Michel, 1996 (1962).

## BIBLIOGRAPHY

——. *Intégrisme et catholicisme intégral. Un réseau secret international antimoderniste: la 'Sapinière' (1909–1921)*. Paris: Casterman, 1969.
Preus, J. Samuel. *Spinoza and the Irrelevance of Biblical Authority*. Cambridge: Cambridge University Press, 2001.
Ramage, Matthew. "In the Beginning: Aquinas, Benedict XVI, and the Book of Genesis." In *Reading Sacred Scripture with Thomas Aquinas: Hermeneutical Tools, Theological Questions and New Perspectives*, edited by Piotr Roszak and Jörgen Vijgen, 481–506. Madrid: Fédération Internationale des Instituts d'Études Médiévales, 2015.
Rasmussen, Tarald. "Bridging the Middle Ages and the Renaissance: *Biblia Pauperum*, their Genre and Hermeneutical Significance." In *Hebrew Bible/Old Testament: The History of Its Interpretation II: From the Renaissance to the Enlightenment*, edited by Magne Sæbø, 76–93. Göttingen: Vandenhoeck & Ruprecht, 2008.
Raurell, Frederic. "Mètode d'aproximació de la Bíblia en el *Jesús de Natzaret* de Joseph Ratzinger/Benet XVI." *Revista Catalana de Teologia* 32 (2007) 435–58.
Raymond of Capua. *Life of Saint Catherine of Siena*. Translated by the Ladies of the Sacred Heart. New York: Kenedy & Sons, 1862.
Reinhardt, Elisabeth. "Thomas Aquinas as Interpreter of Scripture in Light of his Inauguration Lectures." In *Reading Sacred Scripture with Thomas Aquinas: Hermeneutical Tools, Theological Questions and New Perspectives*, edited by Piotr Roszak and Jörgen Vijgen, 71–90. Madrid: Fédération Internationale des Instituts d'Études Médiévales, 2015.
Remer, Gary. "After Machiavelli and Hobbes: James Harrington's Commonwealth of Israel." In *Political Hebraism: Judaic Sources in Early Modern Political Thought*, edited by Gordon Schochet et al., 207–30. Jerusalem: Shalem, 2008.
Rendsburg, Gary A. *The Redaction of Genesis*. Winona Lake, IN: Eisenbrauns, 1986.
Reventlow, Henning Graf. *Epochen der Bibelauslegung Band III: Renaissance, Reformation, Humanismus*. Munich: Beck, 1997.
——. *History of Biblical Interpretation Volume 4: From the Enlightenment to the Twentieth Century*. Translated by Leo G. Perdue. Atlanta: Society of Biblical Literature, 2010.
Rohls, Jan. "Historical, Cultural and Philosophical Aspects of the Nineteenth Century with Special Regard to Biblical Interpretation." In *Hebrew Bible/Old Testament: The History of Its Interpretation Volume III: From Modernism to Post-Modernism (The Nineteenth and Twentieth Centuries) Part 1: The Nineteenth Century—A Century of Modernism and Historicism*, edited by Magne Sæbø, 31–63. Göttingen: Vandenhoeck & Ruprecht, 2013.
Roszak, Piotr, and Jörgen Vijgen, eds. *Reading Sacred Scripture with Thomas Aquinas: Hermeneutical Tools, Theological Questions and New Perspectives*. Madrid: Fédération Internationale des Instituts d'Études Médiévales, 2015.
Rummel, Erika. "The Textual and Hermeneutical Work of Desiderius Erasmus of Rotterdam." In *Hebrew Bible/Old Testament: The History of Its Interpretation II: From the Renaissance to the Enlightenment*, edited by Magne Sæbø, 215–30. Göttingen: Vandenhoeck & Ruprecht, 2008.
Sæbø, Magne. "From the Renaissance to the Enlightenment—Aspects of the Cultural and Ideological Framework of Scriptural Interpretation." In *Hebrew Bible/Old Testament: The History of Its Interpretation II: From the Renaissance to the Enlightenment*, edited by Magne Sæbø, 21–45. Göttingen: Vandenhoeck & Ruprecht, 2008.
——, ed. *Hebrew Bible/Old Testament: The History of Its Interpretation II: From the Renaissance to the Enlightenment*. Göttingen: Vandenhoeck & Ruprecht, 2008.

## BIBLIOGRAPHY

Sanders, James A. *From Sacred Story to Sacred Text.* Philadelphia: Fortress, 1987.

Scheeben, Matthias Joseph. *Die Mysterien des Christentums: Wesen Bedeutung und Zusammenhang derselben nach der in ihrem übernatürlichen Charakter gegebenen Perspektive dargestellt.* Freiburg im Breisgau: Herder, 1941.

———. *The Mysteries of Christianity.* Translated by Cyril Vollert, SJ. London: Herder, 1946.

Schelkens, Karim, et al. *Aggiornamento?: Catholicism from Gregory XVI to Benedict XVI.* Leiden: Brill, 2013.

Schneiders, Sandra M. *Jesus Risen in Our Midst: Essays on the Resurrection of Jesus in the Fourth Gospel.* Collegeville, MN: Liturgical, 2013.

———. *The Revelatory Text: Interpreting the New Testament as Sacred Scripture.* Collegeville, MN: Michael Glazier, 1999.

———. *Written That You May Believe: Encountering Jesus in the Fourth Gospel.* Rev. and exp. ed. New York: Crossroad, 2003.

Schochet, Gordon, et al., eds. *Political Hebraism: Judaic Sources in Early Modern Political Thought.* Jerusalem: Shalem, 2008.

Schüssler Fiorenza, Elizabeth. *Bread Not Stone: The Challenge of Feminist Biblical Interpretation.* Boston: Beacon, 1985.

———. *In Memory of Her: A Feminist Theological Reconstruction of Christian Origins.* New York: Crossroad, 1983.

———. *Jesus and the Politics of Interpretation.* New York: Continuum, 2000.

———. *Sharing Her Word: Feminist Biblical Interpretation in Context.* Boston: Beacon, 1998.

Scroggs, Robin. *The Last Adam: A Study in Pauline Anthropology.* Philadelphia: Fortress, 1966.

Segovia, Fernando F. "Liberation Hermeneutics: Revisiting the Foundations in Latin America." In *Towards a New Heaven and a New Earth: Essays in Honor of Elizabeth Schüssler Fiorenza's 65th Birthday,* edited by Fernando F. Segovia, 106–32. Maryknoll, NY: Orbis, 2003.

———. "Postcolonial Biblical Criticism: Critiques and Challenges." *Biblical Interpretation* 19 (2011) 91–101.

———. "Postcolonial Criticism and the Gospel of Matthew." In *Methods for Matthew,* edited by Mark Allan Powell, 194–237. Cambridge: Cambridge University Press, 2009.

Sheehan, Jonathan. *The Enlightenment Bible: Translation, Scholarship, Culture.* Princeton: Princeton University Press, 2005.

Sheppard, Gerald T. *Wisdom as a Hermeneutical Construct: A Study in the Sapientializing of the Old Testament.* Berlin: Walter de Gruyter, 1980.

Shuger, Debora Kuller. *The Renaissance Bible: Scholarship, Sacrifice, and Subjectivity.* Berkeley: University of California, 1994.

Simon, Christian. "History As a Case-Study of the Relations Between University Professors and the State in Germany." In *Biblical Studies and the Shifting of Paradigms, 1850–1914,* edited by Henning Graf Reventlow and William Farmer, 168–96. Sheffield: Sheffield Academic, 1995.

Simonetti, Manlio. *Lettera e/o allegoria. Un contributo alla storia dell'esegesi patristica.* Rome: Institutum Patristicum "Augustinianum," 1985.

Smalley, Beryl. *The Study of the Bible in the Middle Ages.* 3rd ed. Oxford: Blackwell, 1983 (1941).

# BIBLIOGRAPHY

Spinoza. *Œuvres III: Tractatus Theologico-Politicus/Traité théologico-politique*. 2nd ed. Edited by Pierre-François Moreau. Text established by Fokke Akkerman. Translated and notes by Jacqueline Lagrée and Pierre-François Moreau. Paris: Presses universitaires de France, 2012.

Stager, Lawrence E. "Jerusalem and the Garden of Eden." In *Eretz-Israel: Archaeological, Historical and Geographical Studies: Volume Twenty Six: Frank Moore Cross Volume*, edited by Baruch A. Levine et al., 183–94. Jerusalem: Israel Exploration Society with Hebrew Union College—Jewish Institute of Religion, 1999.

Stallsworth, Paul T. "The Story of an Encounter." In *Biblical Interpretation in Crisis: The Ratzinger Conference on Bible and Church*, edited by Richard John Neuhaus, 102–90. Grand Rapids: Eerdmans, 1989.

Stammberger, Ralf M.W. "Die Exegese des Oktateuch bei Hugo von Saint-Victor." In *Bibel und Exegese in der Abtei Saint-Victor zu Paris: Form und Funktion eines Grundtextes im europäischen Rahmen*, edited by Rainer Berndt, 235–57. Münster: Aschendorff, 2009.

Stewart, Bryan A. *Priests of My People: Levitical Paradigms for Early Christian Ministers*. New York: Peter Lang, 2015.

Stuhlmueller, Carroll, CP. *Thirsting for the Lord: Essays in Biblical Spirituality*. Staten Island, NY: Alba House, 1977.

Suarez, Federico. *Joseph of Nazareth*. Princeton: Scepter, 2004.

Swartz, Michael D. "Ritual about Myth about Ritual: Towards an Understanding of the Avodah in the Rabbinic Period." *Journal of Jewish Thought and Philosophy* 6 (1997) 135–55.

Sweeney, Marvin A. *I and II Kings: A Commentary*. Louisville: Westminster John Knox, 2007.

Tábet, Miguel Ángel. "Cristología e historicidad de los evangelios en la constitución 'Dei verbum.'" In *Cristo, Hijo de Dios y Redentor del Hombre: III Simposio Internacional de Teología de la Universidad de Navarra*, edited by Lucas F. Mateo Seco et al., 299–324. Pamplona: Servicio de Publicaciones de la Universidad de Navarra, 1982.

Talar, C. J. T. "Between Science and Myth: Alfred Loisy on Genesis." *Mythos* 7 (2013) 27–41.

———. "Innovation and Biblical Interpretation." In *Catholicism Contending with Modernity: Roman Catholic Modernism and Anti-Modernism in Historical Context*, edited by Darrell Jodock, 191–211. Cambridge: Cambridge University Press, 2000.

———. *(Re)reading, Reception, and Rhetoric: Approaches to Roman Catholic Modernism*. New York: Peter Lang, 1999.

Tanner, Norman P., SJ, ed. *Decrees of the Ecumenical Councils Volume Two: Trent to Vatican II*. Washington, DC: Georgetown University Press, 1990.

Tavard, George H. "Blondel's *Action* and the Problem of the University." In *Catholicism Contending with Modernity: Roman Catholic Modernism and Anti-Modernism in Historical Context*, edited by Darrell Jodock, 142–68. Cambridge: Cambridge University Press, 2000.

Taylor Coolman, Boyd. "*Pulchrum Esse*: The Beauty of Scripture, the Beauty of the Soul, and the Art of Exegesis in Hugh of St. Victor." *Traditio* 58 (2003) 175–200.

———. *The Theology of Hugh of St. Victor: An Interpretation*. Cambridge: Cambridge University Press, 2010.

Taylor Coolman, Holly. "Romans 9-11: Rereading Aquinas on the Jews." In *Reading Romans with St. Thomas Aquinas*, edited by Matthew Levering and Michael Dauphinais, 101-12. Washington, DC: The Catholic University of America Press, 2012.

Théobald, Christoph. "L'exégèse catholique au moment de la crise moderniste." In *Le monde contemporain et la Bible*, edited by Claude Savart and Jean-Noël Aletti, 387-439. Paris: Beauchesne, 1985.

Thomson, Rodney Malcolm. "The English Reception of the Writings of Hugh of St. Victor." In *Bibel und Exegese in der Abtei Saint-Victor zu Paris: Form und Funktion eines Grundtextes im europäischen Rahmen*, edited by Rainer Berndt, 527-37. Münster: Aschendorff, 2009.

Tilley, Maureen A. "Understanding Augustine Misunderstanding Tyconius." *Studia Patristica* 27 (1993) 405-08.

Turner, Denys. *Eros and Allegory: Medieval Exegesis of the Song of Songs*. With a foreword by Bernard McGinn. Kalamazoo: Cistercian, 1995.

van der Coelen, Peter. "Pictures for the People?: Bible Illustrations and their Audience." In *Lay Bibles in Europe 1450-1800*, edited by M. Lamberigts and A.A. den Hollander, 185-205. Leuven: Leuven University and Peeters, 2006.

van 't Spijker, Ineke. "'Ad commovendos affectus': Exegesis and the Affects in Hugh of Saint-Victor." In *Bibel und Exegese in der Abtei Saint-Victor zu Paris: Form und Funktion eines Grundtextes im europäischen Rahmen*, edited by Rainer Berndt, 215-34. Münster: Aschendorff, 2009.

———. "The Literal and the Spiritual: Richard Saint-Victor and the Multiple Meaning of Scripture." In *The Multiple Meaning of Scripture: The Role of Exegesis in Early-Christian and Medieval Culture*, edited by Ineke van 't Spijker, 225-48. Leiden: Brill, 2009.

Vanderjagt, Arjo. "*Ad fontes!* The Early Humanist Concern for the *Hebraica veritas*." In *Hebrew Bible/Old Testament: The History of Its Interpretation II: From the Renaissance to the Enlightenment*, edited by Magne Sæbø, 154-89. Göttingen: Vandenhoeck & Ruprecht, 2008.

Vanhoye, Albert. "Passé et présent de la Commission Biblique." *Gregorianum* 74 (1993) 261-75.

Vázquez de Prada, Andrés. *The Founder of Opus Dei: The Life of St. Josemaría Escrivá Vol. II: God and Daring*. New York: Scepter, 2003.

———. *Sir Tomás Moro. Lord Canciller de Inglaterra*. 8th ed. Madrid: Rialp, 2004.

Vereb, Jerome-Michael. *"Because He Was a German!": Cardinal Bea and the Origins of Roman Catholic Engagement in the Ecumenical Movement*. Grand Rapids: Eerdmans, 2006.

Vervenne, Marc. "Genesis 1, 1-2, 4: The Compositional Texture of the Priestly Overture to the Pentateuch." In *Studies in the Book of Genesis: Literature, Redaction and History*, edited by A. Wénin, 35-79. Leuven: Leuven University Press, 2001.

Viviano, Benedict Thomas. *Catholic Hermeneutics Today: Critical Essays*. Eugene, OR: Cascade, 2014.

Vogt, Hermann J. "Origen of Alexandria (185-253)." In *Handbook of Patristic Exegesis: The Bible in Ancient Christianity*, edited by Charles Kannengiesser, 536-74. Leiden: Brill, 2006.

von Balthasar, Hans Urs. "Theologie und Heiligkeit." In *Verbum Caro. Skizzen zur Theologie 1*, by Hans Urs von Balthasar, 195-224. Einsiedeln: Johannes, 1960.

———. "Theologie und Heiligkeit." *Wort und Wahrheit* 3 (1948) 881–97.

———. "Theology and Sanctity." In *Explorations in Theology Volume 1: The Word Made Flesh*, by Hans Urs von Balthasar, 181–86. San Francisco: Ignatius, 1989.

Waldstein, Michael Maria. "*Analogia Verbi*: The Truth of Scripture in Rudolf Bultmann and Raymond Brown." *Letter and Spirit* 6 (2010) 93–140.

———. "The Analogy of Mission and Obedience: A Central Point in the Relation between *Theologia* and *Oikonomia* in St. Thomas Aquinas's *Commentary on John*." In *Reading John with St. Thomas Aquinas: Theological Exegesis and Speculative Theology*, edited by Michael Dauphinais and Matthew Levering, 92–114. Washington, DC: The Catholic University of America Press, 2005.

———. "The Foundations of Bultmann's Work." *Communio* 14 (1987) 115–45.

———. "The Self-Critique of the Historical-Critical Method: Cardinal Ratzinger's Erasmus Lecture." *Modern Theology* 28 (2012) 732–47.

———. "The Trinitarian, Spousal, and Ecclesial Logic of Justification." In *Reading Romans with St. Thomas Aquinas*, edited by Matthew Levering and Michael Dauphinais, 274–87. Washington, DC: The Catholic University of America Press, 2012.

Walton, John H. *Genesis 1 as Ancient Cosmology*. Winona Lake, IN: Eisenbrauns, 2011.

Watts, Rikki E. "On the Edge of the Millennium: Making Sense of Genesis 1." In *Living in the Lamblight: Christianity and Contemporary Challenges to the Gospel*, edited by Hans Boersma, 129–51. Vancouver: Regent College, 2001.

Wegemer, Gerard. "Introduction." In *The Life of Pico Della Mirandola: 'A Very Spectacle To All,'* by St. Thomas More, vii–xxii. New York: Scepter, 2010.

———. "Introduction." In *The Sadness of Christ: And Final Prayers and Benedictions*, by St. Thomas More, v–xxi. New York: Scepter, 1993.

———. *Thomas More: A Portrait of Courage*. Princeton: Scepter, 1995.

Weinfeld, Moshe. "Sabbath, Temple and Enthronement of the Lord—The Problem of the Sitz im Leben of Genesis 1:1–2:3." In *Mélanges bibliques et orientaux en l'honneur de M. Henri Cazelles*, edited by A. Caquot and M. Delcor, 501–12. Kevelaer: Butzon & Bercker, 1981.

Weismann, Francisco José. "Principios de exégesis bíblica en el *De Doctrina Christiana* de San Agustín." *Cuadernos monásticos* 80 (1987) 61–73.

Wenham, Gordon J. "The Coherence of the Flood Narrative." *Vetus Testamentum* 28 (1978) 336–48.

———. *Genesis 1–15*. Waco, TX: Word, 1987.

———. "Sanctuary Symbolism in the Garden of Eden Story." In *Proceedings of the Ninth World Congress of Jewish Studies, Division A: The Period of the Bible*, 19–25. Jerusalem: World Union of Jewish Studies, 1986.

———. "Sanctuary Symbolism in the Garden of Eden Story." In *"I Studied Inscriptions from before the Flood": Ancient Near Eastern, Literary, and Linguistic Approaches to Genesis 1–11*, edited by Richard S. Hess and David Toshio Tsumura, 399–404. Winona Lake, IN: Eisenbrauns, 1994.

White, Hugh C. "The Initiation Legend of Ishmael." *Zeitschrift für die alttestamentliche Wissenschaft* 87 (1975) 267–306.

Whybray, R. N. *The Making of the Pentateuch: A Methodological Study*. Sheffield: Sheffield Academic Press, 1999.

Wiener, Aharon. *The Prophet Elijah in the Development of Judaism: A Depth-Psychological Study*. London: Routledge & Kegan Paul, 1978.

# BIBLIOGRAPHY

Wilken, Robert Louis. "Allegory and the Interpretation of the Old Testament in the 21st Century." *Letter and Spirit* 1 (2005) 11–21.

———. "'Bread from Both Tables': Scripture and Tradition in the 21st Century Church." Inaugural Fr. Ronald Lawler Memorial Lecture, Letter & Spirit Conference, Saturday, December 10, 2005.

———. *The First Thousand Years: A Global History of Christianity*. New Haven, CT: Yale University Press, 2012.

———. "*In Dominico Eloquio*: Learning the Lord's Style of Language." *Communio* 24 (1997) 846–66.

———. "Interpreting the Bible as Bible." Society of Biblical Literature Annual Meeting, Theological Hermeneutics of Christian Scripture Unit. Boston, November 22, 2008.

———. "Interpreting Job Allegorically: The *Moralia* of Gregory the Great." *Pro Ecclesia* 10 (2001) 213–26.

———. *The Spirit of Early Christian Thought: Seeking the Face of God*. New Haven, CT: Yale University Press, 2003.

Williamson, Peter S. "Catholic Principles for Interpreting Scripture." *Catholic Biblical Quarterly* 65 (2003) 327–49.

———. *Catholic Principles for Interpreting Scripture: A Study of the Pontifical Biblical Commission's The Interpretation of the Bible in the Church*. Rome: Editrice Pontificio Istituto Biblico, 2001.

———. "The Place of History in Catholic Exegesis: An Examination of the Pontifical Biblical Commission's The Interpretation of the Bible in the Church." In *"Behind" the Text: History and Biblical Interpretation*, edited by Craig Bartholomew et al., 196–226. Grand Rapids: Zondervan, 2003.

Wise, Michael Owen. "*4QFlorilegium* and the Temple of Adam." *Revue de Qumran* 15 (1991) 126–32.

Wiseman, P. J. *Ancient Records and the Structure of Genesis: A Case for Literary Unity*. Nashville: Thomas Nelson, 1985.

Witherup, Ronald D., SS. "The Incarnate Word Revealed: The Pastoral Writings of Raymond E. Brown." In *Life in Abundance: Studies in John's Gospel in Tribute to Raymond E. Brown*, edited by John R. Donahue, 238–52. Collegeville, MN: Liturgical, 2005.

———. "Raymond E. Brown, S.S., and Catholic Exegesis in the Twentieth Century: A Retrospective." *U.S. Catholic Historian* 31 (2013) 1–26.

Witherup, Ronald D., SS, and Michael L. Barré, SS. "Biography and Bibliography of the Publications of Raymond E. Brown, S.S." In *Life in Abundance: Studies in John's Gospel in Tribute to Raymond E. Brown*, edited by John R. Donahue, 253–90. Collegeville, MN: Liturgical, 2005.

Witter, Henning Bernhard. *Jura Israelitarum in Palaestiniam terrram Chananaeam, commentatione perpetua in Genesin demonstrate*. Hildesheim: Schröder, 1711.

Whybray, R. N. *The Making of the Pentateuch: A Methodological Study*. Sheffield: Journal for the Study of the Old Testament, 1987.

Wilken, Robert L. "Interpreting Job Allegorically: The 'Moralia' of Gregory the Great." *Pro Ecclesia* 10 (2001) 213–26.

———. "Origen, Augustine, and Thomas: Interpreters of the Letter to the Romans." In *Reading Romans with St. Thomas Aquinas*, edited by Matthew Levering and Michael Dauphinais, 288–301. Washington, DC: The Catholic University of America Press, 2012.

———. *The Spirit of Early Christian Thought: Seeking the Face of God.* New Haven, CT: Yale University Press, 2003.

Woodbridge, John D. "Richard Simon le 'père de la critique biblique.'" In *Le Grand Siècle et la Bible*, ed. J.-R. Armogathe, 193–206. Paris: Beauchesne, 1986.

Wright, William M., IV. "A 'New Synthesis': Joseph Ratzinger's *Jesus of Nazareth*." *Nova et Vetera* 7 (2009) 35–66.

———. "Patristic Biblical Hermeneutics in Joseph Ratzinger's *Jesus of Nazareth*." *Letter and Spirit* 7 (2011) 191–207.

Wright, William M., IV, and Francis Martin. *Encountering the Living God in Scripture: Theological and Philosophical Principles.* Grand Rapids: Baker Academic, 2019.

Young, Robin Darling. *In Procession before the World: Martyrdom as Public Liturgy in Early Christianity.* Milwaukee: Marquette University Press, 2001.

Younger, K. Lawson, Jr. *Ancient Conquest Accounts: A Study in Ancient Near Eastern and Biblical History Writing.* Sheffield: Journal for the Study of the Old Testament, 1990.

Zac, Sylvain. *Spinoza et l'interprétation de l'Écriture.* Paris: Presses universitaires de France, 1965.

Zumstein, Jean. "Alfred Loisy, commentateur de l'évangile selon Jean." *Mythos* 7 (2013) 43–58.

# Author Index

Abrahams, Israel, 124
Ackroyd, Peter, 100n49, 101n51, 101n53, 119
Akkerman, Fokke, 144
Aletti, Jean-Noël, 145
Alexander, T. Desmond, 128
Ames, Frank Ritchel, 128
Amsler, Frédéric, 20n50, 119
Anderson, Gary A., 38n22, 45n49, 56n93, 57n98, 119
Anderson, Justin, xi
Aquinas, St. Thomas, 3, 9, 11, 61n6, 91, 94n25, 119
Armogathe, J.-R., 148
Arnaldez, Roger, 16n38, 119
Arnold, Claus, 20n53, 119
Arnold, Duane W.H., 124
Asad, Talal, 14n26, 65, 119
Ashley, J. Matthew, 121
Astruc, Jean, 17, 19, 35, 119
Augustine, Saint, 9-10, 117, 119
Auvray, Paul, 14n28, 119
Averbeck, Richard E., 37n17, 49-50, 51n77, 120

Baglow, Christopher, 12n21, 91n9, 120
Baldovin, John F., SJ, 67n34, 120
Balentine, Samuel E., 45nn48-50, 120
Bar, S., 123
Barber, Michael, 3n12, 45n49, 48n55, 62n10, 120
Barré, SS, Michael L., 147

Barron, Caroline M., 100n49, 101n53, 120
Barthélemy, Dominique, 14n28, 120
Bartholomew, Craig G., 125, 130, 147
Bataillon, Louis-Jacques, 11n20, 120-22, 125, 140
Bauks, Michaela, 36n9, 45n49, 120
Bea, Augustin, 19, 23n65, 24, 25n71, 121
Beale, G. K., 38n22, 40n30, 45n49, 48n55, 49n59, 51nn78-79, 52, 53nn85-86, 54n87, 56nn93-94, 57nn97-98, 121
Béchard, Dean P., SJ, 121, 133, 141
Bellamah, Timothy, 11n20, 12n21, 121
Ben-Dov, Jonathan, 38n22, 39n30, 121
Benedict XVI, Pope (Joseph Ratzinger), 1-3, 5, 7, 9n8, 12, 22-25, 30-31, 32n97, 45n49, 61, 63, 64n21, 67, 68n37, 71, 73, 90, 91nn10-12, 92, 100, 112, 121
Benin, Stephen D., 10n12, 122
Berglar, Peter, 100n49, 101n51, 101n53, 101n55, 122
Bergsma, John, x-xi, 3n12, 17n41, 37, 62n10, 78n1, 122
Berman, Joshua, 17n41, 122
Berndt, Rainer, 11-12n20, 122, 127, 132, 137, 140, 144-45
Bernier, Jean, 14n27, 122
Betz, John R., 7n2, 122
Bieringer, Reimund, 25n71, 123
Binder, Susanne, 17n41, 123
Blank, Reiner, 30n90, 123

## AUTHOR INDEX

Blenkinsopp, Joseph, 36n9, 36n11, 45n49, 123
Bloch-Smith, Elizabeth, 38n20, 38n22, 123
Boersma, Hans, 146
Boyle, John F., 12n21, 123
Branick, Vincent, x
Bright, Pamela, 9n11, 123–24
Bronner, Leah, 81n5, 123
Brown, Raymond E., SS, 27–28, 123
Brown, Stephen, 11, 12n21, 123
Bucur, Bogdan, xi
Bullivant, Stephen, 139
Bunta, Silviu, x, 37n15, 45n47, 48n55, 53n87, 124
Burigana, Riccardo, 25n71, 124
Burns, J. Patout, 9n10, 124
Burtchaell, James Tunstead, CSC, 19n48, 124

Callender, Dexter E., Jr, 38n21, 44n43, 51n79, 54n87, 56nn93–94, 124
Candler, Peter M., Jr, 64nn20–21, 65–67, 124
Caquot, A., 146
Carl, Fr. Scott, 7n3, 124, 128, 141
Carlson, R. A., 79n2, 124
Carruthers, Mary, 67n34, 124
Cassuto, Umberto, 19, 35n7, 36n10, 40n33, 41–43, 45n49, 124
Catry, Patrick, 10n15, 124
Catto, Jeremy, 13n22, 124
Cavalletti, Sofia, 62n12, 124
Cavanaugh, William T., 13n26, 14, 15n30, 67n34, 124
Chavalas, Mark W., 120
Childs, Brevard S., 63, 68n38, 125
Clark, Mark J., 11n16, 125
Cogan, Mordechai, 86nn21–22, 125
Cohn, Robert L., 79n2, 125
Colin, Pierre, 20n49, 125
Connor, Robert A., xi, 93n19, 125
Cooke, Bernard, 141
Coogan, Michael D., 123
Cook, Johann, 43nn41–42, 125
Coote, Robert E., 85n17, 125
Corbon, Jean, 67n34, 70n45, 72n60, 125

Crim, Keith, 129
Currid, John D., 19n46, 51n80, 125
Curtis, Cathy, 100n49, 101n51, 125

Dahan, Gilbert, 8n5, 11n16, 11n20, 12n21, 125–26, 135–36
Daly, Gabriel, OSA, 20n49, 126
Dauphinais, Michael, 12n21, 123, 126–27, 131, 135, 145–47
D'Costa, Gavin, 64n21, 67n34, 67n36, 126
de Gaiffier, Baudouin, 119
de Lubac, Henri, 8n5, 61, 126
de Wette, Wilhelm Martin Leberecht, 17, 126
DeConick, April D., 79n3, 126, 135
Delcor, M., 146
Delmas, Sophie, 11n16, 126
den Hollander, A. A., 145
Despland, Michel, 127
Donahue, John R., SJ, 27n77, 126, 147
Doyle, Dennis, x
Duffy, Eamon, 64nn20–21, 66, 126
Duffy, Kevin, 27n77, 126
Dulaey, Martine, 9n11, 126
Dulles, Avery, SJ, 25n71, 126
Dunn, Matthew W. I., 27n77, 127
Dupuy, B.-D., 129

Egger, Christoph, 12n20, 127
Emery, Gilles, OP, 12n21, 127
Erasmus, Desiderius, 101–2, 127
Escrivá, St. Josemaría, 75n72, 94, 105n69, 106nn71–72, 110n95, 127, 133
Eubank, Nathan, 3n12, 127
Evans, C. Stephen, 129
Evans, Craig A., 128

Fagerberg, David W., 39, 59, 67n36, 69, 72n57, 127
Farkasfalvy, Denis, OCist, 8n6, 25n71, 127
Farmer, William R., 17n40, 127, 143
Feil, Ernst, 13–14n26, 127
Fishbane, Michael, 10, 48n58, 128
Fisher, Loren R., 37n17, 51, 128

## AUTHOR INDEX

Fitzmyer, SJ, Joseph A., 27–28, 29n83, 121, 128, 133, 141
Flannery, Frances, 79n2, 128
Fletcher-Louis, Crispin H. T., 36n11, 37, 38n21, 39n24, 39n26, 40, 44n43, 45n49, 47, 48n58, 53n87, 54–55, 56nn92–93, 128
Fogarty, Gerald P., SJ, 24, 26n74, 27nn76–77, 128
Frampton, Travis L., 13, 128
Freedman, Bernice, v, xi
Freedman, R. David, 16n38, 128

Gabrielli, Timothy R., 138
Gadenz, Pablo T., ix, xi, 3n12, 7nn2–3, 128
Gaeta, Giancarlo, 9n11, 128
Gage, Warren Austin, 54n87, 56n93, 129
Galil, Gershon, 136
García de Haro, Ramón, 20n49, 129
Gathercole, Simon, 128
Gelardini, Gabriella, 130
Gese, Hartmut, 54, 129
Gibert, Pierre, 14n27, 119, 129
Gilbert, Maurice, SJ, 26n72, 86n20, 129
Gittlen, Barry M., 123
Glazov, Gregory, xi
Goering, Joseph W., 123
Golitzin, Hieromonk Alexander, 70n45, 129
Gordon, Cyrus H., 19, 129
Goshen-Gottstein, M.H., 16, 129
Gosse, Bernard, 38n21, 54n87, 56n93, 129
Greenberg, Moshe, 133
Greer, David, xi
Gregory the Great, Pope, 10, 60–61, 129
Gregory, Russell, 84n11, 129
Grelot, Pierre, 25n71, 129
Greschat, Katharina, 10n15, 129
Grillmeier, Alois, 25n71, 129
Grisez, Germain, 7n2, 129
Gross, Michael B., 17n40, 129
Guardini, Romano, 121
Guigo II, 92n16, 129

Hahn, Scott W., x, 2n7, 3–4, 6n1, 7nn2–3, 8–9nn6–7, 10, 12n21, 13n23, 14nn27–28, 15n31, 17, 30n89, 32, 35n8, 36, 37n16, 38–39, 40n31, 45n49, 48n55, 52n84, 57n97, 60n3, 61–62, 63n15, 64n19, 68, 69n41, 70nn45–46, 71nn53–54, 72, 75n73, 90n2, 90nn4–6, 92–94, 112, 113n1, 115, 129–31
Hall, Mable, v, xii
Hall, Walt, v, xi
Hallo, William W., 37n17, 50nn66–73, 51nn74–77, 131
Halpern, Baruch, 125
Haran, Menahem, 45n49, 131
Hatch, Derek C., 138
Hauser, Alan J., 81n5, 129, 131
Healy, Mary, 12n21, 131
Heitz, Carol, 67n34, 131
Helmer, Christine, 139
Herr, Denise Dick, 79n2, 131
Heschel, Abraham Joshua, 70, 74, 131
Hess, Richard S., 34n2, 37n19, 131, 137, 146
Hill, Harvey, 20n49–50, 20n52, 21n57, 131
Hill, William F., SS, 26n75, 131
Himmelfarb, Martha, 38n21, 33n87, 54n88, 131
Hoffmeier, James K., 17n41, 18n44, 19n46, 37n18, 131
Holmes, Jeremy, 12n21, 132, 138
Hosse, Josef, 121
Huizenga, Leroy A., 3n12, 91n13, 132
Huizinga, Johan, 64n21, 132
Hultgren, Stephen, 38n22, 56n94, 132
Hünermann, Peter, 121
Hupfeld, Hermann W., 35, 132
Hurowitz, Victor (Avigdor), 18n44, 37n15, 37n17, 132

Illich, Ivan, 64n21, 65n23, 132
Iversen, Gunilla, 12n20, 132
Izquierdo, César, 19n49, 132

Jagersma, H., 81, 132
Janowski, Bernd, 37n17, 39n30, 132

## AUTHOR INDEX

Jarick, John, 140
Jeffrey, David Lyle, 129
Jodock, Darrell, 19n49, 126, 131–34, 137, 144
John Paul II, Pope, 68n37, 71, 73n64, 74–76, 93n19, 110, 133
Johnson, Luke Timothy, 29, 73, 133
Johnston, Eric, ix
Jones, Andrew Willard, ix, 13n26, 15, 133
Jones, Lindsay, 67n34, 133
Jones, Meirav, 135

Kannengiesser, Charles, 145
Kauffman, Christopher J., 26n75, 133
Kaufmann, Yehezkel, 19n47, 133
Kearney, Peter J., 36n9, 36n11, 45nn49–50, 48n55, 49nn59–60, 133
Keating, Daniel, 12n21, 134
Keinänen, Jyrki, 79n2, 81n5, 84n11, 86n21, 134
Kelle, Brad E., 128
Kelly, Henry Ansgar, 95n27, 100n49, 134
Kenis, Leo, 119, 123
Kikawada, Isaac M., 19n47, 134
Kincaid, John, 12n21, 131
King, Joshua, 139
Kitchen, Kenneth A., 19n47, 125, 134
Kleinhans, Arduin, 23, 134
Kline, Meredith G., 45n49, 46, 52, 56n93–94, 57n98, 134
Knoch, Wendelin, 12n20, 134
Kozar, SM, Joseph, xi
Kruggel, James C., 25n71, 134
Kugel, James L., 26, 29–30, 85n16, 134
Kurtz, Paul Michael, 17n40, 134
Kurz, William S., SJ, 133

Lagrée, Jacqueline, 144
Lamb, Matthew L., 127, 136
Lamberigts, M., 123–24, 145
Laplanche, François, 119
Lasnoski, Kent, 138
Lawler, Thomas, 137
Lawrie, Douglas, 79n2, 83n10, 84n15, 86n21, 134
Lazarus-Yafeh, Hava, 16n38, 134
Lease, Gary, 19n49, 20n54, 134

Leclercq, Jean, 65n23, 65n25, 134
Legaspi, Michael C., 17n40, 18, 64n20, 135
Leithart, Peter J., 83n9, 86n22, 135
Leonard, SJ, William J., 136
Levenson, Jon D., 14, 17n40, 30, 36nn10–11, 37nn15–16, 38n21, 39n30, 41–44, 45nn49–50, 48, 49n59, 51n79, 52n82, 53–54n87, 56n93, 87n23, 125, 135
Levering, Matthew, 8n6, 12n21, 67n34, 123, 126–27, 131, 135–36, 145–47
Levine, Baruch A., 144
Lieber, Andrea, 87n24, 135
Lobrichon, Guy, 11n16, 135
Logan, George M., 100n49, 120, 125, 135–36
Loisy, Alfred, 2, 20–21
Lorberbaum, Menachem, 16n37, 135
Losito, Giacomo, 20n53, 119
Luscombe, David, 11, 135

Machinist, Peter, 18n45, 136
Macierowski, E.M., 126
Madigan, Kevin, 11, 140
Malcolm, Noel, 14n27, 16n35, 136
Mâle, Emile, 67n34, 136
Maly, Eugene H., 44n44, 136
Mammitzsch, Ulrich, 132
Marenbon, John, 123
Marshall, Peter, 100n49, 136
Martens, Peter W., 9n9, 136
Martin, Francis, 3n12, 10n12, 25n71, 136, 148
Mateo Seco, Lucas F., 144
Mazza, Enrico, 70n45, 136
McAuliffe, Jane Dammen, 123
McConica, James, 100n49, 101n51, 136
McCutcheon, Elizabeth, 101n51, 136
McDermott, Ryan, 8n5, 136
McDonald, Lee M., 64n19, 68n38, 136
McGinn, Bernard, 145
McGovern, Thomas James, 25n71, 136
Mégier, Elisabeth, 12n20, 137
Mesguich, Sophie Kessler, 13n22, 137
Meyers, Carol L., 40n33, 49n59, 53n87, 137

## AUTHOR INDEX

Michaelis, Johann David, 18, 35n7, 137
Millard, A.R., 132
Miller, Athanasius, 23, 137
Minnis, Alastair, 8n5, 137
Mirri, F. Saverio, 14nn27-28, 137
Misner, Paul, 20n49, 137
Misrahi, Catharine, 134
Momigliano, Arnaldo, 17n40, 137
Monson, John M., 56n93, 137
More, Thomas, Saint, 5, 89, 94–107, 108nn81–89, 109–12, 114, 137
Moreau, Pierre-François, 144
Morey, James H., 11n16, 137
Morrow, Jeffrey L., 2nn5-8, 3n10, 5n15, 6n1, 13n26, 14nn27-28, 15n31, 17nn39-40, 18n43, 19n49, 20nn50-51, 23n65, 26nn74-75, 27nn76-77, 28n79, 32n97, 35n8, 60n2, 60n4, 61n9, 64nn20-22, 70n48, 74nn67-68, 90n2, 112n99, 130, 137
Morrow, Maria C., ix–xi
Morrow, Morty, v, xii
Müller, Sascha, 14n27, 139
Munro, J. Iverach, 17n41, 139
Murphy, Bill, ix
Murphy, Roland E., 27, 29, 140

Nahkola, Aulikki, 17, 18n42, 35n6, 140
Nakamura, Hideki, 12n20, 140
Narváez, Mauricio, 12n21, 140
Nelson, Eric, 16n37, 140
Neuhaus, Richard John, 144
Neuman, Kalman, 16n37, 140
Newman, Carey C., 128
Nielsen, Lauge O., 12n20, 140
Nussey, Dora, 136

Ocker, Christopher, 11, 12n20, 140
Ockham, William of, 13n23, 15, 16n34, 140
O'Connell, Matthew J., 125, 136
O'Connell, Marvin R., 20n49, 20n52, 21–22, 140
Olsen, Derek A., 8n6, 140
O'Malley, John W., 24n67, 140
Ong, Walter J., SJ., 64n21, 140
Osiek, Carolyn, 29, 140

Ossandón Widow, Juan Carlos, 27n77, 140
Ouellet, Cardinal Marc, 30n93, 31, 33, 140
Oz-Salzberger, Fania, 135

Pasto, James, 17n40, 141
Payton, Rodney J., 132
Pelikan, Jaroslav, 13, 141
Penco, Gregorio, 10n15, 141
Perdue, Leo G., 142
Perreau-Saussine, Emile, 16n37, 141
Persidok, Andrzej, 8n5, 141
Peters, Tiemo Rainer, 121
Pickstock, Catherine, 64n20, 67n34, 141
Pietsch, Andreas Nikolaus, 14n27, 141
Pitre, Brant, xi, 3n12, 7nn2-3, 35n5, 39n26, 62n10, 78n1, 84nn12-13, 85nn18-19, 122, 141
Pius XI, Pope, 112, 141
Pius XII, Pope, 23, 73
Popkin, R.H., 14n27, 141
Portier, William L., x, 15, 19n49, 20–21, 141
Poulat, Émile, 20n49, 21n60, 141
Powell, Mark Allan, 143
Preus, J. Samuel, 14n27, 142

Quinn, Arthur, 19n47, 134

Ramage, Matthew, 12n21, 142
Rasmussen, Tarald, 13n22, 142
Raurell, Frederic, 71n54, 142
Raymond of Capua, 105n70, 142
Reinhardt, Elisabeth, 12n21, 142
Remer, Gary, 16n37, 142
Rendsburg, Gary A., 19n47, 35n7, 142
Reventlow, Henning Graf, 13n22, 64n22, 127, 142–43
Rice, Joseph, xi
Rocha, Biff, x–xi
Rohls, Jan, 17n40, 142
Roszak, Piotr, 12n21, 120–21, 126, 132, 134–35, 140, 142
Rummel, Erika, 13n22, 142
Ruse, Michael, 139
Ryan, Archbishop Dermot J., 121

## AUTHOR INDEX

Sæbø, Magne, 13n22, 122, 124, 137, 142, 145
Sanders, James A., 68n38, 136, 143
Savart, Claude, 145
Saward, John, 122
Scheeben, Matthias Joseph, 70n45, 143
Schelkens, Karim, 24n67, 143
Schneiders, Sandra M., 28, 143
Schochet, Gordon, 16n37, 135, 140–43
Schüssler Fiorenza, Elizabeth, 28, 143
Scott, Jamie, 131
Scroggs, Robin, 57n98, 143
Sebanc, Mark, 126
Segovia, Fernando F., 28, 143
Sheehan, Jonathan, 17n40, 143
Sheppard, Gerald T., 54n88, 143
Shuger, Debora Kuller, 13n22, 143
Simon, Christian, 17n40, 143
Simonetti, Manlio, 9n9, 143
Simpson-Housley, Paul, 131
Smalley, Beryl, 8n5, 12n20, 143
Smith, Stephen, 137
Söding, Thomas, 121
Sommer, Benjamin, xi
Spinoza, Baruch, 14–17, 19, 35n7, 144
Stager, Lawrence E., 38nn21–22, 56, 144
Stallsworth, Paul T., 1n2, 64n21, 90n3, 144
Stammberger, Ralf M.W., 12n20, 144
Stewart, Bryan A., 62n12, 144
Stone, Michael E., 123
Strugnell, John, 123
Stuhlmueller, Carroll, CP, 27, 68n38, 144
Suarez, Federico, 75n73, 76, 144
Swartz, Michael D., 38n22, 144
Sweeney, Marvin A., 85n17, 86n21, 144

Tábet, Miguel Ángel, 25n71, 144
Talar, C. J. T., 20nn49–50, 144
Tanner, Norman P., SJ, 68n37, 70n47, 93n20, 144
Tavard, George H., 20n49, 144
Taylor, Henry, 121
Taylor Coolman, Boyd, 12n20, 144
Taylor Coolman, Holly, 12n21, 145
Théobald, Christoph, 20n50, 145
Thomson, Rodney Malcolm, 12n20, 145

Tilley, Maureen A., 9n11, 145
Trollinger, William, x
Tsumura, David Toshio, 34n2, 37n19, 131, 146
Turner, Denys, 65n23, 69, 145

Urban, Claus, 121

Vallée, Gérard, 127
van der Coelen, Peter, 64n22, 145
van der Wall, Ernestine, 119
van 't Spijker, Ineke, 12n20, 145
Vanderjagt, Arjo, 13n22, 145
Vanhoye, Albert, 22n63, 145
Vázquez de Prada, Andrés, 100n49, 101n51, 101n53, 106n72, 145
Vereb, Jerome-Michael, 24n67, 145
Vervenne, Marc, 39n28, 44n44, 145
Vijgen, Jörgen, 12n21, 120–21, 126, 132, 134–35, 140, 142
Viviano, Benedict Thomas, 24n67, 145
Vogt, Hermann J., 9n9, 145
Vollert, SJ, Cyril, 143
von Balthasar, Hans Urs, 72n59, 145–46
Vorgrimler, Herbert, 121–22

Waldstein, Michael, 7nn2–3, 9n8, 12n21, 27, 30nn89–90, 90n2, 133, 146
Walfish, Barry D., 123
Walker, Adrian, 122
Walton, John H., 19n46, 52, 146
Watts, Rikki E., 37nn17–18, 146
Wegemer, Gerard, 96, 100n49, 101nn51–56, 102, 103n59, 104, 105nn66–67, 110, 112n102, 146
Weinandy, Thomas, 120
Weinfeld, Moshe, 33n2, 35, 36n9, 36nn11–12, 39–40, 44, 45nn46–47, 45nn49–50, 46, 47n53, 48n58, 49nn59–60, 51n78, 52n82, 146
Weismann, Francisco José, 9n10, 146
Wenham, Gordon J., 19n47, 33–34n2, 37, 38n20, 39n30, 40n34, 43, 45n49, 48n58, 53nn86–87, 56, 57nn96–98, 137, 146
Wénin, A., 120, 125, 129, 145
Werner, Winter Jade, 139

## AUTHOR INDEX

White, Hugh C., 83n9, 146
Whybray, R. N., 19, 35n7, 146
Wicks, SJ, Jared, ix
Wiener, Aharon, 86n20, 146
Wiker, Benjamin, 13n23, 14nn27–28, 15n31, 17, 90n2, 130
Wilken, Robert Louis, 1, 8n6, 10n15, 12n21, 61n6, 61n9, 62, 67n33, 68n38, 76, 77n79, 90n4, 126, 147
Williamson, Peter S., 29n83, 147
Wise, Michael Owen, 38n22, 56n94, 147
Wiseman, P. J., 19n47, 147
Witherup, Ronald D., SS., 27n77, 147

Witter, Henning Bernhard, 35, 147
Woodbridge, John D., 14n27, 148
Wright, William M., IV, 3n12, 7n3, 148

Yocum, Sandra, x
Young, Gordon D., 120
Young, Robin Darling, 91n7, 148
Younger, K. Lawson, Jr., 19n46, 37n17, 50nn66–73, 51nn74–77, 120, 131, 148

Zac, Sylvain, 14n27, 148
Zumstein, Jean, 20n50, 148

# Subject Index

Adam, 33, 38–39, 51, 53, 54n87, 55, 57, 79

Baltimore Catechism, 34, 120
Benedict XV, Pope, 22
Benigni, Umberto, 21–22

Catechism of the Catholic Church, 2, 9n8, 12, 34–35, 70n45, 91–92, 124
Comestor, Peter, 11

*Dei Verbum*, 1, 6–7, 18, 24–25, 32, 68n37, 70n47
*Dies Domini*, 71, 133
*Divino Afflante Spiritu*, 23–24, 27

Eichhorn, Johann Gottfried, 19
Elijah, 4, 79–89, 114
Enlightenment, 17–18
Eucharist, 4, 9, 64, 69–71, 73–74, 76, 78–79, 84n12, 88, 91n7, 93, 114
Eve, 39n25, 55

Garden of Eden, 33, 38–39, 42, 50, 52–54, 56–58, 74
Glossa Ordinaria, 10
Gratian, 11
Gudea Cylinders, 37, 44, 49–52

hermeneutics, 1, 4, 6, 9, 10n12, 14n27, 16, 29n83, 30–31, 59–62, 68–69, 71–73, 76, 78, 90, 112–14

historical critical method, 2, 25, 28, 31–32, 79
historical criticism, ix, 2–3, 14–16, 17n40, 20, 22, 26–28, 30, 90
Hobbes, Thomas, 14, 16, 35n7

Joseph, St., 4, 60, 72–77, 114

La Peyrère, Isaac, 14, 16, 35n7
*Lamentabili Sane Exitu*, 20, 23
Leo XIII, Pope, 20, 23
liturgy, 8–9, 33, 39–40, 44n43, 45n48, 47, 59–74, 77–78, 90, 91n7, 111, 113–14
liturgical hermeneutic, 4, 59–60, 62, 68, 69n45, 71–72, 76, 78, 90, 113
liturgical interpretation, 4, 78
Lombard, Peter, 11
*Lumen Gentium*, 70, 101

martyrdom, 5, 89, 91n7, 92–94, 104, 110–12
martyrological interpretation, 5, 88–89, 92, 95, 110–11, 114
Modernism, 2, 4, 7, 19–24, 27
mystagogical interpretation, 4, 78, 89, 91–92, 110–11, 114
mystagogy, 70n45–46, 89, 91–93

*Pascendi Dominici Gregis*, 20–21, 23
Paul VI, Pope St., 22
Pius X, Pope St., 20–21, 23, 29–30

## SUBJECT INDEX

Pontifical Biblical Commission, 22–23, 26, 29n83, 63, 64n21, 141
*Providentissimus Deus*, 20, 23–24

*Redemptoris Custos*, 73n64, 74, 75nn70–71, 75n74, 76n78, 133
Reformation, 12–13, 15, 59n1, 66
Renan, Ernest, 20

Sabbath, 36, 40, 45–48, 56, 70–71
Simon, Richard, 14, 16, 35n7
Sodalitium Pianum, 21
*Spiritus Paraclitus*, 22

Tyconius, 9
typology, 4, 9–10, 70n45, 77–79, 83, 88–89, 91–92, 110–11, 114

Vatican I, 19
Vatican II, 1, 3–4, 6–7, 22–24, 27–28, 32–33, 68n37, 70, 93n20
*Verbum Domini*, 2, 5, 7, 9n8, 12, 24, 25n70, 30, 71, 73n63, 91n10, 92n16, 100, 122
Victorines, 4, 11

Wellhausen, Julius, 17n41, 18–19

# Scripture Index

## Gen

| | |
|---|---|
| 1 | 4, 34, 36, 39–40, 42, 43n41, 44–45, 50–52, 54–55, 73, 114 |
| 1:1 | 35, 36n10, 37, 39–40, 43, 44n43, 50, 55 |
| 1:2 | 40, 54 |
| 1:3 | 50, 54 |
| 1:4 | 50 |
| 1:3–5 | 39n26, 47, 55 |
| 1:6 | 50, 54 |
| 1:6–8 | 43, 55 |
| 1:9 | 43, 50, 55 |
| 1:10 | 50 |
| 1:11 | 50, 54 |
| 1:12 | 50 |
| 1:13 | 55 |
| 1:14 | 50, 54–55 |
| 1:15 | 50 |
| 1:18 | 50 |
| 1:19 | 55 |
| 1:20 | 43, 50, 55 |
| 1:22 | 50 |
| 1:23 | 55 |
| 1:24 | 50, 56 |
| 1:25 | 50 |
| 1:26 | 50, 73 |
| 1:31 | 46, 50–51, 53, 56 |
| 1–2 | 39, 45n48, 46 |
| 1–3 | 4, 33–35, 38, 40, 45, 58–60, 70n48, 76–77, 79, 90, 113 |
| 2 | 37–38, 57n98 |
| 2:1 | 44, 45n46, 46, 51 |
| 2:2 | 46, 55 |
| 2:3 | 46, 50 |
| 2:1–3 | 43, 45n48, 51, 56 |
| 2:3 | 35, 36n10, 37, 39, 43, 73 |
| 2:4 | 35, 44n43 |
| 2:7 | 38n22 |
| 2:9 | 50 |
| 2:15 | 38n22, 57n97, 74 |
| 2:17 | 50 |
| 2:25 | 55 |
| 2–3 | 40, 42, 52 |
| 3 | 37–38 |
| 3:8 | 38, 53 |
| 3:19 | 55 |
| 3:24 | 35, 38 |
| 14:8 | 38n22 |

## Exod

| | |
|---|---|
| 13:21 | 54 |
| 13:22 | 54 |
| 14:21 | 84 |
| 16:4 | 84 |
| 16:18 | 84 |
| 16:25 | 85 |
| 24 | 87n24 |

## Exod (cont.)

| | |
|---|---|
| 24:11 | 87n24 |
| 24:16 | 36 |
| 25:1 | 47 |
| 25:18 | 38 |
| 25:20 | 38 |
| 25:22 | 38 |
| 25–29 | 55 |
| 25–31 | 55 |
| 25–40 | 47 |
| 26:31 | 38n20 |
| 27:20 | 39n26 |
| 27:21 | 39n26 |
| 30:7–8 | 39n26 |
| 30:11 | 47, 55 |
| 30:16 | 47, 55 |
| 30:17 | 55 |
| 30:21 | 55 |
| 30:22 | 47, 55 |
| 30:33 | 55 |
| 30:34 | 47, 55 |
| 30:38 | 55 |
| 31:1 | 56 |
| 31:11 | 47, 56 |
| 31:12 | 47, 56 |
| 31:17 | 47, 56 |
| 32:31 | 84 |
| 36:8 | 38n20 |
| 36:35 | 38n20 |
| 37:7 | 38 |
| 37:9 | 38 |
| 39–40 | 45 |
| 39:32 | 46 |
| 39:43 | 46 |
| 40:9 | 46 |
| 40:33 | 46 |
| 40:38 | 54 |

## Lev

| | |
|---|---|
| 25:3–7 | 48 |
| 26:12 | 38, 53 |

## Num

| | |
|---|---|
| 3:7–8 | 38, 57 |
| 7:89 | 38 |
| 8:25 | 57 |
| 8:26 | 38, 57 |
| 11:8 | 86 |
| 14:14 | 54 |
| 18:5–6 | 38, 57 |

## Deut

| | |
|---|---|
| 1:33 | 54 |
| 9:9 | 85 |
| 16:13 | 48 |
| 18:15 | 84 |
| 18:19 | 84 |
| 23:14 | 38, 53 |

## 1 Kgs

| | |
|---|---|
| 6:27 | 38 |
| 6:28 | 38 |
| 6:29 | 38n20 |
| 6:32 | 38n20 |
| 6:35 | 38n20 |
| 6:38 | 48 |
| 7:29 | 38n20 |
| 7:36 | 38n20 |
| 8:2 | 48 |
| 8:6 | 38 |
| 8:31 | 48 |
| 8:53 | 48 |
| 17 | 86 |
| 17–19 | 79, 83 |
| 17:1 | 85n16 |
| 17:6 | 85n16 |
| 17:10 | 84 |
| 17:16 | 84 |
| 17:17 | 87, 85n16 |
| 17:24 | 87, 85n16 |
| 18:27 | 81 |
| 18:41 | 82 |
| 19 | 84, 86n22 |

## SCRIPTURE INDEX

| | |
|---|---|
| 19:3–8 | 4, 78–80, 87, 89, 114 |
| 19:4 | 82 |
| 19:5 | 82, 85n16 |
| 19:6 | 86 |
| 19:7 | 82 |
| 19:8 | 85 |

### 2 Kgs

| | |
|---|---|
| 2:8 | 84 |
| 2:11 | 80 |

### 1 Chr

| | |
|---|---|
| 22:9 | 48 |
| 23:32 | 57 |

### Neh

| | |
|---|---|
| 9:12 | 54 |
| 9:16 | 54 |
| 9:19 | 54 |

### Esth

| | |
|---|---|
| 1:6 | 86n22 |

### Job

| | |
|---|---|
| 3:13 | 81 |

### Pss

| | |
|---|---|
| 13:4 | 81 |
| 77:25 | 84 |
| 78:25 | 84n12 |
| 90:2–4 | 74 |
| 90:12 | 74 |
| 90:14 | 74 |
| 90:16 | 74 |
| 104 | 44 |
| 132:13 | 48 |
| 132:14 | 48 |

### Sir

| | |
|---|---|
| 24 | 38, 54 |
| 24:3 | 54 |
| 24:4 | 54 |
| 24:6 | 54 |
| 24:3–6 | 54 |
| 24:12 | 54 |
| 24:17 | 54 |
| 24:22 | 55 |

### Jer

| | |
|---|---|
| 51:39 | 81 |

### Ezek

| | |
|---|---|
| 28 | 38, 51, 53 |
| 40:17 | 86n22 |
| 44:14 | 57 |

### Dan

| | |
|---|---|
| 12:2 | 81 |

### Mal

| | |
|---|---|
| 3:22 | 85n20 |
| 3:23 | 85 |
| 3:24 | 85n20 |
| 4:4–5 | 86n20 |

## SCRIPTURE INDEX

### Matt

| | |
|---|---|
| 13:54 | 74 |
| 13:55 | 74 |
| 13:58 | 74 |

### Mark

| | |
|---|---|
| 5:41 | 82n8 |

### Luke

| | |
|---|---|
| 8:54 | 82n8 |

### John

| | |
|---|---|
| 3:1–21 | 70n46 |
| 11 | 83 |

| | |
|---|---|
| 11:11 | 83 |
| 16:33 | 117 |

### 1 Cor

| | |
|---|---|
| 10:1–4 | 84 |
| 11:30 | 81 |
| 15:6 | 81 |
| 15:18 | 81 |

### Eph

| | |
|---|---|
| 5:14 | 82 |

### 2 Tim

| | |
|---|---|
| 3:16 | 92 |

www.ingramcontent.com/pod-product-compliance
Lightning Source LLC
Chambersburg PA
CBHW050817160426
43192CB00010B/1796